INTRODUCTION TO
LOGIC PROGRAMMING

This is volume 21 in A.P.I.C. Studies in Data Processing
General Editors: Fraser Duncan and M. J. R. Shave
A complete list of titles in this series appears at the end of this volume

INTRODUCTION TO LOGIC PROGRAMMING

Christopher John Hogger

Department of Computing
Imperial College of Science and Technology
London, United Kingdom

1984

ACADEMIC PRESS, INC.
Harcourt Brace Jovanovich, Publishers
London   Orlando   San Diego
New York   Austin   Montreal   Sydney
Tokyo   Toronto

ACADEMIC PRESS INC. (LONDON) LTD.
24-28 Oval Road,
London NW1 7DX

United States Edition published by
ACADEMIC PRESS, INC.
Orlando, Florida 32887

British Library Cataloguing in Publication Data

Hogger, Christopher John
 Introduction to logic programming.—(APIC
 studies in data processing)
 1. Electronic digital computers—Programming
 2. Logic, Symbolic and mathematical
 I. Title II. Series
 001.64'2'015113   QA76.6

Library of Congress Cataloging in Publication Data

Hogger, Christopher John.
 Introduction to logic programming.

 Bibliography: p.
 Includes index.
 1. Electronic digital computers—Programming.   2. Logic,
Symbolic and mathematical.   I. Title.
QA76.6.H624   1984   001.64'2   84-14533
ISBN 0–12–352090–8 (Hardbound, Alk. Paper)
ISBN 0–12–352092–4 (Paperback, Alk. Paper)

PRINTED IN THE UNITED STATES OF AMERICA

85 86 87 88   9 8 7 6 5 4 3 2

CONTENTS

FOREWORD

This book is a major contribution to logic programming. It sets out for the first time in one place a comprehensive yet accessible introduction to all aspects of our subject. It covers a sound middle ground between the practical introductions to PROLOG by Clocksin and Mellish and by Clark and McCabe on the one side, and more general treatments of computational logic like Robinson's and mine on the other.

It covers two important aspects of logic programming which are to be found in no other place: derivation of logic programs from logic specifications and implementation of PROLOG. The first of these is a major contribution of logic programming to classical problems of software engineering, in which the author himself has played a significant and pioneering role. The second is a topic of great theoretical and commercial interest, and many devotees of PROLOG will be grateful for this accessible account of this hitherto esoteric subject.

This beautifully written book will be a joy to both novices and experts. It will help waken the novice to the wider world of logic programming which lies beyond PROLOG, and it will help stir the logic programming expert to greater understanding and further enthusiasm for our subject.

Imperial College, London   Robert Kowalski
May 1984

PREFACE

It is widely expected that symbolic logic will serve as the core programming formalism for the next generation of computer systems. The identification of this role for logic in Japan's Fifth Generation Project has stimulated world-wide interest in logic programming, although even beforehand it was becoming clear that this fascinating formalism was destined to make substantial contributions to the theory and practice of computing.

The advancement of logic programming was, until this recent growth of interest, confined to just a few research centres, with the result that the existing literature base describing the subject is still rather small. A few texts are already available based upon specific implementations, and others are expected shortly: for the most part these books are intended as tutorial introductions to program writing. In addition, collections of advanced research papers for computer science specialists have been published in book form. This leaves a rather large gap between the two extremes of expository level, and the chief purpose of this book is to close the gap a little.

In the book's first half, logic programming is introduced at a tutorial level but supplemented with more background and foundational material than would normally be expected in a programmer's guide. The level of presentation here is consistent with a first-year undergraduate course in computing science. The second half deals with more advanced aspects of logic as a computational formalism. It aims to gather together, simplify and interpret selected themes from a somewhat disunited, and often technically very difficult, research literature and to survey current developments in theory and application. It is intended to be of use for explanatory and reference purposes both to undergraduates taking specialized course options in logic programming and to researchers comparatively new to the field.

My endeavours in writing this book owe much to the privilege of work-ing in the company of other researchers in logic programming in the Comput-ing Department of Imperial College. In particular I gratefully acknowledge the encouragement afforded by both Robert Kowalski and Keith Clark to persist in the completion of my task. My thanks also go to Maarten van Emden and John Lloyd for reading and commenting upon the greater part of the manuscript. The daunting task of keeping abreast of new activities and research publications in the field was much ameliorated by the excellent series of Logic Programming Newsletters edited by Luis Moniz Pereira at the University of Lisbon, and I am sure that my own appreciation of his good work in this is shared by the rest of the logic programming community.

MEANINGS OF PRINCIPAL SYMBOLS

SYMBOL	MEANING
, (comma)	and
∨	or
¬	not
←	if
↔	if and only if
iff	if and only if
∀	for all
∃	for some (there exists)
:=	is assigned
⊨	logically implies
⊢	admits a proof of
~	not provable
|	such that
□	success (by contradiction)
■	failure
≠	not identical to
⊕	vector sum
△	assert if provable (generate lemma)
∈	belongs to (is a member of)
⊆	is a subset of
∪	set union
∅	empty set

INTRODUCTION

The subject of this book is the use of symbolic logic as a programming language. At the time of writing, this use of logic has a history of no more than twelve years, and is still unfamiliar in detail to much of the programming community. This situation is likely to change rapidly owing to the recent identification of logic programming as the key formalism for the next generation of computers.

Logic programming differs fundamentally from conventional programming in requiring us to describe the logical structure of problems rather than making us prescribe how the computer is to go about solving them. People with no previous computing experience tend to believe that programming is, and always has been, a naturally logical business, and when introduced to languages like BASIC are often surprised or even dismayed to find that this is not really the case. Instead they discover that the traditional way of writing programs pays much homage to the computer's internal mechanisms, which, whilst certainly having a rationale of their own, do not seem to derive straightforwardly from the original conception of the problem. Conversely, programmers trained only in the use of conventional languages can experience comparable problems of adjustment when introduced to logic programming. Instinctively anxious to control the machine efficiently, they are subject to a vague sense of deprivation when getting used to a language possessing no machine-oriented features; they may suffer the programmer's equivalent of withdrawal symptoms following a long spell of addictive devotion to the assignment statement.

These adjustments are not always easy, as I know from my own experience. Two memories still stand out clearly: first, as a science undergraduate in an introductory FORTRAN course, being able to accept descriptions of the effects of individual statements upon the machine but uncertain as to how they should be knitted together in a manner consistent with the problem's logical structure; second, as a teacher of FORTRAN some years later, being shown my first logic programming statement and being unclear as to how it could contribute to an algorithmic solution of a problem on a machine. A definite effort is needed to overcome long-term conditioning to one view of computation.

The first logic programming statement I was ever shown stated "you are healthy if you eat porridge." This sentence of everyday language becomes a sentence of symbolic logic when arranged in the more structured style

$$\textbf{healthy}(u) \quad \textbf{if} \quad \textbf{eat}(u, PORRIDGE)$$

This format exposes all the principal constituents of the language as we shall use it for programming purposes: individual objects ($PORRIDGE$), variables (u) standing for any objects, propositions like **healthy**(u) and **eat**(u, $PORRIDGE$) about objects, and connectives (**if**) relating the propositions. This sentence might form part of an "expert system" program offering advice (in this example, of questionable worth) about personal nutrition. We can just as easily state something having a more numerical flavour such as

$$\textbf{even-number}(u) \quad \textbf{if} \quad \textbf{divisible}(u, 2)$$

How can logical descriptions of this sort be used to make a computer solve a problem? Consider an analogy. You wish to undertake a car journey having decided the origin, destination and possibly other defining features of the route. Getting the car to traverse this route entails multifarious decisions, many of them petty and repetitious, about vehicle-handling and motoring protocols. It is now proposed that the journey be accomplished without your having to make any of these decisions. How is this possible? By engaging someone else to do the driving and telling him the requirements of the route.

The logic programmer's 'driver' is the logic interpreter. This is a program which knows how to exploit the computer in order to infer the consequences of any set of logic sentences. The programmer's responsibility is to ensure that the given sentences are both correct and sufficiently informative to make the desired consequences inferrable.

Let's consider a more concrete example. Imagine that some piece of equipment exhibits a three-light display monitor; each light is either ON or OFF. Various ON/OFF combinations on this display periodically determine whether some switch on the equipment is to be set to ON or OFF by a human operator. Using logic we can write a collection of simple assertions

$$R1 : \quad \textbf{rule}(ON, \quad ON, OFF, ON)$$
$$R2 : \quad \textbf{rule}(OFF, \quad ON, ON, OFF)$$
$$\vdots$$
$$\text{etc.}$$

where each proposition **rule**(*w*,   *x*, *y*, *z*) is read as saying that the switch is to be set to the state *w* when the display's state is *x*, *y*, *z*. Jointly these sentences can be used as a decision table. Suppose we wish to store this table in a computer so that the operator can interrogate it in order to find out which state *w* is the appropriate response to some *x*, *y*, *z* displayed on the monitor. Given a logic interpreter implemented on the computer, the operator need only ask whether a particular proposition is a consequence of (implied by) the stored sentences. For example, he can type in the logic query

$$? \textbf{rule}(w, \quad ON, OFF, ON)$$

which asks which value of *w* makes **rule**(*w*,   *ON*, *OFF*, *ON*) such a consequence. According to R1 this value is *ON* and so the interpreter will autonomously discover this and print out *w* := *ON*.

Many other queries are answerable on the same basis (that is, without altering the stored sentences) by simply posing them to the interpreter. The query ? **rule**(*OFF*,   *x*, *y*, *z*) returns all states *x*, *y*, *z* of the display requiring the *OFF* response. The query ? **rule**(*OFF*,   *ON*, *ON*, *OFF*) merely asks for confirmation that *OFF* is a correct response to the display *ON*, *ON*, *OFF*; the interpreter just answers "*YES*" (because of R2). The query ? **rule**(*w*,   *x*, *y*, *z*) elicits a printout of the entire decision table. The query ? **rule**(*w1*,   *x*, *y*, *z*), **rule**(*w2*,   *x*, *y*, *z*), *w1* ≠ *w2* instigates a table-consistency check by asking whether any displays *x*, *y*, *z* have multiple occurrences in the table with contradictory responses. If we store in the machine two further sentences

$$S1 : \quad \textbf{state}(ON)$$
$$S2 : \quad \textbf{state}(OFF)$$

then the query ? **state**(*x*), **state**(*y*), **state**(*z*), ∼**rule**(*w*,   *x*, *y*, *z*) instigates a table-completeness check by asking whether any displays *x*, *y*, *z* have been omitted from the table (∼ means 'not') and, if so, tells us what they are.

In short, every possible query that is logically answerable using the stored sentences *will* be answered by the interpreter using logical inference. In virtually every other programming language each new problem to be solved using a fixed corpus of knowledge requires the laborious construction of new code, and the more complicated the derivation of the problem's solution, the more complicated that code needs to be. This inflexibility of programs in the face of changing goals must detract significantly from programming productivity.

Now it would be wrong to give the false impression that logic frees the programmer from pragmatic considerations. In realistic applications it is often necessary in the interests of acceptable execution performance to structure the input sentences with due regard for the interpreter's deductive strategy and for the particular query being posed. So the programmer will normally need to think about the algorithmic quality of what he writes as well as its descriptive quality. Nonetheless the important point is that the program statements (i.e., the input logic sentences) will always be logical descriptions of the problem itself and not of the execution process: the exact assumptions made about the problem will always be directly apparent from the program text. Throughout the book much emphasis will be placed upon this point and the ramifications it has for programming methodology and the wider issues of software engineering.

Logic programming has been successfully taught to young children using informal notions of logical implication and inference. Such informality is extremely useful for enabling naive users to assimilate the basic principles relatively painlessly. However, a more precise treatment is necessary for a proper appreciation of the formalism's historical and theoretical foundations. With this in mind, the first chapter aims to provide a reasonably precise and self-contained account of logic as a language for problem solving, explaining sentence structure, implication and inference. The second chapter has a more computational flavour, dealing mostly with the procedural interpretation of logic and showing how familiar algorithmic processes are elicited from programs by the interpreter. Chapters III and IV describe pragmatic and stylistic considerations in the structuring of programs and data. This first half of the book is therefore chiefly concerned with how to understand and construct logic programs.

The second half of the book is written more for the computer scientist and is consequently more technical. Chapters V and VI discuss the specification, verification and synthesis of programs, whilst Chapter VII outlines the elementary features of typical logic implementations. The last chapter surveys the main contributions of logic programming to computing generally: it covers important results in the theory of logic programming, describes some of the work underway in knowledge-based applications and explains the role of logic in the forthcoming fifth generation computer systems.

I REPRESENTATION AND REASONING

A logic program consists of sentences expressing knowledge relevant to the problem that the program is intended to solve. The formulation of this knowledge makes use of two basic concepts: the existence of discrete objects, referred to here as *individuals*; and the existence of *relations* between them. The individuals considered in the context of a particular problem jointly constitute the *domain* of that problem. For example, if the problem is to solve an algebraic equation, then the domain may consist of—or at least include—the real numbers.

In order to be represented by a symbolic system such as logic, both individuals and relations must be given *names*. Naming is just a preliminary task in creating symbolic models representing what we know. The main task is to construct *sentences* expressing various logical properties of the named relations. Reasoning about some problem posed on the domain can be achieved by manipulating these sentences using logical *inference*. In a typical logic programming environment the programmer invents the sentences forming his program and the computer then performs the necessary inference to solve the problem. For this to be accomplished effectively the programmer must be sufficiently skilled both in representing knowledge and in understanding how it will be processed on the machine. In this chapter we introduce the language of *first-order logic* and show how it serves as a tool for representation and reasoning, and hence for computational problem solving.

I.1. Individuals

Individuals may be any objects at all. Examples are numbers, geometrical figures, equations and computer programs. Very often it suffices to give them simple names like

1   2   ONE   TWO   CIRCLE   EQUATION-1   PROGRAM-2

chosen from some prescribed vocabulary. These names are indivisible (or unstructured) and are conventionally called *constants*. Any number of these may, if desired, simultaneously name a particular individual. So *ONE* and *1* could both name the individual known as the first positive integer. The choice of names is arbitrary, and so the first positive integer could (perversely) be named *3* if so desired.

Sometimes it is convenient to give individuals composite (structured) names like

TWICE(2)   PLUS(1, 2)

Each of these consists of an *n-tuple* prefixed by a *functor* (or function symbol). An *n*-tuple is just any ordered collection of *n* names, so (*1, 2*) is an example of a *2*-tuple. The enclosing parentheses serve only to clarify the start and end of the *n*-tuple and can be omitted when convenient. A *2*-tuple can be called, more simply, a *pair*, whilst a *3*-tuple can be called a *triplet*. Functors like *TWICE* and *PLUS* are also chosen arbitrarily from another prescribed vocabulary. Each one can only prefix *n*-tuples for a particular value of *n*, and is then said to be an *n-place* (or *n*-ary) *functor*. So in the present context, *TWICE* is a *1*-place (or *1*-ary or 'unary') functor whilst *PLUS* is a *2*-place (or *2*-ary or 'binary') functor.

Functors enable the construction of arbitrarily elaborate names like

PLUS(TWICE(2), PLUS(1, TWICE(1)))

This name, which might be given to the seventh positive integer [because it can be viewed as $2 * 2 + (1 + 2 * 1) = 7$], indicates that individual's dependence upon two other individuals, respectively named *TWICE(2)* and *PLUS(1, TWICE(1))*. The outermost *PLUS* essentially names that dependence.

I.2. Relations

A symbol like *TWICE* has no intrinsic meaning and so does not, in its own right, correspond to our intuitive idea of 'twice'. Fundamentally that idea refers to a particular set of pairs of numbers which, for simplicity's sake, we will restrict here to the natural numbers. One way of capturing the idea is to choose names *1, 2, 3, . . .* etc. for the numbers and then collect them into pairs to form the set shown below, which has been given the name **twice**.

$$\textbf{twice} = \{(1, 2), (2, 4), (3, 6), \ldots \text{etc.}\}$$

The occurrence in this set of any pair (x, y) can then signify 'twice x equals y' and the entire set can be considered to encompass the entire concept of 'twice'.

This set is an example of a relation. An *n-place* (or *n*-ary) *relation* is just any set of *n*-tuples for some particular value of *n*. So **twice** here names a 2-place (or 2-ary or binary) relation; it *relates* the individuals named within each *n*-tuple belonging to it. Note that we are under no obligation to choose *n*-tuples having some kind of internal dependence. If we wish, we can construct a relation which contains the pair (*tomorrow's weather, height of the Eiffel Tower*).

Every idea is representable in indefinitely many ways. For example, we could define another, more general relation named **equals** containing such pairs as

$$(TWICE(1), 2) \qquad (TWICE(2), 4) \qquad (ONCE(1), 1) \qquad (THRICE(2), 6)$$

Then the occurrence of any pair (x, y) in **equals** can signify 'x equals y'. In particular, a pair $(TWICE(x), y)$ in **equals** can signify 'twice x equals y'. Then the idea 'twice' is represented by the set of all such pairs belonging to **equals**.

The degree to which a relation represents an idea depends not upon the evocative nature of symbols like **twice** but rather upon the logical features of the relation itself. So if our **twice** relation is to represent faithfully the intuitive meaning of twice then it must not contain a pair (x, x) for any instance of x. This is just one of many features, deriving from the laws of integer arithmetic, which the relation must satisfy to fulfil its intended role.

Some facts can be represented using only sets of *1*-tuples. For instance, the property of being a negative integer might be represented by the set

$$\{-1, -2, -3, \ldots \text{etc.}\}$$

Such sets are strictly called *properties* rather than *1*-place relations. However, because it can be tedious to maintain a distinction between properties and relations, subsequent discussions about relations can be assumed to refer also to properties.

I.3. Predicates, Connectives and Formulae

In logic, relations are named by *predicate symbols* chosen from a prescribed vocabulary. Knowledge about the relations is then expressed by sentences constructed from predicates, connectives and formulae. An *n-place* (or *n*-ary) *predicate* is formed by prefixing an *n*-tuple with an *n*-place (or *n*-ary) predicate symbol. An example is **twice**(*2, 4*), where **twice** is a *2*-place predicate symbol. The predicate is read as the proposition that the pair (*2, 4*) belongs to the relation named **twice**. We refer to *2* and *4* here as the first and second *arguments* of the predicate **twice**(*2, 4*). More generally, a predicate **p**(*t*), where *t* is some *n*-tuple, can be read informally either as '*t* belongs to relation **p**' or as 'proposition **p** holds true of *t*'.

Logic also provides several *connectives*

$$, \qquad \lor \qquad \neg \qquad \leftarrow \qquad \leftrightarrow$$

which are respectively pronounced 'and', 'or', 'not', 'if' and 'if and only if'. They are used to construct formulae by connecting predicates or other formulae.

Formulae of a simple kind are defined by the rules

(i)   any predicate is a formula;
(ii)   if **F1** and **F2** are formulae, then so are

$$\text{(F1)} \qquad \textbf{F1}, \textbf{F2} \qquad \textbf{F1} \leftarrow \textbf{F2}$$
$$\neg \textbf{F1} \qquad \textbf{F1} \lor \textbf{F2} \qquad \textbf{F1} \leftrightarrow \textbf{F2}$$

Later on the definition of a formula will be extended to admit occurrences of variables in predicate arguments. Rules (i) and (ii) provide only for the construction of *variable-free formulae*.

Observe that rule (ii) provides the *punctuation symbols* (and) so that we can distinguish, for example,

$$\textbf{F1} \leftarrow (\textbf{F2}, \textbf{F3}) \qquad \text{from} \qquad (\textbf{F1} \leftarrow \textbf{F2}), \textbf{F3}$$

and

$$\neg(\textbf{F2}, \textbf{F3}) \qquad \text{from} \qquad (\neg\textbf{F2}), \textbf{F3}$$

The use of these symbols can be reduced, without introducing ambiguity, by adopting the convention that $\neg$ binds more strongly than the other connectives whilst , and $\lor$ bind more strongly than $\leftarrow$ and $\leftrightarrow$. Then it is possible to write

$$\textbf{F1} \leftarrow \textbf{F2}, \textbf{F3} \qquad \text{in place of} \qquad \textbf{F1} \leftarrow (\textbf{F2}, \textbf{F3})$$

and

$$\neg\textbf{F2}, \textbf{F3} \qquad \text{in place of} \qquad (\neg\textbf{F2}), \textbf{F3}$$

In addition it is permitted to write

$$\textbf{F1}, \textbf{F2}, \textbf{F3} \qquad \text{in place of} \qquad (\textbf{F1}, \textbf{F2}), \textbf{F3} \quad \text{or} \quad \textbf{F1}, (\textbf{F2}, \textbf{F3})$$

and

$$\textbf{F1} \lor \textbf{F2} \lor \textbf{F3} \qquad \text{in place of} \qquad (\textbf{F1} \lor \textbf{F2}) \lor \textbf{F3} \quad \text{or} \quad \textbf{F1} \lor (\textbf{F2} \lor \textbf{F3})$$

The most frequently used connectives in logic programming are 'and', 'not' and 'if'. These are typically used to construct formulae such as

positive$(6) \leftarrow$ **negative**(-2) , **negative**(-3) , **times**$(-2, -3, 6)$

This formula is an example of a *variable-free sentence* and can be read as saying

$$6 \text{ is positive } \textbf{if} \quad -2 \text{ is negative } \textbf{and}$$
$$-3 \text{ is negative } \textbf{and}$$
$$-2 \text{ times } -3 \text{ is } 6$$

This is a moderately complicated sentence. The simplest sentences consist of single predicates or single negated predicates like

negative(-1) and $\neg$**positive**(-1)

The general structure of sentences will be described after the discussion of variables.

I.4. Variables

Very often it is required to make statements about 'all' individuals. The precise meaning of 'all' will be clarified later, in Section I.7 which deals with the interpretation of sentences. One such statement is

$$\text{for all } x \text{ and } y, \ (TWICE(x), y) \text{ belongs to } \textbf{equals}$$
$$\textbf{if} \quad (x, y) \text{ belongs to } \textbf{twice}$$

One way of expressing this in logic is by writing a variable-free sentence to deal with each choice of x and y encompassed by the intended meaning of 'all', as shown below.

equals$(TWICE(1), 2) \leftarrow$ **twice**$(1, 2)$
equals$(TWICE(2), 4) \leftarrow$ **twice**$(2, 4)$
$\vdots$
etc.

Clearly this is too cumbersome to be practical. The use of variables allows a generalised sentence to be written instead, namely

equals$(TWICE(x), y) \leftarrow$ **twice**(x, y)

where x and y are chosen from a prescribed vocabulary of *variables*. The notion of an n-tuple, and hence of a formula and a sentence, is therefore being generalised by permitting variables in place of specific names. Variables are distinguished from constants in this book by the convention that they begin with lower-case letters as in

$$x \quad y \quad i \quad j \quad alpha \quad abc123$$

The role of a variable in a sentence is governed by its mode of *quantification*, which may be either *universal* or *existential*. The kind intended in the example above is universal and can be indicated explicitly using the symbol ∀, which is pronounced 'for all'. So to make the intention clear the sentence should be written strictly as

$$(\forall x \forall y)(\textbf{equals}(TWICE(x), y) \leftarrow \textbf{twice}(x, y))$$

Existential quantification is used when it is required to refer to 'some' (at least one) individual. The symbol ∃, which is pronounced 'there exists', is used to indicate this requirement. For example, consider a simple definition in set theory

for all y, y is a non-empty set **if and only if**
there exists some x such that x belongs to y

This can be expressed in logic by the sentence

$$(\forall y)(\textbf{non-empty}(y) \leftrightarrow (\exists x)\textbf{belongs}(x, y))$$

The expressions $(\forall y)$ and $(\exists x)$ are respectively called universal and existential *quantifiers*. The *scope* of each one is the formula to which it is prefixed. So the scope of $(\forall y)$ above is the formula

$$(\textbf{non-empty}(y) \leftrightarrow (\exists x)\textbf{belongs}(x, y))$$

whilst the scope of $(\exists x)$ is the formula $\textbf{belongs}(x, y)$.

I.5. Sentences

With the introduction of variables it is now possible to extend the definitions of predicate and formula. Predicates are now allowed to contain terms as their arguments rather than just specific names, subject to the definitions

(i)   a *term* is either a constant or a variable or an n-tuple of terms prefixed by a functor;

(ii)   a *predicate* is an n-tuple of terms prefixed by a predicate symbol.

Formulae are now allowed to contain quantifiers in accordance with

(iii)   a *formula* is either a predicate or has one of the forms

$$\textbf{(F1)}\quad \textbf{F1 , F2}\qquad \textbf{F1} \leftarrow \textbf{F2}$$
$$\neg\textbf{F1}\quad \textbf{F1} \vee \textbf{F2}\qquad \textbf{F1} \leftrightarrow \textbf{F2}\qquad Q\textbf{F1}$$

where **F1** and **F2** are any formulae and Q is any quantifier.

Finally, a sentence is defined by

(iv)   a *sentence* is a formula in which every occurrence of a variable (if any) is within the scope of a quantifier for that variable.

For presentation's sake it is customary to omit outermost universal quantifiers as in the example

$$\textbf{non-empty}(y) \leftrightarrow (\exists x)\textbf{belongs}(x, y)$$

Here the variable y is apparently unquantified, and therefore it is assumed to be universally quantified by an unwritten outermost $(\forall y)$. Thus the assumed sentence conforms to rule (iv) above. Terms, predicates, formulae and sentences which contain no variables are said to be variable-free or *ground*.

The set of all sentences constructible from rules (i)–(iv) constitutes the *language of first-order logic*. In this language, terms provide the means of referring to the individuals of interest, using either specific names like *PLUS(1, 2)* or generalised names like *PLUS(x, TWICE(PLUS(2, TWICE(y))))*. Predicates express relations between the individuals denoted by terms, and sentences describe the logical properties of these relations. All computational problems (problems solvable by a computer) can be formulated in this language. In any particular logic programming implementation, conventions will exist which describe exactly the kinds of sentence allowable in programs together with the vocabularies available for constructing names.

I.6. Examples of Representation

The following examples demonstrate the use of sentences for describing some familiar data structures and their properties.

Example 1:   To describe a list $L = (A, B, C, D)$.

(a)   A dot can be used as a 2-place functor to construct terms of the form $.(u, y)$. Such a term can name a list having some u as its first member whilst y denotes the rest of the list. The term's readability can be improved by adopting the parenthesis-free *infix notation u.y* instead of the *prefix notation .(u, y)*. The constant *NIL* can name the empty list and the predicate **list**(z, x) can express that z is a name for list x. Then one sentence

$$\textbf{list}(L, A.B.C.D.NIL)$$

suffices to describe L as the list (A, B, C, D). Essentially it associates two names L and $A.B.C.D.NIL$ with the same list; the second one is more informative in showing that the list consists of individuals named A, B, C, D and *NIL*.

  (b)   Another way is to use a predicate **m**(u, i, x) to express that element u occupies position i in list x. The four sentences

$$\textbf{m}(A, 1, L)$$
$$\textbf{m}(B, 2, L)$$
$$\textbf{m}(C, 3, L)$$
$$\textbf{m}(D, 4, L)$$

jointly provide an alternative description of L. They are reminiscent of, though not strictly analogous to, the conventional programmer's method of assigning elements to a linear array L using statements like

$$L(1) := \text{`}A\text{'}$$
$$L(2) := \text{`}B\text{'}$$
$$L(3) := \text{`}C\text{'}$$
$$L(4) := \text{`}D\text{'}$$

  (c)   Yet another way is to use a predicate **consec**(u, v, x) to express that elements u and v are consecutive in list x, with u preceding v. The three sentences

$$\textbf{consec}(A, B, L)$$
$$\textbf{consec}(B, C, L)$$
$$\textbf{consec}(C, D, L)$$

also jointly describe L.

  Example 2.   To describe the matrix

$$M = \begin{bmatrix} 1 & 2 \\ 3 & 4 \end{bmatrix}$$

  (a)   Use a predicate **elem**(u, i, j, x) to express that u is the element in row i

and column j of matrix x. So M is described by the four sentences

$$\textbf{elem}(1, 1, 1, M)$$
$$\textbf{elem}(2, 1, 2, M)$$
$$\textbf{elem}(3, 2, 1, M)$$
$$\textbf{elem}(4, 2, 2, M)$$

(b)   Another possibility is to use a predicate $\textbf{row}(i, z, x)$ to express that the ith row of matrix x is the list of elements z. Then two sentences suffice, these being

$$\textbf{row}(1, 1.2.NIL, M)$$
$$\textbf{row}(2, 3.4.NIL, M)$$

(c)   Analogously describe M columnwise using

$$\textbf{col}(1, 1.3.NIL, M)$$
$$\textbf{col}(2, 2.4.NIL, M)$$

Example 3.   To describe the membership relation $\in$ between an element u and a list x using each of the three list representations shown in Example 1; the predicate $\in(u, x)$, meaning that u is a member of x, can be written in the more readable infix notation $u \in x$.

(a) $u \in x \leftrightarrow (\exists v \exists y)(\textbf{list}(x, v.y), (u = v \lor u \in y))$

Here $=$ names the *identity relation*, which contains all pairs of identical individuals.

(b) $u \in x \leftrightarrow (\exists i)\textbf{m}(u, i, x)$

(c) $u \in x \leftrightarrow (\exists v)\textbf{consec}(u, v, x) \lor (\exists v)\textbf{consec}(v, u, x)$
$$\lor \textbf{list}(x, u.NIL)$$

Observe that in method (c) it is not possible to use only the **consec** relation because it cannot deal with a unit list (one having just one member)— hence the use of the **list** relation as well.

Example 4.   To describe the relationship between a matrix and its transpose for each of the three previous matrix representations; the functor T can be used to give the name $T(x)$ to the transpose of matrix x.

(a) $\textbf{elem}(u, i, j, T(x)) \leftrightarrow \textbf{elem}(u, j, i, x)$
(b) $\textbf{row}(i, z, T(x)) \leftrightarrow \textbf{col}(i, z, x)$
(c) $\textbf{col}(i, z, T(x)) \leftrightarrow \textbf{row}(i, z, x)$

In all these examples there is scope for questioning the sense in which the sentences actually represent the intended ideas and for asking whether they do so correctly and completely. One can also ask what role they serve in solving computational problems and why one set of sentences might be preferred to another. These questions will be dealt with presently in the discussions of the interpretation of sentences, their manipulation by logical inference and their assessment in terms of computational utility.

Before meeting these topics, the reader who is new to logic should first practise reading logical sentences and correlating them informally with the kind of statements found in more familiar symbolic systems such as conventional mathematics and natural language. Logic is just one reasonably simple and uniform notation for expressing ideas like that in Example 3(c), where it formalizes the intuition that an element belongs to a list if and only if it either precedes or succeeds another member or else is the only member.

I.7. Interpretation of Sentences

The usual sequel to representing knowledge in a formal system like logic is the operation of some precise reasoning process which explores the logical consequences of the knowledge. The fundamental notion underlying this reasoning is that of *logical implication*. We talk about some conclusion being logically implied by some set of assumptions. Informally this is understood to mean that if the assumptions are 'true' according to any interpretation of them, then so must be the conclusion. Contrary to popular supposition, the intuitive ideas of truth and falsity are not intrinsic features of logic. Nevertheless, the association of those ideas with logic provides a useful way of describing the relationships between sentences. Here we explain the notion of interpretation in order to construct a precise concept of logical implication.

It will be helpful in what follows to focus upon a specific example. Suppose then that we begin with two sentences

$$\textbf{positive}(ONE)$$

and

$$(\forall x)(\textbf{positive}(TWICE(x)) \leftarrow \textbf{positive}(x))$$

It so happens that these logically imply a third sentence

$$\textbf{positive}(TWICE(ONE))$$

This fact can be made to appear obvious by paraphrasing the sentences in

English to form the argument

> **if** it is true that
> > *ONE* is positive
> > **and** for all x, twice x is positive   **if** x is positive
> **then** it is true that
> > twice *ONE* is positive

The apparent obviousness of the implication is due to our natural facility for reasoning informally in everyday language. Moreover, the symbols used in the sentences automatically evoke the familiar ideas of numbers and their arithmetical properties. We can easily satisfy ourselves that the implication is sound by associating the first two sentences with laws of arithmetic that we already hold to be true, and then applying commonsense reasoning in order to conclude the truth of the third sentence.

This superficial treatment is often sufficient for deciding whether or not particular conclusions follow from given assumptions. Yet it is clearly susceptible to the imprecision of natural language interpretation. For instance, what *exactly* is meant by 'if', 'and', 'for all' and 'true'? Does the soundness of the implication depend upon interpreting the sentences as laws of arithmetic? Other examples might not be obvious and could force us to consider these questions very carefully.

The formal treatment of logical implication is very simple conceptually but is somewhat laborious to describe. At this stage the reader may, without significant disadvantage, proceed straightaway to Section I.9, which deals with logical inference, and rely there upon his informal notion of implication. The rest of this section and the next one can be read later if a more thorough understanding is required.

The principal task in formally defining logical implication is to establish a precise concept of interpretation. In order to interpret a set S of sentences we begin by choosing a *domain of discourse*, which is just any non-empty set D of individuals. The motivation here is to provide individuals to correspond to the names occurring in S. Next, the functors and predicate symbols in S are in turn associated with chosen functions and relations defined on D. Consequently the sentences in S can be interpreted as statements about D. Then to say that a sentence in S is true (or false), according to the chosen interpretation, is to say that the corresponding statement made about D is true (or false). In this way sentences acquire a truth-functional meaning by association with the external world of individuals. These ideas can be made very precise after the following preliminaries:

(i)   for each $n \geqslant 1$, let D^n denote the set of all possible n-tuples of individuals chosen from D;

(ii)   a *mapping* (strictly a many-to-1 mapping) from one set to another is a set of pairs (x, y) such that x belongs to the first set and y to the second and every member of x appears exactly once as the first argument of some pair; we say that the mapping *maps* x to y;

(iii)   a *truth-value*, or simply *value*, is either of the two symbols t and f, pronounced 'true' and 'false'.

An *interpretation* of S over domain D then consists of three *associations* A1, A2 and A3, where

A1 associates some individual in D with each constant in S;

A2 associates some mapping from D^n to D with each n-place functor in S;

A3 associates some mapping from D^n to the set $\{t, f\}$ with each n-place predicate symbol in S.

As a simple example let S contain the sentences presented earlier,

positive(*ONE*)

$(\forall x)(\textbf{positive}(TWICE(x)) \leftarrow \textbf{positive}(x))$

Now freely choose the following domain and associations:

D is the set of natural numbers *1, 2, 3,* ... etc.;

A1 associates *1* with *ONE*;

A2 associates $\{(1, 2), (2, 4), (3, 6), \dots \text{ etc.}\}$ with *TWICE*;

A3 associates $\{(1, t), (2, t), (3, t), \dots \text{ etc.}\}$ with **positive**.

The interpretation of S is now complete, although it may not seem to have achieved very much. The interpretation does not become significant until it has been used to *evaluate* each sentence in S to one of the values t or f. This is achieved by evaluating the sentences' constituent formulae using the following rules, in which **F** is any formula within the sentence under consideration.

(a)   **F** is a variable-free predicate: replace each constant in **F** by the individual which A1 associates with it, and then replace each structured term by the individual to which its n-tuple is mapped according to A2; these replacements leave the predicate in the form $\textbf{p}(d)$ where d is an n-tuple of individuals; the value of **F** is then the value to which d is mapped by A3 for the predicate symbol **p**.

(b)   **F** has the form $(\forall x)\textbf{F}'$, where **F**′ is a formula in which x appears: the value of **F** is t if t is the value of every instance of **F**′ obtainable by uniformly replacing all its occurrences of x by an individual in D, but is otherwise f.

(c)   **F** has the form $(\exists x)\textbf{F}'$, where **F**′ is a formula in which **x** appears:

the value of **F** is t if t is the value of at least one instance of **F′** obtainable by uniformly replacing all its occurrences of x by an individual in **D**, but is otherwise f.

(d) **F** has the form $\neg$ **F1** or **F1** , **F2** or **F1** $\vee$ **F2** or **F1** $\leftarrow$ **F2** or **F1** $\leftrightarrow$ **F2**, where **F1** and **F2** are formulae: the value of **F** is looked up from the 'truth-table' below according to the values of **F1** and **F2**.

F1	F2	¬ F1	F1 , F2	F1 ∨ F2	F1 ← F2	F1 ↔ F2
t	t	f	t	t	t	t
t	f	f	f	t	t	f
f	t	t	f	t	f	f
f	f	t	f	f	t	t

Observe that rules (b) and (c) make precise the meanings of 'for all' and 'some' by referring them to the domain **D**, whilst rule (d) defines the connectives so as to make their meanings close to their counterparts in natural language.

The application of these rules can be clarified by considering our example with the suggested interpretation. The first sentence

positive(ONE)

is a formula of type (a). Using A1 we replace ONE by the individual 1 to produce **positive**(1). According to A3 the tuple 1 is mapped to t, which is therefore the value of the first sentence.

The second sentence is a formula of type (b) where **F′** is

positive($TWICE(x)$) $\leftarrow$ **positive**(x)

An instance of **F′** must be evaluated for every choice of x in **D**. Consider just one instance obtained by choosing 1 for x; thus

positive($TWICE(1)$) $\leftarrow$ **positive**(1)

The value of **positive**(1) using rule (a) is t. The value of **positive**($TWICE(1)$) is that of **positive**(2) because, for the functor $TWICE$, the tuple 1 is mapped to 2 according to A2 and so the structured term $TWICE(1)$ is replaced by 2. The value of **positive**(2) using rule (a) is also t. Therefore the entire instance of **F′** has the form **F1** $\leftarrow$ **F2**, where both **F1** and **F2** have the value t. Applying rule (d), the instance finally evaluates to t. Moreover, *all other instances* also have this value, no matter which individual from **D** is substituted for x, and so the value of the second sentence according to rule (b) is also t.

In this example, then, each sentence of S evaluates to t for the given interpretation. However, other choices for D, A1, A2 and A3 can be found which lead to different evaluations. As we emphasized at the beginning of this section, sentences are not inherently 'true' or 'false'. The values t and f are no more than symbols assigned to sentences by this particular method of interpretation. This is not to say that those values have no significance; their role will become clear in the next section.

I.8. Logical Implication

The concept of logical implication can now be made very precise. An interpretation over some domain D is said to *satisfy* a sentence if and only if it makes that sentence evaluate to t. It satisfies a set S of sentences if and only if it satisfies each sentence in S. Then we say that S *logically implies*, or simply *implies*, some sentence s if and only if, for all possible domains, every interpretation which satisfies S also satisfies s.

Referring again to the example, it has already been shown that the set S is satisfied by the chosen domain and interpretation. It will be easily found (useful exercise for the reader) that the third sentence

s :   **positive**(*TWICE*(*ONE*))

is also satisfied. Furthermore, it turns out that *every* interpretation which satisfies S also satisfies s, no matter which domain is chosen, and therefore we say that the set

positive(*ONE*)

$(\forall x)(\textbf{positive}(TWICE(x)) \leftarrow \textbf{positive}(x))$

logically implies the sentence

positive(*TWICE*(*ONE*))

This relationship is summarized by the notation S ⊨ s where ⊨ is pronounced 'logically implies'.

The significance of the ⊨ relationship is that, when S ⊨ s holds, it does so by virtue of the internal composition of the sentences themselves, irrespective of what their constituents might denote according to some interpretation of them. It is therefore independent of any connection which might be asserted between the language and the world of individuals. The use of value-assigning interpretations as defined above is just one way of constructing a concept of logical implication which is ultimately independent of the interpretations.

The relevance of logical implication to logic programming lies in the way that problems are formulated and solved. Consider the typical problem of solving some equations. In logic programming a set S of sentences could be composed which described the equations and the criteria for their solution. The computer then derives from S another sentence s, stating the equations' solution, which is implied by S. Thus the logical basis of problem solving is made much more explicit here than it is in the use of conventional programming languages.

From a practical point of view, it is fortunate that in order to establish S ⊨ s it is not necessary to investigate various domains and interpretations. Much easier methods exist which rely upon *logical inference*. It is therefore not important that the reader should fully grasp the formal definitions presented so far. In fact almost all aspects of the logic programming formalism could be presented without even referring to logical implication, although this would entail some loss of insight.

I.9. Logical Inference

Logical inference is the process of deriving a sentence s from a set S of sentences by applying one or more *inference rules*, usually with the motive of showing that S ⊨ s (S implies s). A very simple method of derivation, upon which the normal way of processing logic programs depends, is introduced here, and makes use of just one inference rule called *resolution*. Each application of the rule is called an *inference step* and, for our purposes, deals with sentences of just three kinds called *denials*, *assertions* and *implications* (with the latter not to be confused with logical implication). Their structures are shown below, where A, A_1, ..., A_n, B_1, ..., B_m are any predicates:

$$\text{denial}: \quad \neg (A_1, \ldots, A_n)$$
$$\text{assertion}: \quad A$$
$$\text{implication}: \quad A \leftarrow B_1, \ldots, B_m$$

In an implication the predicate on the left of the ← is called the *consequent*; those on the right of the ← are called the *antecedents*. An assertion can be viewed as an implication having no antecedents.

Resolution can be introduced most easily by first considering one of its simplest forms. Suppose we begin with a denial and an implication

$$\text{denial} \quad \text{S1}: \quad \neg A$$
$$\text{implication S2}: \quad A \leftarrow B$$

where the predicate A in S1 is identical to the consequent A in S2. A single resolution inference step derives from S1 and S2 the new sentence

$$s: \quad \neg B$$

In this step S1 and S2 are called the *parents* and s is the *resolvent* obtained by *resolving* the parents. Resolution in this simple case corresponds to a standard (and for our purposes very important) propositional inference rule called *modus tollens*, the essence of which is the argument

assuming **not A** and **A if B**
infer **not B**

The reader who has not previously met *modus tollens* should be quite satisfied about the intuitive reasonableness of this argument before proceeding further.

Consider next an even simpler case in which S1 is a denial and S2 is an assertion

denial   S1 :   ¬A
assertion S2 :   A

From these parents a resolution step derives as resolvent the *empty denial*

s :   □

which is denoted by the symbol □ and signifies a *contradiction*. So resolution is reasoning here as follows:

assuming   **not A** and **A**
infer a contradiction

In order to comprehend the purpose of such inferences in the context of problem solving, consider a simple problem posed upon the logic of giving and receiving. Suppose a predicate **gives**(x, y, z) expresses 'x gives y to z', whilst another predicate **receives**(y, z) expresses 'y receives z'. Suppose further that some knowledge about the two relations is expressed in two sentences

S2 : **receives**$(YOU, POWER) \leftarrow$ **gives**$(LOGIC, POWER, YOU)$
S3 : **gives**$(LOGIC, POWER, YOU)$

The problem to be solved is to answer the question

do *YOU* receive *POWER*?

When using a conventional logic programming system, such a question is posed as a denial

S1 :   ¬ **receives**$(YOU, POWER)$

and the system is challenged to refute the denial using the other sentences; the denial is refuted by showing that its assumption leads to a contradiction.

This approach is especially common in mathematics and is known as *reductio ad absurdum*, or *proof by contradiction*.

Imagine then that a logic program is composed of the three sentences S1, S2 and S3 and submitted to a resolution inference system implemented on the computer. The system resolves S1 and S2 to produce the resolvent

$$s : \quad \neg \textbf{gives}(LOGIC, POWER, YOU)$$

and resolves this in turn with S3 to yield a contradiction

$$s' : \quad \square$$

Two inference steps have therefore been sufficient to show that the input sentences S1, S2 and S3 are contradictory. Assuming that S2 and S3 are not retractable and not in themselves contradictory, it follows that they jointly contradict S1, which is equivalent to their affirming the negation of S1, namely

$$\textbf{receives}(YOU, POWER)$$

The answer to the original problem is therefore 'yes'.

Resolution which generates chains of denials, such as $(S1, s, s')$ in the example, is called *top-down resolution*; this terminology is explained in Section I.14.

Realistic programs usually contain sentences of greater complexity than those shown above. For instance, denials may have several predicates and implications may have several antecedents. So a more general case is where the parents have the form

$$S1 : \quad \neg (\textbf{A}_1, \ldots, \textbf{A}_n)$$
$$S2 : \quad \textbf{A}_k \leftarrow \textbf{B}_1, \ldots, \textbf{B}_m \quad (\text{where } 1 \leqslant k \leqslant n)$$

Here some predicate $\textbf{A}_k$ in the denial S1 is identical to the consequent of the implication S2. In this event the inference step just replaces $\textbf{A}_k$ in S1 by the antecedents of S2 to produce as resolvent the denial

$$s : \quad \neg (\textbf{A}_1, \ldots, \textbf{A}_{k-1}, \textbf{B}_1, \ldots, \textbf{B}_m, \textbf{A}_{k+1}, \ldots, \textbf{A}_n)$$

Comprehension of this may be aided by considering a simple case where $n = 3$ and $m = 1$ and paraphrasing it informally:

> assuming it is **not (dark and Winter and cold)**
> and it is **Winter if January**
> infer it is **not (dark and January and cold)**

In the case in which the denial has the same form as S1 above but S2 is just an assertion

$$S2 : \quad \textbf{A}_k$$

where A_k is one of S1's predicates, the inference step merely deletes A_k from S1 to produce the resolvent

$$s : \quad \neg (A_1, \ldots, A_{k-1}, A_{k+1}, \ldots, A_n)$$

as in the informal example

> assuming it is **not** (**dark and Winter and cold**)
> and it is **Winter**
> infer it is **not** (**dark and cold**)

In all the cases examined so far, the precondition for the step to be possible is that some predicate in the denial S1 is *identical* to the consequent predicate of the implication or assertion S2. However, resolution is much more general than this, as the next section demonstrates.

I.10. General Top-Down Resolution

Consider the following two parent sentences:

> S1 : $\neg$ **receives**(YOU, y)
> S2 :   **receives**$(x, POWER) \leftarrow$ **gives**$(z, POWER, x)$

These contain three variables x, y and z which are (implicitly) universally quantified. Thus S1 declares that

> for all y, YOU do   **not**   receive y

Recall that Section I.7 treated 'for all' as meaning 'for all individuals in whatever domain is chosen for interpreting the sentences'. Now in any interpretation of S1 and S2 over that domain, at least one such individual will be associated with the name $POWER$, and therefore an immediate consequence of S1 is the more specific sentence dealing with just that individual, namely

> S1′ : $\neg$ **receives**$(YOU, POWER)$

that is

> YOU do   **not**   receive $POWER$

A similar treatment of S2, choosing for x an individual named YOU yields the more specific sentence

> S2′ :   **receives**$(YOU, POWER) \leftarrow$ **gives**$(z, POWER, YOU)$

that is,

> for all z, YOU receive $POWER$ **if** z gives $POWER$ to YOU

We now have two sentences S1′ and S2′ which conform to the precondition that the denial has a predicate identical to the implication's consequent, and so their resolvent is

$$\text{s} : \quad \neg\,\textbf{gives}(z, POWER, YOU)$$

The identical predicate **receives**(YOU, $POWER$) is called a *common instance* of the parent predicates

$$\textbf{receives}(YOU, y)$$

and

$$\textbf{receives}(x, POWER)$$

and is defined as follows.

A *substitution* Θ is a set of assignments of terms to variables, with no variable being assigned more than one term. Its application to any expression **E**, such as a predicate, consists of replacing variables in **E** by the terms which Θ assigns to them. Any variables in **E** not mentioned in Θ are left unchanged, and any assignments in Θ to variables not occurring in **E** are not applied. The result of applying Θ to **E** is denoted by **E**Θ and is called a *substitution instance* of **E**. If the application of Θ to two expressions **E1** and **E2** yields identical substitution instances then **E1**Θ = **E2**Θ is the *common instance* of **E1** and **E2**, and Θ is then called a *unifier* (or unifying substitution) for **E1** and **E2**.

In our example the parent predicates possess the unifier

$$\Theta = \{x := YOU, y := POWER\}$$

which assigns the terms YOU and $POWER$ to the variables x and y, respectively. In practice unifiers can usually be determined easily by inspection, by comparing the predicates' corresponding arguments in turn and noting the assignments of terms to their variables which would make them identical. Systematic algorithms are available (see Chapter VII) for dealing with difficult cases and for implementation on the computer. At this stage it will probably be helpful to look at some simple examples of unification and resolution listed below.

(i) Parent predicates $\textbf{p}(5)$ and $\textbf{p}(5)$;
    unifier Θ = the empty set (no variables substituted);
    common instance $\textbf{p}(5)$.

(ii) Parent predicates $\textbf{p}(x)$ and $\textbf{p}(5)$;
    unifier $\Theta = \{x := 5\}$;
    common instance $\textbf{p}(x)\Theta = \textbf{p}(5)\Theta = \textbf{p}(5)$.

(iii) Parent predicates $\textbf{p}(x)$ and $\textbf{p}(y)$;
    unifier $\Theta = \{x := y\}$;
    common instance $\textbf{p}(y)$.

(iv)   Parent predicates $\mathbf{p}(x, x)$ and $\mathbf{p}(5, y)$;
comparing first arguments gives $x := 5$, then comparing second arguments gives $y := x$, so net effect is $y := 5$;
unifier $\Theta = \{x := 5, y := 5\}$;
common instance $\mathbf{p}(5, 5)$.

(v)   Parent predicates $\mathbf{p}(f(x), f(5), x)$ and $\mathbf{p}(z, f(y), y)$; comparing left to right and seeking the 'net effect' as in the previous example gives unifier $\Theta = \{z := f(5), y := 5, x := 5\}$;
common instance $\mathbf{p}(f(5), f(5), 5)$.

(vi)   Parent sentences S1 : $\neg \mathbf{p}(5, y)$
$$\text{S2 :}\qquad \mathbf{p}(x, x) \leftarrow \mathbf{q}(x);$$
unifier Θ of parent predicates $= \{x := 5, y := 5\}$;
resolvent s : $\neg \mathbf{q}(5)$;
upon the assumption of S2, to deny (by S1) that y exists such that $\mathbf{p}(5, y)$ holds is to choose $y := 5$ and deny (by s) that $\mathbf{q}(5)$ holds.

In general, when a unifier of two predicates exists it is not necessarily the only one possible. We next consider a case in which several unifiers exist. The parent sentences this time are

$$\text{S1 :} \quad \neg \mathbf{ord}(1.x)$$
$$\text{S2 :} \quad \mathbf{ord}(u.v.y) \leftarrow u < v, \mathbf{ord}(v.y)$$

Here S2 expresses a property of ordered lists like $(1, 2, 3)$ where the lists are represented by structured terms constructed using the dot functor and the constant *NIL* (recall Section I.6). The predicate symbol $<$ names the ordering relation. A list of the form $u.v.y$ has u and v as its first and second members, and y is the list of remaining members. S2 declares that such a list is ordered if $u < v$ and the sublist $v.y$ is ordered. S1 denies that a list of the form $1.x$ is ordered, for all x.

In order to see if the parents are resolvable, we seek a unifier for the predicates

$$\mathbf{ord}(1.x) \qquad \text{and} \qquad \mathbf{ord}(u.v.y)$$

The predicate symbols being equal, it remains to unify the arguments $1.x$ and $u.v.y$. It should be easy to see that the unifier

$$\Theta = \{u := 1, x := v.y\}$$

will suffice. The adequacy of Θ is perhaps clarified by considering its application when the two terms are written in their prefix form, namely $.(1, x)$ and $.(u, .(v, y))$. This choice of Θ produces from S1 and S2 the resolvent

$$\text{s :} \quad \neg(1 < v, \mathbf{ord}(v.y))$$

as the reader can confirm by applying Θ to S1 and S2 to produce more specific sentences S1′ and S2′ as in the previous example, and then resolving these directly.

Another possible unifier for S1 and S2 is

$$\Theta' = \{u := 1, x := 2.NIL, v := 2, y := NIL\}$$

This leads to a different resolvent,

$$s' : \quad \neg(1 < 2, \mathbf{ord}(2.NIL))$$

The unifier Θ is *more general* than Θ' in the sense that Θ makes a less specific assignment of terms to variables than Θ' does. In fact Θ is the *most general unifier* which is capable of unifying the two **ord** predicates: it only requires the term assigned to x to have the form $v.y$ where v and y remain unassigned, whereas every other unifier would, like Θ', further constrain that term by assigning terms to v and/or y. When using resolution we invariably use the most general unifier, which always exists uniquely when the predicates are unifiable.

The details of the general top-down resolution inference step, which caters for all the examples previously shown, can now be summarized as follows.

Step 1:   To avoid confusion, first ensure that no variable occurs in both the denial S1 and the implication S2; this may require replacing some variables by new ones, which in no way alters what the parents express.

Step 2:   Choose a predicate in the denial whose predicate symbol is identical to that in the implication's consequent; if this is impossible, then so is the inference step.

Step 3:   Determine the most general unifier Θ for the selected predicate in S1 and the consequent of S2; if this is impossible, then so is the inference step.

Step 4:   Replace the selected predicate in S1 by the antecedents of S2—or, if S2 is an assertion, just delete that predicate; the result is a new denial (possibly the empty denial).

Step 5:   Apply Θ to the entire new denial; this is more economical than first applying Θ to the parents and then resolving them using the common instance, as in earlier examples; the result is the resolvent s of S1 and S2.

The significance of the material presented in this section is that all computational problems can be formulated using only denials, implications and assertions, and all those which are solvable can be solved using general top-down resolution.

I.11. Problem Solving

The problem-solving capability of resolution will now be illustrated by a complete example. The problem considered is one which investigates the consecutivity of members in lists represented by terms. The relation of interest is described by using the predicate **consec**(u, v, x), which expresses that u and v are consecutive members of list x, with u preceding v.

Two sentences are sufficient for describing the **consec** relation. The first is an assertion which declares the consecutivity of any list's first two members; thus

$$S1 : \quad \textbf{consec}(u, v, u.v.x)$$

and the second is an implication describing consecutivity amongst the list's other members; thus

$$S2 : \quad \textbf{consec}(u, v, w.y) \leftarrow \textbf{consec}(u, v, y)$$

Perhaps the easiest way to comprehend their descriptive adequacy is to imagine that one wished to demonstrate that two given elements u and v were indeed consecutive members of a given list. Then one would either show the list to have the form $u.v.x$ or else show it to have the form $w.y$ and demonstrate that u and v were consecutive in y. S1 and S2 correspond to these alternatives and are clearly exhaustive.

Composing S1 and S2 is the first task in dealing with the problem; it consists of the formulation of our *assumptions* about the problem domain. In general there can be a great many assumptions.

The second task is that of expressing the particular problem posed on the domain. The problem can always be expressed as a *query* about one or more relations defined on the domain. For our example, the problem chosen is that of showing that 3 and 4 are consecutive members of the list $(1, 2, 3, 4, 5)$, which is equivalent to querying whether **consec**$(3, 4, 1.2.3.4.5.NIL)$ is implied by the assumptions S1 and S2.

In the customary way, then, the query is posed as an *initial denial*

$$D1 : \quad \neg\,\textbf{consec}(3, 4, 1.2.3.4.5.NIL)$$

The composition of both the assumptions and the initial denial completes the programmer's task of *problem formulation*. The sentences composed declare everything he wishes to state and ask about this particular problem.

The final, third task is carried out by the computer, which attempts to solve the problem by generating a proof by contradiction. More specifically, it generates a *top-down derivation*. This is a sequence of denials (D1, ..., Dn) starting with the initial denial. If a derivation can be generated which ends with $Dn = \square$, then it is said to be a *successful derivation*, and immediately yields a solution to the original problem.

The derivation is developed by resolving each successive denial, starting with D1, with another parent sentence chosen from the assumption set $S = \{S1, S2\}$; the resolvent becomes the next denial in the derivation. The present example proceeds as follows.

	Denial	Parents
D1 :	$\neg$ **consec**(3, 4, 1.2.3.4.5.NIL)	none
D2 :	$\neg$ **consec**(3, 4, 2.3.4.5.NIL)	D1, S2
D3 :	$\neg$ **consec**(3, 4, 3.4.5.NIL)	D2, S2
D4 :	$\square$	D3, S1

The derivation (D1, D2, D3, D4) is successful in that it terminates with $\square$. The reason why it solves the problem is that the theory of resolution contains the following important result:

S implies $\neg$ D1 if and only if $\square$ is derivable from S and D1

In the present example, $\neg$ D1 is equivalent to **consec**(3, 4, 1.2.3.4.5.NIL) and deriving $\square$ confirms that this conclusion is implied by the assumption set S.

Independently of the resolution theorem, we normally assume that S is internally consistent (equivalently, satisfiable), because if it were not then this would mean that the assumptions made about the problem domain were mutually contradictory no matter how they were interpreted—in which event a resolution demonstration that they (vacuously) implied $\neg$ D1 would have no straightforward problem-solving interpretation. The consistency of S is guaranteed whenever it contains only implications and/or assertions; this is the case for all standard logic programs.

Another way of viewing a successful derivation uses the fact (also established by resolution theory) that every resolvent is logically implied by its parents. By tracing through the chain of such implications entailed in the derivation above, it becomes apparent that D1 and S jointly imply $\square$. The empty denial is conventionally evaluated as 'false' in every interpretation. If D1 and S imply $\square$, then no interpretation can satisfy both of them, because if it did then $\square$ would need to have the value 'true'. It follows from this that any interpretation which satisfies S must make D1 'false' and hence make $\neg$ D1 'true', thus establishing $S \models \neg$ D1.

It does not matter if these explanations appear rather complicated upon first reading. It is only necessary to hold on to the essential result that deriving the empty denial by resolution inference steps signifies that the assumptions in S imply the conclusion $\neg$ D1. This conclusion directly answers the query posed initially by D1 and is therefore a statement of the problem's solution. Because the initial denial has been refuted, the successful derivation is called a *refutation*. Methods of generating refutations are called *refutation procedures*.

I.12. Answer Extraction

In the example just examined, the answer to the problem posed is simply 'yes': the predicate **consec**$(3, 4, 1.2.3.4.5.NIL)$ holds according to the given assumptions. More often, answers are required which tell us the particular arguments for which certain predicates hold, those arguments not being fully known at the stage of problem formulation. It turns out that answers of this kind are extractable from the unifiers entailed in the derivations generated from the input program.

As an example consider another consecutivity problem—that of *discovering* which member z, if any, follows 3 consecutively in the list $(1, 2, 3, 4, 5)$. It will be shown that the answer 4 emerges naturally from the application of resolution. The appropriate initial denial this time is

$$D1 : \quad \neg \, \textbf{consec}(3, z, 1.2.3.4.5.NIL)$$

which, for all z, denies that z is consecutive to 3 in $1.2.3.4.5.NIL$. Insofar as z occurs in D1, it is called a '*problem variable*'. D1 can be regarded as a query as to whether any instance of z exists which makes the predicate hold.

Using the same assumptions

$$S1 : \quad \textbf{consec}(u, v, u.v.x)$$
$$S2 : \quad \textbf{consec}(u, v, w.y) \leftarrow \textbf{consec}(u, v, y)$$

as before, we can generate the following refutation:

	Denial	Parents
D1 :	$\neg \, \textbf{consec}(3, z, 1.2.3.4.5.NIL)$	none
D2 :	$\neg \, \textbf{consec}(3, z, \quad 2.3.4.5.NIL)$	D1, S2
D3 :	$\neg \, \textbf{consec}(3, z, \quad\quad 3.4.5.NIL)$	D2, S2
D4 :	$\square$	D3, S1

This shows that the assumptions imply $\neg$D1. When written in full, D1 is the sentence

$$(\forall z) \, \neg \, \textbf{consec}(3, z, 1.2.3.4.5.NIL)$$

and is logically equivalent to

$$\neg \, (\exists z)\textbf{consec}(3, z, 1.2.3.4.5.NIL)$$

(Two sentences are *logically equivalent* when each implies the other.) Consequently the assumptions imply the negation of this, which is just

$$(\exists z)\textbf{consec}(3, z, 1.2.3.4.5.NIL)$$

and so establish the existence of some member z consecutive to 3 in the list $(1, 2, 3, 4, 5)$. In order to discover what this member is, it is necessary to inspect the derivation's *binding history*. This is the set of all those assignments generated by unification which contribute to the binding of terms to the problem variables. (When a term is assigned to a variable we say that it *binds* the variable or, equivalently, that the variable becomes *bound* to the term.) The (most general) unifiers entailed in the example are shown below against the denials which arise from them.

Denial	Unifier
D2	$\{u := 3, v := z, w := 1, y := 2.3.4.5.NIL\}$
D3	$\{u := 3, v := z, w := 2, y := 3.4.5.NIL\}$
D4	$\{u := 3, v := z, z := 4, x := 5.NIL\}$

The problem variable z in D1 remains unbound during the first inference step, because the first unifier assigns no term to it. The binding history therefore remains empty immediately after this step, and likewise immediately after the second step. The third step, however, entails a unifier which binds z to 4, so that the binding history is then $\{z := 4\}$. The latter is furthermore the *final* state of the binding history when the derivation terminates. Thus the refutation and the final state of the problem variable establish that the assumptions imply the answer

$$\textbf{consec}(3, z, 1.2.3.4.5.NIL) \qquad \text{where } z := 4,$$

that is,

$$\textbf{consec}(3, 4, 1.2.3.4.5.NIL)$$

The process of recovering the values of the problem variables from the binding history of a derivation is called *answer extraction*, and in a logic programming implementation is carried out automatically by the computer.

Performing unification and answer extraction by hand requires some care. In particular, the process of renaming variables in parent sentences in order to ensure that they have no common variables when resolved should be carried out as follows.

Before each step,

if   renaming is necessary
then   only rename variables in the parent assumption and do so such that its new variables are distinct from those in the parent denial and from all those referred to in the current binding history.

This rule protects against all possible muddles to do with the identities of variables.

Confusion can also arise in the circumstance in which the predicates to be unified each contain a variable in some common argument position. This was the case in the first step in the example, the predicates being

$$\textbf{consec}(3, z, 1.2.3.4.5.NIL)$$

and

$$\textbf{consec}(u, v, w.y)$$

The second argument of each predicate is a variable. The question arises whether z should be assigned to v, or v to z. Previously we took the former option, but the unifier for the first step might just as well have been $\{u := 3, z := v, w := 1, y := 2.3.4.5.NIL\}$, which assigns v to z. This is really the same unifier, and it does not matter in principle which form is used. In practice the latter one produces a less compact binding history and also makes some renaming of variables necessary; the derivation which this option produces is shown below, together with the binding history.

Denial		Parents
D1 :	$\neg\,\textbf{consec}(3, z, 1.2.3.4.5.NIL)$	none
D2 :	$\neg\,\textbf{consec}(3, v,\ \ \ 2.3.4.5.NIL)$	D1, S2
D3 :	$\neg\,\textbf{consec}(3, v'\ \ \ \ 3.4.5.NIL)$	D2, S2 with v renamed v'
D4 :	$\square$	D3, S1 with v renamed v''

Denial	Current binding history
D1	empty (z initially unbound)
D2	$\{z := v\}$
D3	$\{z := v, v := v'\}$
D4	$\{z := v, v := v', v' := v'', v'' := 4\}$

The value finally bound to z is still 4 as before, but is here expressed through a chain of variable-to-variable bindings accumulated in the binding history. As a general rule, whenever a decision must be made about how to treat a variable-to-variable binding, the simplest outcome is obtained by choosing the denial variable to be the assigned term. So in the example it is preferable to choose $v := z$ rather than $z := v$. This rule also has a much more profound justification in terms of run-time memory conservation in logic programming implementations, as discussed in Chapter VII.

With enough practice at performing top-down inference manually, it becomes instinctive to choose, at each step, such renamings and unifiers as are necessary in order to maintain a reasonably compact and intelligible binding history. This skill is comparable to that of streamlining the presentation of a lengthy mathematical proof by periodically transforming names and tidying up accumulated substitutions. Failure to perform this well may produce a less elegant derivation but does not invalidate the end result.

I.13. Summary

Programming in logic requires the programmer to have a clear understanding of the relations pertinent to the problem whose solution is sought. Moreover, he must be able to express that understanding by stating relevant logical properties of those relations in the simple language of assertions and implications. The problem itself can always be viewed as a query about the contents of the relations and is posed initially as a denial open to refutation.

Once the assumptions and the query have been formulated, they are submitted as input to a programmed resolution system implemented on the computer. The system attempts to answer the query by generating an appropriate refutation. If the query is answerable on the basis of the knowledge encoded by the input assumptions, then the answer is inevitably discoverable by the system.

Responsibility for the derivation's development and for the management of the binding history and answer extraction may be given entirely to the system or may be shared with the programmer, depending upon the particular implementation. Any solution computed has the desirable property of being logically implied by the given assumptions, and the entire computation is directly comprehensible as a process of rational and systematic reasoning. Very few existing programming formalisms possess these qualities.

I.14. Background

The foundations of symbolic logic were developed, somewhat unsystematically, by Boole, De Morgan and others in the last century. The modern, systematic formulation of first-order logic is owed primarily to Frege. The relationship between logic and mathematics was first investigated comprehensively in the celebrated work *Principia Mathematica* by Whitehead and Russell in 1910, who demonstrated the adequacy of logic for deriving much of mathematics. Excellent introductions to the history and foundations of modern logic are given in the books by De Long (1970), Hodges (1977) and Robinson (1979).

For a long time, the semantics or 'meaning' of logic remained a matter of much confusion, but eventually was largely clarified by Tarski; a lucid account of the modern view of logical proof and implication is given in his paper (Tarski, 1969). In particular, the precise concept of an interpretation as defined in Section I.7 played a crucial role in this clarification. When an interpretation satisfies a set of sentences it is called a *model* for that set, and the treatment of logic's semantics in terms of models is known is known as *model theory*. The importance of the *model-theoretic semantics* to logic programming is discussed in Chapter VIII.

The combination of a set of inference rules with a strategy for applying them yields an algorithm called a *proof procedure*, and can clearly be encoded as a computer program. The process of executing such a program in order to generate logical inferences from logic sentences supplied as data is called *automatic theorem proving*. The study of automatic theorem proving during the last three decades, which has been very considerable, reflects much earlier aspirations toward the systematization of mathematical proof. The earliest programmed proof procedures were therefore applied most notably to mathematical theorem proving and were motivated by the hope that computers would provide proofs of significant theorems whose proofs were too lengthy or too difficult to be undertaken by non-mechanical methods; computers could then be expected to accelerate the pace of mathematical discovery.

Apart from potentially contributing to the extension of mathematical knowledge, automatic theorem proving has also assumed importance in those aspects of artificial intelligence which deal with the manipulation of knowledge by logical inference. There it has been applied successfully to such tasks as question answering, game playing and state-space problem solving. Its success in these fields is due to the sufficient expressiveness of logic for representing knowledge and the power of logical inference for processing it.

The discovery of the resolution rule by Robinson (1965) represented a major advance in the practicality of automatic theorem proving and followed a long history of efforts by many researchers to devise systematic and efficient proof procedures for first-order logic. Resolution possesses the important properties of *soundness* and *completeness*. It is sound in the sense that if it derives $\square$ from assumptions S and denial D then $S \vDash \neg D$ necessarily holds. It is complete in the sense that if $S \vDash \neg D$ holds then $\square$ is necessarily derivable. The completeness and efficiency of various resolution systems are discussed in a paper by Kowalski and Kuehner (1971).

Despite the properties just mentioned, resolution is not unaffected by certain limitations on provability imposed by the nature of logic itself. A fundamental problem associated with a formal logical system is the 'validity problem'. A sentence in the system is *valid* if and only if it is satisfied by all interpretations over all domains; the validity problem is that of *deciding* whether or not any given sentence is valid. It affects logic programming in that the task of showing $S \vDash \neg D$ is equivalent to that of showing that the sentence $(\neg D \leftarrow S^*)$ is valid, where S^* is the conjunction (the result of connecting by 'and') of all the sentences in S. It was proved both by Church and by Turing in 1936 [see the book by Davis (1958) for a detailed account of these discoveries] that for first-order logic this problem is only *partially solvable*: no algorithm exists which is capable of deciding, for all possible choices of S and D, whether or not $S \vDash \neg D$ holds; but algorithms do fortunately exist which always demonstrate $S \vDash \neg D$ for the cases in which it does hold. These algorithms are called *partial decision procedures*. The significance of all this is that if we composed, inadvertently or otherwise, a logic program admitting no refutation (that is, an unsolvable program) and submitted it to a resolution-based partial decision procedure implemented on the computer, then the ensuing execution might never terminate in its futile attempt to derive $\square$. Such an inconclusive outcome is always necessarily possible with such a system and is a direct consequence of the Church–Turing result.

In practice non-termination sometimes arises anyway even when solvable programs are executed because, as is explained in Chapter V, a standard logic programming implementation uses a particular control strategy which causes the system not to exploit fully the completeness of resolution. Consequently a refutation which is derivable in principle may, depending upon the circumstances, never actually be generated, because execution first becomes trapped in some other non-terminating derivation. Non-termination is therefore as much an occupational hazard in logic programming as it is in conventional programming, though for not quite the same reasons.

Resolution is more general than the version of it presented earlier in the chapter. In fact it applies to all sentences known as *clauses*, which have the form

$$A_1 \vee \cdots \vee A_n \leftarrow B_1, \ldots, B_m$$

It can be shown that every set of sentences in first-order logic can be converted to a set of clauses having identical satisfiability properties. A simple conversion algorithm is given in the book by Nilsson (1971). The theory of resolution derives fundamentally from earlier studies by Herbrand (1930) of proof procedures for clausal-form logic. The book by Chang and Lee (1973) provides a clear introduction to the theory and applications of resolution.

Sentences consisting only of denials, assertions or implications form a subclass of clausal form and are called *Horn clauses*. The logic programming language is sometimes referred to as 'the Horn-clause subset of logic'. Horn clauses are practicable for virtually all problem-solving purposes. A discussion of their sufficiency from the viewpoint of computability theory is given in Chapter VIII.

The derivation of successive denials is just one way of using resolution to solve problems posed in Horn-clause logic, and is called *top-down resolution*. At present it is the most important mode of resolution used in logic programming. Another mode, which generates successive assertions instead, is called *bottom-up resolution*. Other modes can be prescribed which mix the former two in various ways. The top-down/bottom-up terminology describes the direction in which inference steps are pursued between assumptions and conclusions. Top-down inference begins with the intended conclusion of the problem, represented in negated form by the initial denial, and attempts to solve it by deriving a new intended conclusion (the next denial) and solving that in turn. This mode always pursues the particular problem first posed to it. Bottom-up inference proceeds in the opposite direction, generating new assertions by resolving old ones with implications. This mode is not inherently directed toward any particular intended conclusion and so tends to be much harder to control effectively. It can be viewed as 'assumption-directed' problem solving in contrast to the 'goal-directed' nature of the top-down mode. The first comprehensive investigation of general problem solving in clausal-form logic was made by Kowalski (1974a) and illustrates many different styles of both representation and reasoning. A fuller and more up-to-date account is provided by his book *Logic for Problem Solving* (1979a).

II LOGIC PROGRAMS

In the previous chapter the theoretical basis of logic programming was explained by using theorem-proving concepts and terminology. The operational features of logic programs, however, can be described in terms of computational notions already familiar in conventional programming languages. These features include data assignment, input and output, procedure calling, testing and branching, iteration and recursion. All of these, and some more exotic mechanisms, emanate directly and naturally from the resolution process previously described and so, happily, do not require the introduction of any further technicalities. The purpose of this chapter, then, is simply to identify the computational effects of applying resolution to logic programs and so give the reader some feeling of practical command over the formalism.

II.1. Programs, Computations and Executions

We begin by restating the general structure of logic programs and establishing some notational and terminological conventions. Precise ideas of 'computation' and 'execution' are also introduced, and these provide all the necessary basic ingredients for explaining the computational behaviour of programs.

II.1.1. Program Statements

A variety of notations are now in use for writing logic programs. Some of them reflect conventions in clausal-form theorem proving which predated logic programming. More modern ones are designed for the convenience of logic program interpreters or programmers or, ideally, both. We shall consider a few of these notations briefly before fixing the particular one used throughout the rest of this book.

The *signed literal notation*, now considered rather antiquated, recognises that a general clause like

$$\mathbf{P} \vee \mathbf{Q} \leftarrow \mathbf{R}, \mathbf{S}, \mathbf{T}$$

is logically equivalent to

$$\mathbf{P} \vee \mathbf{Q} \vee \neg \mathbf{R} \vee \neg \mathbf{S} \vee \neg \mathbf{T}$$

Predicates and negated predicates are also known as *positive literals* and *negative literals*, respectively, and therefore an alternative way of writing the above clause is

$$+\mathbf{P} + \mathbf{Q} - \mathbf{R} - \mathbf{S} - \mathbf{T}$$

Using this signed literal notation, a logic program such as

$$\neg (\mathbf{A}, \mathbf{B})$$
$$\mathbf{A} \leftarrow \mathbf{B}, \mathbf{C}$$
$$\mathbf{B}$$
$$\mathbf{C}$$

would be written

$$-\mathbf{A} - \mathbf{B}$$
$$+\mathbf{A} - \mathbf{B} - \mathbf{C}$$
$$+\mathbf{B}$$
$$+\mathbf{C}$$

This has a certain algebraic neatness but loses the intuitive flavour of denials, assertions and (especially) implications.

The more modern *arrow notation* uses ← in place of ¬ in a denial, and appends ← to each assertion. The program above would then be written as

$$\leftarrow \mathbf{A}, \mathbf{B}$$
$$\mathbf{A} \leftarrow \mathbf{B}, \mathbf{C}$$
$$\mathbf{B} \leftarrow$$
$$\mathbf{C} \leftarrow$$

All logic program sentences can then be viewed as having the form

$$\mathbf{P} \leftarrow \mathbf{Q}, \mathbf{R}, \ldots \text{etc.}$$

where the constituents on either side of the arrow may be either present or absent. Although this notation is very uniform and has proved quite popular, it does suffer a certain austerity.

For our purposes henceforth, a rather less severe notation will be used. The symbol ? is written instead of ¬ in a denial in order to emphasize that the denial is essentially a query. In an implication the connective **if** is written instead of ←. This notation is quite close to some of those used in existing implementations, and gives the example program the following appearance:

$$? \mathbf{A}, \mathbf{B}$$
$$\mathbf{A} \quad \text{if} \quad \mathbf{B}, \mathbf{C}$$
$$\mathbf{B}$$
$$\mathbf{C}$$

Some systems also use the symbol & to denote the 'and' connective, but it gives a rather cluttered appearance to long sentences; here we shall retain the comma instead.

In future all sentences making up a program will be called *statements*. The denial will be called the *goal*. So when a program contains a goal such as

$$? \mathbf{A}(x), \mathbf{B}(y)$$

we say that the goal (or purpose) of the program is to answer the query 'for which instances (values) of x and y do $\mathbf{A}(x)$ **and** $\mathbf{B}(y)$ hold?'

Implications and assertions will in future both be called *procedures*. Each one is said to be a procedure 'for' the particular predicate symbol with which it begins. For example, the statement

$$\mathbf{A}(x) \quad \text{if} \quad \mathbf{B}(x), \mathbf{C}(x)$$

is a procedure for **A**.

II.1.2. Program Structure and Purpose

The structure of a standard logic program is

program = goal and any number of procedures

No limitations are imposed upon either the number or the length of statements.

The order in which procedures appear in a program has no logical significance, since each one states some fact about the problem independently of the others. It is usual, though, to collect procedures for the same predicate symbol into a group, which is then called a *procedure set* for that symbol, as in the example

$$\mathbf{A}(x) \quad \text{if} \quad \mathbf{B}(x), \mathbf{C}(x)$$
$$\mathbf{A}(x) \quad \text{if} \quad \mathbf{C}(y), \mathbf{D}(x, y)$$
$$\mathbf{B}(x) \quad \text{if} \quad \mathbf{D}(x, x)$$
$$\mathbf{B}(x) \quad \text{if} \quad \mathbf{C}(x)$$
$$\vdots$$

etc.

This has at least two procedure sets, one for **A** and one for **B**. (Some people prefer to apply the word 'procedure' to what we have called a procedure set; they then refer to the separate sentences within it as 'clauses'. In earlier times procedure sets were sometimes called 'partitions'.) In later sections it will be seen that the order in which procedures appear within their procedure set *does* matter purely on the grounds of computational efficiency. Likewise the ordering of the predicates in both goals and procedures influences efficiency but has no logical significance.

In order to discuss examples of programs it is useful sometimes to label their statements for the sake of easy reference in the text. These labels are arbitrary and are separated from the statements by colons. They are *not* constituents of the statements themselves; that is, they are not features of the logic programming language.

Here is the consecutivity program considered in the previous chapter, now written in our new notation:

> goal   G1 :   ? **consec**$(3, z, 1.2.3.4.5.NIL)$
> procedures C1 :   **consec**$(u, v, u.v.x)$
>   C2 :   **consec**$(u, v, w.y)$ **if** **consec**(u, v, y)

It has one procedure set for **consec**, and the two procedures in it have been labeled C1 and C2. The initial goal bears the label G1. The problem variable z in G1 is now referred to as a *goal variable*.

The purpose of the program is to *solve* the goal G1 using only the procedures C1 and C2. In problem-oriented terms, solving the goal consists of computing some value t (which will be a term of some kind) for the goal variable z such that t is the member consecutive to 3 in the list $(1, 2, 3, 4, 5)$. In relational terms, it consists of finding an instance t of z which makes the triplet $(3, t, 1.2.3.4.5.NIL)$ belong to the 3-place relation named **consec**. In logical terms, it consists of finding an instance t of z which makes the sentence

$$\mathbf{consec}(3, t, 1.2.3.4.5.NIL)$$

logically implied by the procedures.

II.1.3. Program Execution

Logic programs are executed by submitting them as input to a *logic interpreter*. The interpreter is a program capable of performing resolution inference, usually in the top-down mode. Upon receiving a source logic program, it undertakes the usual steps necessary to interpretive program execution: thus it checks the syntax of the source statements; stores them in central memory in a suitably simplified, compacted and accessible form; sets up an internal representation of the initial goal and then begins the process of developing a derivation by repeatedly resolving the current goal with some parent procedure selected from the stored version of the source program. If it manages to derive $\square$, signifying solution, then it outputs some sort of affirmation together with the values of the goal variables. The printout from the consecutivity program would appear much as follows:

SOLUTION FOUND :
GOAL VARIABLE BINDINGS : $Z := 4$

Some implementations exist which are more like compilers than interpreters. They conduct a pre-execution analysis of the procedures in order to generate machine-code modules incorporating the specific unification steps entailed in their resolution with the goal. These modules are link loaded with a comparatively simple manager module, and the resulting complete object program executes much faster than a true interpreter.

II.1.4. Computations

Rather than using the term 'derivation', we shall henceforth use 'computation' instead. More precisely, a (top-down) *computation* is any derivation beginning with the initial goal which can be generated, by means of (top-down) resolution, from the given program. So a computation is just a sequence of goals each of which, other than the initial one, is generated by resolving the preceding goal with one of the procedures. One possible computation from the consecutivity program is therefore (G1, G2, G3) as follows:

G1 :   ? **consec**$(3, z, 1.2.3.4.5.NIL)$
G2 :   ? **consec**$(3, z, \quad 2.3.4.5.NIL)$
G3 :   ? **consec**$(3, z, \quad 3.4.5.NIL)$

Computations can be variously classified as finite or infinite, successful or unsuccessful and terminated or unterminated. These classifications will be met with later in the chapter. For the moment, it suffices to point out that, in general, a single program can offer numerous distinct computations. In the course of execution, the interpreter attempts to explore *all* of them unless directed otherwise. So if the program has several solutions, that is, admits several computations terminating with $\square$, then the interpreter will not only seek them all but will also seek each one in all possible ways. This means that the interpreter, like any other program executing a *searching* algorithm, must maintain a detailed history of what it has discovered so far and what opportunities still remain open. One of the nicest features of logic programming, distinguishing it from almost all other programming formalisms, is that this burden of managing search processes can be placed wholly upon the interpreter.

II.2. The Procedural Interpretation

The procedural interpretation gives an operational character to logic programs. It consists essentially of viewing goals as sets of procedure calls, each one of which is processed by calling an appropriate procedure. In this respect it is very similar to the procedural semantics of many conventional programming languages. In particular, it contributes to an algorithmic view of logic program execution, complementing the inferential view. The conception of the procedural interpretation was perhaps the most important advance in computational logic which gave credibility to logic as a programming language.

II.2.1. Goal Structure

The procedural interpretation regards a goal

$$? \, A_1, A_2, \ldots \text{etc.}$$

as a collection of *procedure calls* A_1, A_2, ... etc. Each of these calls quotes the *name* of a procedure, which is just the predicate symbol. The predicate's arguments are said to be the *actual parameters* of the call. Thus the goal

$$? \, consec(3, z, 1.2.3.4.5.NIL)$$

contains just one call, which refers to a procedure named **consec** and has three actual parameters *3*, *z* and *1.2.3.4.5.NIL*. A call represents some subproblem waiting to be solved. (Calls are thus sometimes referred to as 'subgoals'.) The reason for describing it as a 'call' is that, when processed during execution, it will call up some procedure having the name quoted which will perform some computational work upon the actual parameters.

II.2.2. Procedure Structure

A procedure represents some *way* of solving a subproblem. For example, the procedure

$$consec(u, v, w.y) \quad \textbf{if} \quad consec(u, v, y)$$

can be read as follows: a subproblem of the form **consec**$(u, v, w.y)$ can be solved by solving the subproblem **consec**(u, v, y). More specifically, it represents some way of solving a call. Thus a call like **consec**$(3, 4, 1.2.3.4.5.NIL)$ can be solved by using the procedure above, provided that the subproblem **consec**$(3, 4, 2.3.4.5.NIL)$ can in turn be solved.

The interaction of goals, calls and procedures will become much clearer in later sections. Meanwhile there is some more terminology to present.

The predicate appearing on the left of **if** in a procedure is referred to as the *procedure heading*. This provides the *name* of the procedure, which is the predicate symbol. The predicate's arguments are said to be the procedure's *formal parameters*. The procedure above, named **consec**, therefore has three such parameters u, v and *w.y*.

The predicates appearing on the right of **if** are referred to as *calls* and jointly constitute the *body* of the procedure. These calls represent the subproblems which would all have to be solved in order for the procedure to solve whatever call had invoked it. In the example the body contains just one such call.

II.2.3. The Procedure-Calling Operation

Each resolution step performed in the course of generating a computation can be viewed as a *procedure-calling* operation. It consists of selecting any call from the current goal, selecting a procedure whose name matches that of the call, unifying the actual and formal parameters (if this is possible), replacing the call by the procedure's body and finally applying the unifier to the result. This produces the next goal. We say that the call has been *activated* and that the procedure has been *invoked*.

Consider an example where the statements have the form

$$\text{goal} \qquad \text{G1} : \quad ? \underline{\textbf{A}}, \textbf{B}$$
$$\text{procedure P1} : \qquad \textbf{A} \quad \textbf{if} \quad \textbf{C}, \textbf{D}$$

and suppose that the underlined call **A** in the goal is the one selected. Suppose further that P1 is the invoked procedure whose heading **A** unifies with the selected call and that the unifier is some Θ. Then the procedure-calling operation generates the next goal

$$\text{G2} : \quad ? \textbf{C}\Theta, \textbf{D}\Theta, \textbf{B}\Theta$$

The step can be understood as follows. Once Θ has been determined, the goal G1 is effectively specialized to an intermediary

$$\text{G1}' : \quad ? \textbf{A}\Theta, \textbf{B}\Theta$$

Note that any solutions of **A**Θ and **B**Θ are solutions of the more general subproblems **A** and **B**. For instance, if the full form of the call **A** is $\textbf{A}(x)$, and Θ is $\{x := f(y)\}$ then **A**Θ is $\textbf{A}(f(y))$; if the latter is solved, perhaps by eventually assigning some term t to y, then the more general call $\textbf{A}(x)$ is thereby solved with the answer $x := f(t)$. Determination of Θ likewise effectively specializes procedure P1 to the form

$$\text{P1'} : \quad \textbf{A}\Theta \quad \text{if} \quad \textbf{C}\Theta, \textbf{D}\Theta$$

which states that the subproblem $\textbf{A}\Theta$ can be solved by solving both $\textbf{C}\Theta$ and $\textbf{D}\Theta$. Therefore G1' can clearly be solved by solving

$$\text{G2} : \quad ?\,\textbf{C}\Theta, \textbf{D}\Theta, \textbf{B}\Theta$$

The process of replacing a call by a procedure body, with such modifications as are necessary to make the actual and formal parameters correspond, is very similar to the way in which the semantics of procedure calling is defined for conventional ALGOL-like languages. The only difference is in the criterion for parameter correspondence; in logic the requirement is that the parameters be structurally matched (unified) whereas other languages impose different criteria. Because of the unifiability requirement, a logic procedure may not be invokable by a call even though it has the correct name. If it is invokable—that is, its heading unifies with the call—then it is said to *respond* to the call.

Recall that unification can also contribute to the computation's binding history (the accumulating goal variable assignments that have to be kept on one side for eventual answer extraction). Suppose the statements written in full are

$$\text{G1} : \quad ?\,\underline{\textbf{A}(x)}, \textbf{B}(z)$$

$$\text{P1} : \quad \textbf{A}(f(y)) \quad \text{if} \quad \textbf{C}(y), \textbf{D}(y)$$

Then the step produces the next goal

$$\text{G2} : \quad ?\,\textbf{C}(y), \textbf{D}(y), \textbf{B}(z)$$

and the unifier $\Theta = \{x := f(y)\}$ contributes the assignment $x := f(y)$ to the binding history, from whence it can be retrieved later for the purpose of extracting the answer finally computed for x. Thus the full general effect of procedure calling can be summarized as

Current goal		Next goal
+	*produces*	+
Procedure		Contribution to binding history

II.2.4. Procedure Entry and Exit

Since every step in a computation entails invoking some procedure and thereby introduces (in general) fresh calls into the goal (from the procedure's body), execution can be regarded as a process of repeated procedure entry and exit. *Procedure entry* occurs at the moment when the procedure's body replaces the invoking call. *Procedure exit* occurs at the moment when all the calls in that body have been solved. (Strictly this describes *successful* exit; the notion of failure exit will be met with later on.)

When a procedure is entered, the calls in its body, if any, are described as the *immediate descendants* of the invoking call. This invoking call becomes *immediately solved* if the step yields no immediate descendants; this occurs whenever the invoked procedure is simply an assertion (having an empty body). More generally, a call becomes *solved* when either (i) it becomes immediately solved or (ii) all of its immediate descendants become solved.

These concepts can be made clear by using the following example. The program is shown with parameters omitted in order to simplify the presentation.

$$
\begin{array}{lll}
\text{goal} & \text{G1}: & ?\,\mathbf{A}, \mathbf{B} \\
\text{procedures P1}: & & \mathbf{A} \quad \text{if} \quad \mathbf{C}, \mathbf{D} \\
\text{P2}: & & \mathbf{C} \quad \text{if} \quad \mathbf{F}, \mathbf{G} \\
\text{P3}: & & \mathbf{F} \\
\text{P4}: & & \mathbf{G} \\
\text{P5}: & & \mathbf{D} \\
\text{P6}: & & \mathbf{B}
\end{array}
$$

Execution would then generate the following computation.

$$
\begin{array}{lll}
& \text{G1}: & ?\,\mathbf{A}, \mathbf{B} \\
\text{enter P1} \ldots & \text{G2}: & ?\,\mathbf{C}, \mathbf{D}, \mathbf{B} \quad \ldots \text{call } \mathbf{A} \text{ activated} \\
& \text{G3}: & ?\,\mathbf{F}, \mathbf{G}, \mathbf{D}, \mathbf{B} \\
& \text{G4}: & ?\,\mathbf{G}, \mathbf{D}, \mathbf{B} \\
& \text{G5}: & ?\,\mathbf{D}, \mathbf{B} \\
\text{exit P1} \ldots & \text{G6}: & ?\,\mathbf{B} \qquad\quad \ldots \text{call } \mathbf{A} \text{ now solved} \\
& \text{G7}: & ? \quad (\text{signifying } \square)
\end{array}
$$

Here procedure P1 is entered when G2 is derived from G1. It provides **C** and **D** as the immediate descendants of the invoking call **A**. When G4 is derived, **F** becomes immediately solved; likewise, **G** becomes immediately solved when G5 is derived, and so at this point **C** becomes solved because **F** and **G** are its immediate descendants. When G6 is derived, the immediate solution of **D** and the earlier solution of **C** cause **A** to become solved, and so procedure P1 is exited at this point. In between entering and exiting P1, execution has also entered and exited P2, P3, P4 and P5 at various moments. Finally, when G7 is derived, **B** is immediately solved; since **A** has already been solved it follows that the initial goal G1 has been completely solved and the computation terminates successfully with the empty goal G7. The emptiness of G7 means that no more calls remain to be solved on behalf of their ancestors.

II.2.5. Call Selection

As a computation develops, the current goal may vary in length depending upon how many calls are introduced by procedure invocation. When several calls exist in the current goal any one of them may be activated in the next step. Deciding which call to activate is called *call selection*; it is one of the aspects of logic program execution which involve making a *choice*.

The effect of this choice can be seen by considering the following program, which asks whether the list $(1, 2, 3)$ is ordered:

$$
\begin{array}{lll}
\text{G1} : & ?\,\textbf{ord}(1.2.3.NIL) \\
\text{ord1} : & \textbf{ord}(NIL) \\
\text{ord2} : & \textbf{ord}(u.NIL) \\
\text{ord3} : & \textbf{ord}(u.v.y) & \textbf{if}\quad u < v, \textbf{ord}(v.y) \\
\text{less1} : & 1 < 2 \\
\text{less2} : & 2 < 3 \\
\end{array}
$$

Now suppose that execution is governed by the rule that in each step the first call is the one activated. In this case the following computation is produced, where activated calls have been underlined.

$$
\begin{array}{lll}
\text{G1} : & ?\,\underline{\textbf{ord}(1.2.3.NIL)} \\
\text{G2} : & ?\,\underline{1 < 2},\ \textbf{ord}(2.3.NIL) & \text{by invoking ord3} \\
\text{G3} : & ?\,\underline{\textbf{ord}(2.3.NIL)} & \text{by invoking less1} \\
\text{G4} : & ?\,\underline{2 < 3},\ \textbf{ord}(3.NIL) & \text{by invoking ord3} \\
\text{G5} : & ?\,\underline{\textbf{ord}(3.NIL)} & \text{by invoking less2} \\
\text{G6} : & ? & \text{by invoking ord2} \\
\end{array}
$$

In effect this rule dictates that the tests for orderedness of consecutive pairs are performed as soon as they appear in the current goal.

II.2.6. Procedure Selection

Another important kind of choice arising at each step during execution concerns which procedure to invoke. In the ordered-list program just examined this sort of choice does not occur, because in each step only one procedure responds to whatever call is activated. By contrast, consider the problem of discovering which member z consecutively follows 2 in the list $(1, 2, 3, 2, 4)$, as formulated by the program

$$
\begin{array}{lll}
\text{G1} : & ?\,\textbf{consec}(2, z, 1.2.3.2.4.NIL) \\
\text{C1} : & \textbf{consec}(u, v, u.v.x) \\
\text{C2} : & \textbf{consec}(u, v, w.y) & \textbf{if}\quad \textbf{consec}(u, v, y) \\
\end{array}
$$

Execution must first invoke C2 to bring the computation to the point

$$\text{G2} : \quad ?\,\textbf{consec}(2, z, \, 2.3.2.4.NIL)$$

but here a choice arises between C1 and C2 for the next invoked procedure, since they both respond. If C1 is selected, then the computation terminates successfully with

$$\text{G3} : \quad ? \qquad \text{and extracted answer } \underline{z := 3}$$

If C2 is selected instead then a different computation is obtained, namely

$$
\begin{aligned}
&\text{G3}' : \quad ?\,\textbf{consec}(2, z, \, 3.2.4.NIL) \\
&\text{G4} : \quad ?\,\textbf{consec}(2, z, \quad 2.4.NIL) \\
&\text{G5} : \quad ? \qquad \text{and extracted answer } \underline{z := 4}
\end{aligned}
$$

Note that G5 was derived by selecting C1. If C2 had been selected instead (it also responds) then the ensuing computation would not have been successful.

This example shows that procedure selection, like call selection, influences the development of computations, and may also generate various answers for the goal variables. This important multiple-computation feature of logic program execution is discussed in greater detail in the next section.

II.3. The Computation Space

It should now be clear to the reader that the execution of a logic program does not necessarily follow just one computational path. The existence of choices at various steps means that several computations may be generated, with potentially differing results. The various kinds of computations and the conditions governing their run-time generation are now examined in turn.

II.3.1. Classifying Computations

Any computation which terminates with the empty goal (denoted by either ? or □) is called *successful* and yields a solution to the initial goal.

If a computation's final goal is such that no procedures respond to the particular call selected for activation from that goal, then it is described as *unsuccessful* and yields no solution. For the sake of clear representation it is customary to append to such a computation the special symbol ∎ to denote *failure*.

Computations which end with either □ or ∎ are described as *terminated*. Computations which end with a goal from which at least one further goal can be derived are described as *unterminated*; these are computations which execution has not yet extended to one of the *conclusions* □ or ■.

All the above are examples of *finite* computations, and are the kinds with which programmers usually wish to deal. However, some programs give rise to *infinite computations* which yield no conclusions.

II.3.2. Total Computation Space

For any given program, the *total computation space* is the set of all computations derivable from it using the standard procedure-calling operation, and encompasses all possible ways of selecting calls and procedures. It can be viewed as the total range of distinct ways in which execution could seek a solution to the program; some of those ways might be successful, some unsuccessful and some infinitely inconclusive. Some may be efficient, some inefficient. Whatever the scale and structure of the space may be, it is determined wholly by the program and the assumption of top-down resolution; the extent to which the space is explored at run time is determined by other factors, in particular the so-called *selection rules*, which are described next.

II.3.3. Effect of Selection Rules

In the *standard mode* of execution, the call selected for activation is always the one which appears first (leftmost) in the current goal. This rule, built into the interpreter, has the effect of confining execution to a selection of computations, called the selected *subspace*, within the total space. Furthermore, all solutions to the program, if any, are computable in this subspace: all successful computations elsewhere in the total space merely yield the same set of solutions but via different paths, so that their excision from the execution process is inconsequential.

These features are illustrated by Fig. II.1, which deals with the ordered-list problem discussed in Section II.2.5. The total computation space can be depicted by a *computation tree* whose root node is the initial goal and whose paths from that node represent the various computations. In the figure lists are shown without their *NIL*s for simplicity's sake. Altogether there are eight terminated computations, all of which are successful; they correspond to the eight distinct ways of solving the problem when call selection is unconstrained. The leftmost path, emphasized by heavy links, depicts the sole computation in the subspace determined by the standard call selection rule. It processes the calls **ord**(*1.2.3.NIL*), *1 < 2*, **ord**(*2.3.NIL*), *2 < 3* and **ord**(*3.NIL*) in that order. The other computations merely process various permutations of this sequence of calls and correspond to different selection

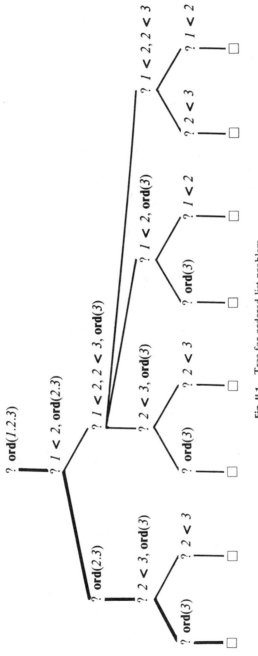

Fig. II.1. Tree for ordered-list problem.

rules. For instance, a rule which always selected the last (rightmost) call in the current goal would confine execution to the subspace depicted by the tree's rightmost path.

In general the selected subspace can contain several computations reflecting alternative choices of responding procedure. (This possibility does not arise in the ordered-list problem because in each step only one procedure responds.) Therefore, once a selection rule has been imposed for activating calls, any *branching* (where paths divide) which remains in the *subtree* depicting the selected subspace is wholly attributable to the existence of choices between responding procedures. Figure II.2 illustrates this for the problem of finding which member z consecutively follows 2 in the list $(1, 2, 3, 2, 4)$, using the program given earlier in Section II.2.6. Here the total tree and the subtree determined by the standard call selection rule happen to be identical, because in each goal there is only one call. In this figure each branch point corresponds to a choice arising between procedures C1 and C2. Observe also that the subtree contains an unsuccessful computation which arises when C2 is always chosen in preference to C1.

If the goal of the consecutivity program had been

$$? \, \mathbf{consec}(4, z, \, 1.2.3.2.4.NIL)$$

then the subtree would show just one computation and this would terminate

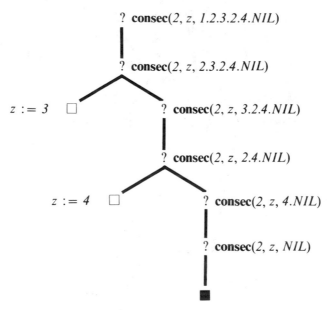

Fig. II.2. Tree for consecutivity program.

unsuccessfully, since the problem has no solution. A program is said to be *unsolvable* when its subspace contains no successful computations; otherwise it is called *solvable*. Note that unsolvability does not arise only when all computations terminate with ■; it arises when all computations are either terminated by ■ or are infinite.

An example of an infinite computation is provided by another consecutivity problem, using the same procedures as before but choosing a different goal:

$$\text{G1}: \quad ?\,\mathbf{consec}(1, 2, z)$$
$$\text{C1}: \quad \mathbf{consec}(u, v, u.v.x)$$
$$\text{C2}: \quad \mathbf{consec}(u, v, w.y) \quad \mathbf{if} \quad \mathbf{consec}(u, v, y)$$

This program seeks lists in which 1 and 2 are consecutive members. Figure II.3. shows the subtree and the assignments made to goal variables.

Once again, branch points occur when both C1 and C2 respond to a call. The paths which branch to the left all terminate successfully to yield various answers

$$z := 1.2.x$$
$$z := w.1.2.x$$
$$z := w.w_2.1.2.x$$
$$z := w.w_2.w_3.1.2.x$$
$$\text{etc.}$$

Each answer is only *partially evaluated* in that it contains variables remaining unbound and which may be assigned arbitrary values. The variables w_2, y_2, w_3, y_3 arise from renaming parent procedure variables in order to meet the requirements of the standard procedure-calling operation. Observe that the

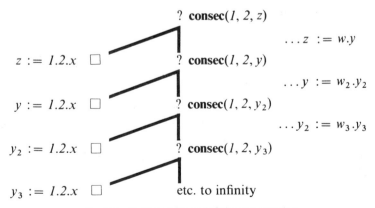

Fig. II.3. Subtree with an infinite computation.

main path in the subtree is infinitely long and is the one pursued when C2 is always invoked in preference to C1.

Assuming that the interpreter is committed to exploring the entire subspace, it will clearly engage in a *non-terminating execution*, because the scope for exploration is here unlimited. Non-terminating execution can sometimes arise even when all computations in the subspace are finite, because certain programs yield subspaces having an infinite *number* of such computations. This condition arises when the interpreter invokes some built-in procedure set (explained in Section II.6) which offers an infinitude of distinct responses to a call, thus introducing an infinitely branched node into the subtree.

II.4. The Standard Control Strategy

Logic program execution is governed primarily by control mechanisms built into the interpreter. The programmer has command over broad details such as the order in which computations are developed, but finer details such as the management of the binding history can be left to the interpreter to sort out.

Our earlier examples have shown that a logic program can yield a variety of computations. This feature is one aspect of the *non-determinism* of logic programs. It also presents the interpreter with the necessity of performing *search* in order not to omit any solutions. In what follows we examine the standard strategy used for controlling search and explain the programmer's influence over it.

II.4.1. Non-Determinism and Search

In its most general sense, non-determinism refers to the absence of factors determining the precise course of execution. Logic is therefore a non-deterministic programming language in that its statements say nothing about this.

An individual program is *non-deterministic* when it admits more than one computation, that is, has a branched computation tree. Such branching has two contributing causes: the existence in goals of several calls capable of activation, and the existence of several procedures capable of responding to particular calls. The former contribution is eliminated by the imposition of a strict order of selection for calls, such as the rule which always chooses the first call in the goal. A rule of this kind 'prunes' redundant paths from the total computation tree, leaving a subtree which still contains all solutions to the program. The other contribution is then manifested by any branching that remains in this subtree, and it is this which poses the need for *search*. Thus we shall henceforth refer to this subtree as the program's *search tree* for the given call selection rule. The search tree does not, of course, exist concretely prior to execution—when we talk of the interpreter *searching* a search tree we really mean that it *constructs* it.

II.4.2. The Computation Rule

A call selection rule is more commonly called a *computation rule*: it fixes the set of computations to be elicited during program execution. The relative rates at which the computations are constructed by the interpreter jointly determine the dynamic shape of the 'search frontier' as it progresses through the search tree. Computations can be developed one at a time (as we shall see presently, this is the usual mode), or in parallel or in some arbitrary mix of these two extremes.

The *standard computation rule* always selects, in each step, the first call in the goal, it being understood that when this call becomes replaced by the invoked procedure body the textual order of the latter's calls is not altered. The resulting search tree is then typically searched *depth first*. That is, the interpreter begins at the root node and then constructs a downward path from it ever deeper through the search tree, developing this particular computation indefinitely unless reaching a terminal node (□ or ■). No other computations are developed unless and until this one has been concluded.

If □ is reached then an answer can be extracted and reported to an output device. If ■ is reached instead, then no report of the failure would normally be announced. Whichever is the case, there may then remain other paths so far unconstructed, branching off from various branch nodes higher in the search tree. When this is so, the interpreter *backtracks* upward through the path just developed seeking the most recent branch node from which some unexplored path still emanates. If none exists then the entire search tree has been constructed and so execution terminates. Otherwise the first alternative new path encountered during backtracking is pursued downward, again using the depth-first principle. In this way a finite search tree will eventually be traversed completely and all solutions found to the program. Figure II.4. shows a depth-first search through the search tree given earlier in Fig. II.2. The arrows indicate the direction of search; those directed upward indicate backtracking.

Knowing the computation rule built into the interpreter, the programmer can decide upon the textual ordering of the calls in his program with due

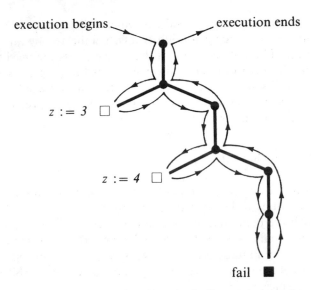

Fig. II.4.   Depth-first backtracking search of a complete search tree.

regard for execution efficiency. He can choose an ordering whose corresponding subspace may contain, in comparison with the total space, fewer failure nodes, or fewer infinite computations, or fewer ways of finding identical solutions, or shorter computations. Quite a lot of experience with one's implementation is necessary in order to assess the precise benefit of choosing a particular ordering. For instance, it is possible that a subspace having just one computation might take longer to explore than another subspace for the same program having many computations of comparable length, because the interpreter might take longer in the former case to realize that there was just one computation than it would take in the latter case to process a more easily bounded set of them. This is in turn due to the fact that the opportunities for exploration are perceived by the interpreter in terms of the number of potentially responding procedures to each call, and the efficiency of determining this is dependent upon the implementation's method of storing, indexing and accessing procedures.

II.4.3. The Search Rule

The depth-first search principle applied to a given search tree does not in itself determine the order in which computations are developed. This is governed instead by the order in which responding procedures are selected. Any rule determining this is known as a *search rule*, because it controls the direction of search taken by the interpreter at each branch point in the search tree. The *standard search rule* chooses responding procedures in the order of appearance in the program text.

Consider the effect of the standard search rule upon the consecutivity program's search tree in Fig. II.4, and suppose that the two procedures appear in the order

$$C1 : \quad \textbf{consec}(u, v, u.v.x)$$
$$C2 : \quad \textbf{consec}(u, v, w.y) \quad \textbf{if} \quad \textbf{consec}(u, v, y)$$

When the interpreter reaches the first branch point it invokes C1 and so produces the solution $z := 3$. It next backtracks to the branch point and remembers that C2, which also responded, has not yet been tried. So C2 is tried next and this path soon leads to another branch point, at which the same order of selection is applied. When the failure node is eventually encountered, backtracking reveals no branch point with unexplored paths, and so the locus of control climbs right back to the root node and execution terminates.

If the textual order of C1 and C2 were reversed, the search tree would, of course, remain unaltered (being determined only by the computation rule). However, the search would proceed in exactly the opposite direction to that shown in Fig. II.4, first encountering the failure node, then the solution $z := 4$ and finally the solution $z := 3$.

In general, the ordering of procedures has little effect upon efficiency provided that the intention is to search the entire search tree. Yet sometimes the programmer is interested in only some part of the search tree. For example, he might only require any one solution rather than all possible solutions. Most implementations therefore provide various additional control devices enabling the programmer to curtail or otherwise modify the search process. It is sometimes easier to write a program which admits many paths and curtail some of them by using control directives than it would be to write a more restrictive program admitting only the paths of interest. This sort of judgement is one of many affecting *programming style*.

The most well-known control directive is the so-called *cut operator*. This is just the symbol / and is written in the program as though it were just another call. When activated it immediately excises all unexplored paths emanating from all branch points encountered since, and possibly including, entry into the particular procedure whose invocation brought this cut into the goal. Thus if C1 and C2 were presented in that order in the program text, but with C1 modified as

$$C1 : \quad \textbf{consec}(u, v, u.v.x) \quad \textbf{if} \quad /$$

then execution would terminate as soon as it discovered the solution $z := 3$, because the activation of / would excise the remaining choice of C2 at the first branch point, thus pruning away the entire unexplored remainder of the search tree.

The cut operator is often quoted as being indispensable to practical logic programming. Undoubtedly useful as it is, however, it does encourage lazy programming style: rather than thinking carefully about how to describe the relation really desired, one can be tempted into writing a possibly much easier description of a super-relation of it and then sprinkling the text with cuts in order to eliminate unwanted tuples. Such undisciplined usage may impair analysis and comprehension of programs.

II.4.4. The Standard Strategy

The *standard strategy* controlling the interpreter's search process consists simply of the standard computation rule combined with the standard search rule. This means that the programmer's chief way of exercising control over execution is in deciding the textual ordering of procedures and calls. Interpreters controlled by the standard strategy are sometimes called 'left-to-right depth-first backtrackers' because that title describes their trajectory through the search tree when the latter is drawn such that the left-to-right order of exits from a branch point corresponds to the first-to-last textual order of the procedures responding at that point.

The cut operator augments the standard strategy as a tool for pruning away unwanted computations, and this is partly why interpreters may not fully exploit the completeness of resolution. Another reason is that the depth-first search principle may cause execution to enter an infinite computation and thence never emerge to deal with the rest of the search tree. Some implementations incorporate 'loop checkers' which attempt to recognise infinite computations, whilst cruder systems may simply impose some arbitrary bound upon the allowable length of a computation. In either case, execution can be liberated from the current path by artificially enforcing backtracking from the offending node, although completeness would then be sacrificed if the abandoned path did happen to terminate successfully.

In many cases, programmers are dealing with problems which only require the pursuit of one computational path, and so need not consider the question of control too closely. On other occasions there may be several answers $a_1, a_2, \ldots$ etc. to find. One can then write a non-deterministic program, each successful computation yielding one answer (as in the consecutivity program). In this event the programmer can either exercise tight control over the course of execution, using the devices of textual ordering and the cut operator, or not worry about it at all, in which case the worst penalty possible is non-termination and the next worse inefficiency. Another possibility is to compose a deterministic program which computes a single answer consisting of a term combining a_1, a_2, ... etc. Whichever option is taken, it should ideally aim to maximize the program's logical simplicity and clarity, and the programmer's productivity, subject to the outcome remaining implementable at an acceptable cost.

II.5. Computational Behaviour

When equipped with an interpreter governed by the standard control strategy, the programmer can evoke many important kinds of computational behaviour simply by choosing appropriate logical structures for his input programs. This section examines the ways in which logic programs behave when executed, comparing them with familiar algorithmic mechanisms.

II.5.1. Data Processing

Most programs are intended for data processing. So it is useful to decide what data processing means in logic programming.

Consider the standard procedure-calling operation. In general, the call will contain some variables, say x_1, x_2, ... etc., and likewise the heading of the invoked procedure may contain some variables, say y_1, y_2, ... etc. It does not matter for present purposes whether these variables are themselves parameters or just occur within parameters.

When the procedure is invoked, the associated *data assignment* (unifier) assigns various terms to some or all of the x_i and y_i variables. We interpret each such term as a *data item*, noting that it is generated by parameter matching. Data items assigned to y_i variables are called *input data* since they are input to the procedure from the call. Those assigned to x_i variables are called *output data* since they are output from the procedure to the call. These notions of input and output are therefore defined in terms of the direction of data flow relative to the procedure.

As an example, consider the step which invokes C2 in response to the first call in goal G1 below:

G1 :   ? **consec**(*2, z, 1.2.3.2.4.NIL*), **consec**(*z, 2, 1.2.3.2.4.NIL*)
C2 :   **consec**(*u, v, w.y*) **if**   **consec**(*u, v, y*)

Relaxing, for demonstration's sake, the customary rule about variable-to-variable bindings, suppose that the data assignment used here is $\{u := 2,$ $z := v, w := 1, y := 2.3.2.4.NIL\}$. The terms *2, 1* and *2.3.2.4.NIL* are the data items which are input to the procedure's y_i variables u, w and y; the term v is the data item which is output to the call's x_i variable z.

Another useful idea is that of *data distribution*. When the procedure is invoked, any input data assigned to a y_i variable is *distributed* to (that is, substituted for) all occurrences of that variable in the procedure body. Simultaneously any output data assigned to an x_i variable is distributed to all the latent calls in the goal. (*Latent calls* are calls still awaiting activation: under the standard computation rule they are all the calls in the current goal after the first one.) After performing these two distributions, the next goal G2 is obtained by replacing the first call in G1 by the distributed body of C2, as shown in Fig. II.5.

Data distribution is just another way of viewing the application of the unifier after replacing the call. From the point of view of the current goal the step feeds data from the procedure via the activated call to the latent calls.

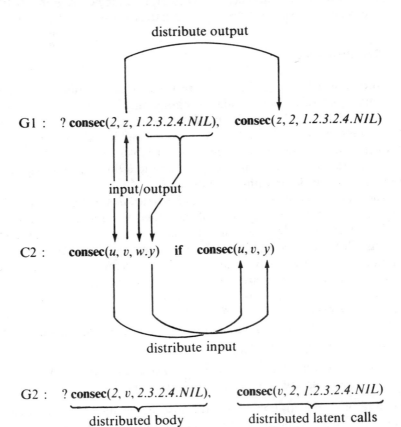

Fig. II.5. Data assignments and distributions in a procedure-calling operation.

This can be made more apparent by pursuing the computation a few steps, assuming that the usual consecutivity procedures C1 and C2 are being used.

G1 :   ? consec$(2, z, 1.2.3.2.4.NIL)$, consec$(z, 2, 1.2.3.2.4.NIL)$
G2 :   ? consec$(2, v,$ $2.3.2.4.NIL)$, consec$(v, 2, 1.2.3.2.4.NIL)$
G3 :   ?   consec$(3, 2, 1.2.3.2.4.NIL)$
G4 :   ?   consec$(3, 2,$ $2.3.2.4.NIL)$
G5 :   ?   consec$(3, 2,$ $3.2.4.NIL)$
G6 :   ?

Observe how the first step distributes the data item v to the variable in G1's latent call, producing G2. The second step distributes 3 to v in G2's latent call, producing G3. Thereafter no variables remain in the goal, so no further distribution of output occurs. The entire computation succeeds in discovering that 3 is the member embedded between two 2's in $(1, 2, 3, 2, 4)$. The answer is extracted from the final state of the binding history, this being $\{z := v, v := 3\}$. Note that the latter can be regarded as a record of the output distributions which have occurred during the computation's development.

   In this example all the data items processed happened to be terms already existing within actual or formal parameters: the computation merely moved them around. On other occasions data items can be computed rather than merely accessed. Consider the invocation of

$$C1 :   \textbf{consec}(u, v, u.v.x)$$

in response to a goal ? consec$(1, 2, z)$. The data assignment $\{u := 1, v := 2, z := 1.2.x\}$ assigns to z the computed term $1.2.x$. This has been constructed from the input data 1 and 2, and then fed back as output data. The interpreter's parameter-matching mechanism therefore behaves as a primitive data processor, being able to assemble or disassemble structured data items according to the patterns in the parameters, which thus serve as templates.

II.5.2. Sequencing

Sequencing, branching and iteration are the most familiar mechanisms used for organizing the flow of computational events. *Sequencing* refers to the execution of several tasks one at a time in a specified order, and is the most elementary mode of control in almost all programming languages.

   In logic programs tasks are arranged in sequence simply by writing calls in a particular textual order. So if some algorithm performed the sequence

read some input x
process x to produce y
print the output y

then the program's goal might be written

$$? \textbf{read}(x), \textbf{process}(x, y), \textbf{print}(y)$$

The interpreter would then automatically perform the three tasks in this order according to the standard computation rule. Alternatively, the same sequence could be specified within some procedure such as

$$\textbf{proc}(x, y) \quad \textbf{if} \quad \textbf{read}(x), \textbf{process}(x, y), \textbf{print}(y)$$

When invoked this would process the three calls in turn: the first might read data for x from some input device and distribute it to the second call; this could then invoke some procedure which returned output data for y, distributing this to the third call, which could transmit it to an output device. The precise details would of course depend upon the procedures provided to respond to the three calls.

It is usually desirable, for efficiency's sake, to choose the appropriate sequence carefully. Consider a simple problem dealing with arithmetical addition, namely that of simultaneously solving the equations

$$x + 1 = 3 \quad \text{and} \quad x + y = 3$$

Using the predicate $\textbf{plus}(x, y, z)$ to express $x + y = z$, one possible goal is

$$? \textbf{plus}(x, 1, 3), \textbf{plus}(x, y, 3)$$

The **plus** relation can be described by a procedure set dealing with any selected range of numbers, say 0, 1, 2 and 3. Here is one possible set:

$$
\begin{aligned}
&\text{P1}: \quad \textbf{plus}(0, z, z) \\
&\text{P2}: \quad \textbf{plus}(z, 0, z) \\
&\text{P3}: \quad \textbf{plus}(1, 1, 2) \\
&\text{P4}: \quad \textbf{plus}(1, 2, 3) \\
&\text{P5}: \quad \textbf{plus}(2, 1, 3)
\end{aligned}
$$

In the course of execution, the interpreter activates the goal's first call and then scans sequentially through P1–P5 seeking the first responding procedure, which is P5. By invoking P5 it assigns 2 to x and the next goal is

$$? \textbf{plus}(2, y, 3)$$

This call is now activated and P1–P5 are again scanned. Once more, P5 is the first responding procedure, and its invocation assigns 1 to y. The computation terminates successfully with the equations' solution $\{x := 2, y := 1\}$ and is a reasonably efficient way of solving the problem.

Suppose instead that the initial goal posed the calls in the reverse order; thus

$$\text{G1} : \quad ? \, \textbf{plus}(x, y, 3), \, \textbf{plus}(x, 1, 3)$$

This produces a much more complicated execution, as follows.

G2 :	? **plus**(0, 1, 3)	by invoking P1; this goal now fails, so backtrack to G1
G2a :	? **plus**(3, 1, 3)	by invoking P2; this goal now fails, so backtrack to G1
G2b :	? **plus**(1, 1, 3)	by invoking P4; this goal now fails, so backtrack to G1
G2c :	? **plus**(2, 1, 3)	by invoking P5; this goal succeeds
G3 :	?	problem solved with answer $\{x := 2, y := 1\}$.

Although this execution is clearly less efficient, the correct answer is nevertheless obtained. The second execution is said to be 'less deterministic' than the first one, in that it has had to explore more computations, most of them ending in failure. Altering the call sequence is equivalent to altering the computation rule, which in turn alters the selected search tree posed to the interpreter.

Usually it is best to aim for the most deterministic behaviour, although this is not always the best policy: much depends upon the details of the various search trees, such as the distribution of failure nodes and the complexity of the binding histories. Often the least-branched search trees arise from call sequences which minimize the number of variables occurring in calls at their instant of activation. This is the case in the example above: the first execution activates the calls **plus**(x, 1, 3) and **plus**(2, y, 3), which each contain just one variable, whereas the second execution activates a call **plus**(x, y, 3) containing two. In general, the more variables an activated call contains, the more procedures are likely to respond to it and hence the greater is the degree of branching in the search tree.

Finally, observe an important contrast with conventional programming, There, the sequence of procedure calls cannot be altered arbitrarily because each procedure usually depends logically upon the assumption that certain parameters communicated to it will have already been assigned data by preceding events; whereas a logic procedure like P1 can be invoked by a call **plus**(0, 1, 1) whose actual parameters are variable-free, or by a call like **plus**(x, y, 1), where x and y are currently unassigned. This feature of logic procedures, absent in almost all other languages, is called *input–output non-determinism* or *invertibility*, meaning that a procedure does not in itself wholly determine which of its formal parameters receive input from the call or which ones return output to it: their input/output status is instead partly determined according to the call which invokes the procedure.

II.5.3. Branching

Branching refers to the circumstance whereby a computational path reaches a point (the branch point) from which further development can proceed in any of several directions. Branching is usually considered in terms of *testing*, that is, applying some test at the branch point in order to decide which direction to take next.

There are several ways of capturing such behaviour in logic programs. All of them rely ultimately upon the use of several procedures sharing the same name: a procedure set can be regarded as a single entity invoked by a call, but offering various internal pathways upon entering it. Suppose we wished to perform some task on objects x, y and z, the action being taken depending upon the status of another object u. More specifically, the task is expressed as follows:

$$\begin{array}{llll} \textbf{if} & u = 1 & \textbf{then} & \text{perform action-1 on } x, y, z \\ \textbf{else} \quad \textbf{if} & u = 2 & \textbf{then} & \text{perform action-2 on } x, y, z \\ & & \textbf{else} & \text{take no action} \end{array}$$

It can be expressed in logic using two procedures sharing the name **task**, as follows:

$$\begin{array}{lll} \text{T1}: & \textbf{task}(1, x, y, z) & \textbf{if} \quad \textbf{action-1}(x, y, z) \\ \text{T2}: & \textbf{task}(2, x, y, z) & \textbf{if} \quad \textbf{action-2}(x, y, z) \end{array}$$

When a call of the form **task**(u, x, y, z) is activated, the ensuing behaviour depends upon the status of u at the moment of activation. If it is just the constant 1, then only T1 responds and so action-1 will be performed; likewise if it is the constant 2 then only T2 responds and so action-2 will be taken. If it is any other non-variable term, then neither responds and so no action is taken. The procedure set therefore achieves the test-and-branch behaviour desired when the discriminator u is already set at the point of call.

The behaviour is rather different if the discriminator u is initially unset when the **task** call is activated, for when u is simply a variable then *both* T1 and T2 respond. In this event *both* action-1 and action-2 will be performed in turn, because the search tree now contains a branch node, all of whose exits are automatically explored by the interpreter.

The testing shown in this example is essentially 'testing by type': the test entails deciding whether the actual and formal parameters share the same structural type in the sense of being unifiable. Procedure calling governed by this kind of test is generally known as 'pattern-directed invocation' and figures in a few other languages (e.g., PLANNER) besides logic.

When the programmer requires a more elaborate test to control the choice of action, the text can be posed as a call within the procedures dealing with the separate possible actions. For example,

$$\text{T1a :} \quad \textbf{task}(u, x, y, z) \quad \textbf{if} \quad \textbf{decide}(u, 1), \textbf{ action-1}(x, y, z)$$
$$\text{T2a :} \quad \textbf{task}(u, x, y, z) \quad \textbf{if} \quad \textbf{decide}(u, 2), \textbf{ action-2}(x, y, z)$$

Here the predicate $\textbf{decide}(u, k)$ is used to express that k is the outcome (1 or 2) appropriate to whatever data has been assigned to u; these data could be as complicated as desired, as could the **decide** procedures provided for analysing them.

Testing and branching are clearly not extra features added to the logic programming formalism, but are instead intrinsic aspects of it. Every procedure-calling operation involves a test on the parameters, and every call can be viewed as a test deciding whether some property holds for some data, for instance, whether data item u demands outcome k. All kinds of algorithmic decision making can be formulated in logic by using these mechanisms.

II.5.4. Iteration

Iteration is customarily viewed as a process which repeatedly executes a program segment; each repetition, or 'iterative step', accomplishes all the computation prescribed by the segment before the next repetition is started. There are two principal ways of achieving this behaviour in logic programming.

One way exploits the inherent iterative behaviour of the interpreter when it scans through a series of procedures seeking one which responds to a call. A simple example is provided by the problem of searching a given list L for a particular element. Suppose $L = (3, 4, 9, 5)$ is represented by procedures M1–M4 below:

$$\text{M1 :} \quad \textbf{m}(3, 1, L)$$
$$\text{M2 :} \quad \textbf{m}(4, 2, L)$$
$$\text{M3 :} \quad \textbf{m}(9, 3, L)$$
$$\text{M4 :} \quad \textbf{m}(5, 4, L)$$

Here (as in Example 1 in Section I.6) the predicate $\textbf{m}(u, i, x)$ means that member u occupies position i in list x. The problem is to find the position i in L, if any, of a given element, say 9. So the appropriate goal is

$$? \, \textbf{m}(9, i, L)$$

As execution proceeds, the interpreter compares 9 with successive members of L in the course of seeking a responding procedure; the comparisons form part of the unifying mechanism. When M3 responds, the computation terminates successfully with the answer $i := 3$. Each step in the scanning of the headings in M1–M4 constitutes an iterative step in an iteration arising from the interpreter's own control strategy. Observe that the programmer has not had to provide constructs specifying how the iteration is to begin, continue or end.

Another way of obtaining iterative behaviour is through the use of an *iterative procedure*. This is a procedure whose body contains exactly one call bearing the same name as the procedure's heading, and this call must also be the last one in the body. It therefore has either of the forms

$$\mathbf{A} \quad \text{if} \quad \mathbf{A}'$$

or

$$\mathbf{A} \quad \text{if} \quad \mathbf{B}_1, \ldots, \mathbf{B}_m, \mathbf{A}'$$

where $\mathbf{A}$ and $\mathbf{A}'$ contain identical procedure names distinct from those in $\mathbf{B}_1, \ldots$ and $\mathbf{B}_m$.

An iterative procedure can be used to solve the problem of adding up a list of numbers like L above to produce a sum y. In each ith iterative step the ith member of L is added to a cumulative sum x, the latter initially being set to 0. When n steps have occurred, where n is the length of L, the final value of x is the answer y. The entire program can be structured as shown below.

G1 :   ? **add**$(0, y, 1, 4, L)$
A1 :   **add**(y, y, i, n, L) **if** $i > n$
A2 :   **add**(x, y, i, n, L) **if** $i \leqslant n$, **m**(u, i, L), **plus**(x, u, x'),
                            plus$(i, 1, i')$, **add**(x', y, i', n, L)

together with procedures M1–M4 defining L and procedures for $>$, $\leqslant$ and **plus**.

As usual, **plus**(u, v, w) expresses $u + v = w$. The predicate **add**(x, y, i, n, L) expresses that x is the sum of all members of L preceding the ith one, whilst y is the result of adding x to the sum of the ith to nth members inclusive.

Procedure A2 is the iterative procedure, and when invoked performs the general iterative step

> check that $i \leqslant n$
> select member u in the ith position of L
> add u to x giving x' (updating the sum)
> add 1 to i giving i' (updating the step count)
> instigate the next iterative step

Procedure A1 just terminates the iteration when the step count i has exceeded n, and the final answer y in the second argument position is forced equal to the cumulative sum in the first argument position. The initial goal G1 injects the necessary initial values of the cumulative sum (0) and the step count (1) into the computation. The ensuing behaviour is indicated below, where, for presentation's sake, many of the intermediate goals have been omitted; filling them in makes a good exercise for the reader. The illustrated goals G1, G6, G11 etc. occur at the moments when new iterative steps are initiated. In each such step, procedure A1 is tried first, because of the standard search rule, and fails whenever $i \leqslant n$—in which event A2 is tried instead. The search tree therefore contains several short failure branches associated with the repeated tests on i. The computation G1–G23 just shows the successful path in the search tree.

$$
\begin{aligned}
&\text{G1}: \quad ?\,\textbf{add}(0, y, 1, 4, L) \\
&\text{G2}: \quad ?\,1 \leqslant 4,\ \textbf{m}(u, 1, L),\ \textbf{plus}(0, u, x'),\ \textbf{plus}(1, 1, i'), \\
&\hspace{9.5em} \textbf{add}(x', y, i', 4, L) \\
&\qquad\qquad \vdots \\
&\text{G6}: \quad ?\,\textbf{add}(3, y, 2, 4, L) \\
&\qquad\qquad \vdots \\
&\text{G11}: \quad ?\,\textbf{add}(7, y, 3, 4, L) \\
&\qquad\qquad \vdots \\
&\text{G16}: \quad ?\,\textbf{add}(16, y, 4, 4, L) \\
&\qquad\qquad \vdots \\
&\text{G21}: \quad ?\,\textbf{add}(21, y, 5, 4, L) \\
&\text{G22}: \quad ?\,5 > 4 \\
&\text{G23}: \quad ? \qquad \text{solved with } y := 21
\end{aligned}
$$

Note that in logic programming it is possible to achieve an algorithmic behaviour which would perhaps best be referred to as 'non-deterministic iteration'. This occurs when either a call **A** or any intermediate calls $\textbf{B}_1, \ldots$ and $\textbf{B}_m$ in the general iterative procedure can be solved in more than one way. In such circumstances the iteration would be 'rewound' (by backtracking) after each solution in order to explore the other alternatives. The example above does not behave like this, provided that the calls to **add**, $>$, $\leqslant$, **m** and **plus** are each solvable in just one way, and produces only the conventional, deterministic mode of iteration.

Here is another brief example to help reinforce the idea of an iterative procedure. Newton's method for computing the approximate square root of a number x begins with an initial guess y. The guess is considered sufficiently accurate if $|x - y^2| \leqslant err$ where err is some specified margin of error. Otherwise a better guess is $\frac{1}{2}(y + x/y)$, which can be computed and similarly subjected to the accuracy test. This method therefore iteratively generates a series of guesses converging upon the exact value of $\sqrt{x}$.

The following program, intended to compute $\sqrt{5}$ from the initial guess 1, uses the predicate **newton**(x, y, z, err) to express that z approximates to $\sqrt{x}$ within a margin err when z is some guess in the series $(y, \frac{1}{2}(y + x/y),$ ... etc.).

G1 : ? **newton**$(5, 1, z, 0.05)$ (choosing $err = 0.05$)
N1 :   **newton**(x, z, z, err) **if** **times**(z, z, zsq), **absdiff**$(x, zsq, diff)$,
                                                    $diff \leqslant err$
N2 :   **newton**(x, y, z, err) **if** **divide**$(x, y, ratio)$, **plus**$(y, ratio, sum)$,
                                                    divide$(sum, 2, y')$, **newton**(x, y', z, err)

together with procedures for **times**, **divide**, **plus**, **absdiff** and $\leqslant$.

The arithmetical predicates have the meanings

$$\begin{aligned}
\textbf{absdiff}(u, v, w) \quad &\text{expresses} \quad |u - v| = w \\
\textbf{plus}(u, v, w) \quad &\text{expresses} \quad u + v = w \\
\textbf{times}(u, v, w) \quad &\text{expresses} \quad u * v = w \\
\textbf{divide}(u, v, w) \quad &\text{expresses} \quad u / v = w
\end{aligned}$$

The first **newton** procedure incorporates the accuracy test; if this fails then the second procedure initiates an iterative step. Execution yields the following successful computation:

$$? \, \textbf{newton}(5, 1, z, 0.05)$$
$$\vdots$$
$$? \, \textbf{newton}(5, 3, z, 0.05)$$
$$\vdots$$
$$? \, \textbf{newton}(5, 2.333, z, 0.05)$$
$$\vdots$$
$$? \, \textbf{newton}(5, 2.238, z, 0.05)$$
$$\vdots$$

? $0.009 \leqslant 0.05$
?   solved with answer $z := 2.238$

II.5.5. Recursion

Recursion is the behaviour obtained when a program segment invokes itself prior to its own completion. In logic programming it is usually achieved by using a *recursive procedure*. This is a procedure whose name occurs in at least one call in the body. (Iterative procedures are thus special cases of recursive ones.)

The problem of computing factorials is often used for illustrating recursion. Let the predicates **fact**(u, v), **minus**(u, v, w) and **times**(u, v, w)

express respectively $u! = v$, $u - v = w$ and $u * v = w$. The following program, which computes $3!$, contains a recursive procedure F2. F1, which terminates the recursive process, is generally called the *base* procedure.

G1 :   ? **fact**$(3, z)$
F1 :   **fact**$(0, 1)$
F2 :   **fact**(x, y) if $x > 0$, **minus**$(x, 1, x')$, **fact**(x', y'),
                                                  times(x, y', y)

In order to compute $3!$ the program computes $2!$ and afterward multiplies this by 3. The calculation of $2!$ similarly leaves a multiplication of $1!$ by 2 pending while $1!$ is being calculated. Therefore several latent calls to **times** representing pending multiplications will accumulate in the current goal until an eventual call to compute $0!$ is solved immediately by F1. Here is an outline of the recursive computation, with some intermediate goals omitted:

? **fact**$(3, z)$
    ⋮
? **fact**$(2, y')$, **times**$(3, y', z)$
    ⋮
? **fact**$(1, y'')$, **times**$(2, y'', y')$, **times**$(3, y', z)$
    ⋮
? **fact**$(0, y''')$, **times**$(1, y''', y'')$, **times**$(2, y'', y')$, **times**$(3, y', z)$
    ⋮   F1 is now invoked, assigning 1 to y''',
    ⋮   and the latent **times** calls are then solved in turn
? **times**$(3, 2, z)$
?   solved with answer $z := 6$

Recursive programs often provide compact and elegant descriptions of the relations of interest, but suffer the run-time drawback of generating an expanding stack of latent calls whose storage requirement may be unacceptable. Usually recursion is employed either when this storage burden is a worthwhile tradeoff for program elegance, or when no practical non-recursive algorithms are available for solving the problem at hand.

II.6. Built-In Facilities

Most programming languages supply a number of procedures and functions having a fixed, internally defined meaning, in order to spare the programmer the inconvenience of having to define elementary and frequently used operations himself. In logic, predicate and function symbols possess no inherently fixed denotation; such meaning as they possess is determined wholly by the programs in which they appear. Nevertheless, certain such symbols can be assigned a fixed meaning within any particular implementation of logic, and indeed virtually all implementations currently in existence do supply a substantial number of these.

II.6.1. Built-In Procedures

The most common kinds of elementary procedure calls are probably those which test for equality and relative magnitude. Many interpreters therefore fix the meaning of predicate symbols like

$$= \quad \neq \quad < \quad \leqslant \quad > \quad \geqslant$$

in accordance with their usual mathematical meaning when applied to real and integer numbers. Thus a programmer writing a procedure

$$\textbf{ord}(u.v.x) \quad \textbf{if} \quad u < v, \textbf{ord}(v.x)$$

has no need to provide additional procedures for $<$. When a call like $1 < 2$ is activated the interpreter simply invokes an internal built-in test to solve the call directly. Its logical effect is exactly as though the programmer had supplied his own procedures

$$0 < 1$$
$$1 < 2$$
$$0 < 2$$
$$\text{etc.}$$

A facility of this kind has to be able to cope with calls having any kind of parameters. Thus the solution of a call $2 < x$, asking which numbers exceed 2, should return appropriate output data to x. Since there are infinitely many answers, the interpreter must deliver these in succession (as though it were successively trying each of the implicitly assumed responding procedures) according to some internally defined precedence. Hence execution of the goal

$$?\, 2 < x, x < 6$$

might return answers in the order $x := 3$, $x := 4$ and $x := 5$.

Whether the interpreter would then continue to generate an infinitude of larger values of x from the first call, all of which would fail to solve the second one, depends upon the precise nature of the implementation. That behaviour could in any case be prevented, if somewhat clumsily, by reposing the problem as

$$? \, 2 < x, \, x < 6, \, \textbf{check}(x)$$
$$\textbf{check}(x) \quad \textbf{if} \quad x \neq 5$$
$$\textbf{check}(5) \quad \textbf{if} \quad /$$

Then as soon as the value *5* is passed to the **check** call, the activation of the /
will excise all the untried possibilities emanating from the $2 < x$ call.

The appropriate library of built-in procedures will naturally vary
according to the intended field of application. An implementation specially
tailored to mathematical work might well provide facilities for processing
vectors, matrices, polynomial expressions, etc., whereas one intended for
database manipulation would need quite different facilities. In this book we
assume that only the six predicate symbols above have fixed meaning.

II.6.2. Built-In Functions

Almost all computing applications require the elementary operations of
arithmetic. Some interpreters therefore assign fixed meaning to certain
predicate symbols like **plus**, **times**, etc. whilst others may assign fixed meaning
to function symbols like $+$ and $*$. The latter arrangement produces the
most compact programs.

As an example of this, consider the following reformulation of the
factorial problem.

$$? \, \textbf{fact}(3, z)$$
$$\textbf{fact}(0, 1)$$
$$\textbf{fact}(x, y) \quad \textbf{if} \quad x > 0, \, \textbf{fact}(x - 1, y'), \, y = x * y'$$

If no special meaning were attached to the function symbols $-$ and $*$ here,
then execution would assign cumbersome terms like $3-1$ and $3-1-1$ to
the program's variables. Moreover, a call $\textbf{fact}(3-1-1-1, y''')$ would
eventually be activated but unable to invoke the first **fact** procedure, since
$3-1-1-1$ and 0 do not match. We clearly intend them both to represent
the number 'zero', but the interpreter does not necessarily know this.

In order to obtain sensible arithmetical behaviour from programs of
this kind, symbols like $-$ and $*$ can be assigned a fixed meaning within the
interpreter. Then at the moment of activating a call with an actual parameter
like $3-1$, the interpreter can immediately evaluate that term in an arithmetical sense, replacing it by a single constant symbol like *2*. Such an
arrangement therefore also assigns special significance to the constants
0, *1*, *2*, ... etc., treating them as conventional numerals instead of arbitrary

uninterpreted symbols. This does not undermine the logical basis of the formalism provided that $0, 1, 2, \ldots$ etc. are consistently processed as though they were only abbreviations constructed by the interpreter in place of more complicated terms.

More elaborate operations, like those capable of 'matching', say, 6 and $3 * x$ to produce the assignment $x := 2$, can also be implemented by using appropriate extensions of the basic unification mechanism, but require careful semantical justification to ensure that execution remains equivalent to logical inference. Throughout this book we shall use only the most innocuous ways of exploiting built-in functions, liberally employing standard arithmetic operators but only permitting arithmetical evaluations of variable-free terms. The factorial program satisfies this restriction and can be processed as follows:

$$? \, \textbf{fact}(3, z)$$
$$? \, \textbf{fact}(3 - 1, y'), \, z = 3 * y'$$
$$? \, \textbf{fact}(2 - 1, y''), \, y' = 2 * y'', \, z = 3 * y'$$
$$? \, \textbf{fact}(1 - 1, y'''), \, y'' = 1 * y''', \, y' = 2 * y'', \, z = 3 * y'$$
$$? \qquad\qquad y'' = 1 * 1, \quad y' = 2 * y'', \, z = 3 * y'$$
$$? \qquad\qquad\qquad\qquad y' = 2 * 1, \quad z = 3 * y'$$
$$? \qquad\qquad\qquad\qquad\qquad\qquad z = 3 * 2$$
$$? \qquad \text{solved with } z := 6$$

In this computation, every time any call is activated in which there occurs a variable-free arithmetic expression, the latter is evaluated and the expression replaced by its value; procedure invocation then proceeds in the normal way.

II.7. Background

Logic programming originated largely from advances in automatic theorem proving, and in particular from the development of the resolution principle. Some of the earliest work relating resolution to computer programming was undertaken by Green (1969), who showed that the answer-extraction mechanism could be used for synthesizing conventional programs by applying resolution to their specifications expressed in clausal-form logic. The synthesizers which were designed for that purpose could be regarded as the precursors of modern logic interpreters.

The general idea of treating logic sentences as program statements, and controlled inference as execution, was explored by Hayes (1973), Sandewall (1973) and others. However, the intelligibility of logic as an executable programming language was especially reinforced by the procedural inter-pretation formulated by Kowalski (1974b). This was the essential advance necessary for the adaptation of theorem-proving concepts to the com-putational techniques already understood by programmers. An excellent overview of the procedural interpretation can be found in the paper by van Emden (1977a).

Advances in implementation technology have also contributed greatly to the presentation of logic as a practical formalism. The first experimental interpreter was implemented by Roussel, Colmerauer and others (1973) at the University of Aix–Marseille in 1972 and given the name PROLOG ('programming in logic'), and has strongly influenced the design of later systems. Following that important first step, more practical implementations were developed by Battani and Meloni (1973), Bruynooghe (1976), Warren (1977a) and Roberts (1977). Since then there has been a very considerable proliferation of PROLOG implementations, covering a wide range of design philosophies, host machines and application environments.

The terms 'logic programming' and 'PROLOG programming' tend to be used interchangeably, yet PROLOG's default strategy, which is the standard strategy defined earlier in the chapter, is by no means the only one available for executing logic programs. For example, an entirely different strategy underlies the 'connection graph' proof procedure developed by Kowalski (1975), which operates using a special scheme of link activation applied to the links in a graph connecting calls to responding procedures. The earliest attempt to implement this method was probably undertaken by Tärnlund (1975a).

In any case, it is important to realise that even PROLOG systems differ considerably amongst themselves on account of the different additional facilities they provide for enriching the programmer's resources. Most interpreters allow various ways of modifying the control strategy, for instance. Sometimes such enhancements to the standard strategy give rise to computations which cannot be wholly justified in terms of logical infer-ence, and the interpreters are then said to be potentially 'impure'; the original Marseille PROLOG is an example of this. Otherwise, when the interpreter always behaves in accordance with strict logical inference (though this need not be using resolution) it is said to be 'pure'; the IC-PROLOG system at Imperial College, London, written by Clark and McCabe (1979a) is pure despite having several sophisticated mechanisms supplementing the standard strategy. A detailed, tutorial account of practical programming with PROLOG systems of the kind developed by Warren (1977a, 1979) and by Clocksin and Mellish (1980) is provided by the first book to deal specifically with logic programming; written by Clocksin and Mellish (1981), this is oriented primarily toward DEC-10 PROLOG.

The extents to which PROLOG both succeeds and fails in realizing the complete ideal of logic as a programming language are discussed in a paper by Kowalski (1981b). Whilst PROLOG is emerging as a new way of thinking about programming, it is nevertheless worth remembering that PROLOG was preceded by new ways of thinking about logic. Kowalski has identified the key advances as, first, the recognition that logic has pragmatic as well as semantic content (by virtue of the procedural interpretation) and, second, that inference can be made goal-directed (by virtue of systems like resolution) in contrast to its traditional reputation for being primarily consequence-oriented. Recent tutorial introductions to both logic programming and PROLOG have been written by Kowalski (1981b, 1983b) and by Sammut and Sammut (1983a,b), whilst collections of advanced research papers have been published by Clark and Tärnlund (1982) and by Warren and van Canaghem (1985). A good coverage of the current research field is provided jointly by the proceedings of the Logic Programming Workshop (1983), the Atlantic City (1984) Symposium and the forthcoming Uppsala (1984) Second International Logic Programming Conference. A new *Journal of Logic Programming*, edited by J. A. Robinson at Syracuse University, New York, is in preparation. A detailed history of the origins of logic programming is set out in a paper by Kowalski (1984).

III PROGRAMMING STYLE

Good 'programming style' contributes to the overall quality of a program, and is as important to successful logic programming as it is to conventional programming. A well-styled program should make the assumptions about the problem clearly perceivable and at the same time should represent a computationally useful algorithm.

In conventional programming these last two objectives are difficult to reconcile, as students of 'structured programming' will know only too well. There, the central difficulty is in deciding how to describe the details of run-time control so as to ensure efficiency without committing the program's logical objectives to obscurity, because these two aspects of the program are interdependent and can impose conflicting requirements.

Possibly the most significant advantage of using logic as a programming language is that the descriptive content of a logic program does not depend upon any assumptions about the execution mechanism. This makes it possible to develop the program's logical and behavioural attributes in a more separable way than can be achieved using the machine-oriented languages now in popular use. The logic programmer can devise various descriptions of the problem of interest and consider how each one responds to the control mechanisms offered by the interpreter at his disposal. The final choice of logic and control should be that which maximizes logical clarity subject to being executable with acceptable efficiency.

When the control options are rather limited, as in standard PROLOG interpreters, the programmer may occasionally be compelled, for efficiency's sake, to construct statements having quite intricate logical structure. Even so, such statements can still be analysed (for example, to assess the correctness of what they assert about the problem) without taking any account at all of their effects upon run-time behaviour. It is this ability to analyse separately the *declarative* and *operational* properties of statements which gives logic its distinctive qualities as a programming language.

This chapter illustrates a variety of styles for the logical construction of programs and considers their practical merits or drawbacks. The ideas and judgements given here derive from empirical studies undertaken during a period when many innovations occurred in implementation technology, and so should not be regarded as having either universal or permanent validity.

In order to discuss examples in a reasonably concise way, a number of assumptions have been made about the interpreter for which the programs are designed. First, it is assumed—except when otherwise stated—to be governed by the standard control strategy and is thus a (virtually) pure PROLOG interpreter. The only slight departure from purity concerns the use of built-in arithmetical functions, whereby variable-free terms like $3 * 2$ are assumed to be evaluable to abbreviations like 6. Second, without affecting purity, certain built-in procedures such as those for $=$, $\neq$ etc. are assumed to be available, so sparing us the tedium of having to append comments to this effect to each program presented.

In some examples the computations generated from programs are discussed but not necessarily illustrated. The reader's assimilation of logic programming will be improved by deriving the computations himself, all of them being straightforward.

III.1. Logic and Control

When a logic program is executed, the resulting behaviour constitutes an *algorithm*. The algorithm can be usefully viewed as a pair (logic, control) whose *logic component* is the set of statements making up the program and whose *control component* is the execution strategy. Thus the first component describes the problem to be solved whilst the second describes a method of solving it.

In many implementations the control component is largely fixed within the interpreter. The programmer can influence the control of execution by choosing the textual ordering of calls and procedures, and by using a number of special devices like the cut operator, but the overall top-down depth-first search principle is usually paramount.

The use of textual ordering is generally insufficient for producing a wide range of useful algorithms from any particular logic component. One ordering may give a good algorithm whilst all others may have no practical merit whatever. Effective logic programming, in the present state of the art, therefore relies mostly upon choosing appropriate logic components to suit the limited control available. One day it might be possible to rely upon one's implementation to devise the most effective control for whatever program is input, thus placing the burden of intelligence upon the machine rather than upon the programmer. Such circumstances will not come about until major advances have been made in the theory of algorithms.

The influence of logical structure upon run-time behaviour can be illustrated by considering the problem of counting the number n of distinct members in some given list, for instance $x = (A, B, C, A, D, B, C, E, A)$. A simple algorithm is that which firstly filters out all duplicates from x to leave a list $y = (A, B, C, D, E)$ and then computes the length $n \ (=5)$ of y. The following program expresses the underlying logic of this algorithm.

Program 1

> ? **count**$(A.B.C.A.D.B.C.E.A.NIL, n)$
> **count**(x, n) **if** **filter**(x, y), **length***$(y, 0, n)$
> **filter**(NIL, NIL)
> **filter**$(u.x, u.y)$ **if** **delete**$(u, u.x, x')$, **filter**(x', y)
> **delete**(u, NIL, NIL)
> **delete**$(u, u.x, z)$ **if** **delete**(u, x, z)
> **delete**$(u, v.x, v.z)$ **if** $u \neq v$, **delete**(u, x, z)
> **length***(NIL, m, m)
> **length***$(u.y, i, m)$ **if** **length***$(y, i+1, m)$

The various predicates are read as follows:

count(x, n)	n distinct members occur in list x;
length*(y, i, m)	the length of list y is $m-i$;
delete(u, x, z)	list z results from deleting all occurrences of u from list x, preserving the relative order of the remaining members;
filter(x, y)	list y results from deleting all duplicates from list x, preserving the relative order of the remaining members

The reader should be satisfied with the declarative content of the procedures before proceeding further; their operational features will then be more readily apparent.

When the program is executed, all counting is deferred until completion of the filtering operation which deletes all duplicates from the input list. The tasks of filtering and counting are performed in sequence owing to the standard control strategy, which holds the call to **length*** latent until the call to **filter** has been solved. The effect of execution can be summarized as follows.

Lists subjected

to filtering	Counts	
$(A, B, C, A, D, B, C, E, A)$	none	list x has its duplicates
$(A, B, C,\quad D, B, C, E\quad)$	none	gradually filtered out to
$(A, B, C,\quad D,\quad C, E\quad)$	none	leave $y = (A, B, C, D, E)$
$(A, B, C,\quad D,\quad\quad E\quad)$	none	

Lists subjected

to counting	Counts	
(A, B, C, D, E)	0	then list y has its length
(B, C, D, E)	1	computed by counting and
(C, D, E)	2	removing successive members
(D, E)	3	until only the empty list
(E)	4	remains, the final count
NIL	5	being $n = 5$

Now compare this with the behaviour of a second program, in which the predicate **count***(x, i, m) expresses that the number of distinct members in list x is $m - i$.

Program 2

> ? **count**$(A.B.C.A.D.B.C.E.A.NIL, n)$
> **count**(x, n) **if**   **count***$(x, 0, n)$
> **count***(NIL, m, m)
> **count***$(u.x, i, m)$ **if**   **delete**$(u, u.x, z)$, **count***$(z, i+1, m)$
> and the same **delete** procedures as before

Execution of this program has the effect of *interleaving* the processes of counting distinct members and deleting duplicates. Each iterative step obtained by invoking the second **count*** procedure finds some new distinct member u in the list, deletes all its occurrences and finally counts it by adding 1 to a counter. This can be summarized as follows.

Lists subjected to simultaneous

counting and deleting	Counts
$(A, B, C, A, D, B, C, E, A)$	0
$(\quad B, C,\quad D, B, C, E\quad)$	1
$(\quad\quad C,\quad D,\quad D, E\quad)$	2
$(\quad\quad\quad D,\quad\quad E\quad)$	3
$(\quad\quad\quad\quad\quad E\quad)$	4
NIL	5

For instance, the second line in this summary shows the state of the data at the moment when the goal has become

$$? \text{ count*}(B.C.D.B.C.E.NIL, 1, n)$$

with A deleted and the count of it (1) held in the second argument position of the **count*** call.

The second program is more concise than the first, but its overall effect is perhaps less clear. It is also more efficient in not having to construct the intermediate list $y = (A, B, C, D, E)$ of distinct members. The two algorithms (Program 1, standard PROLOG) and (Program 2, standard PROLOG) have quite different behaviours despite their common control component, this being due solely to the different logic components; we say that the latter have differing 'pragmatic content' relative to standard PROLOG. Other strategies can be prescribed for these two programs besides the standard one. For example, the IC-PROLOG system at Imperial College is capable of accepting Program 1 as input, together with some minor control annotations, and executing it using a *coroutining* strategy. This strategy can alternately activate calls to **filter** and **length***, thus interleaving the filtering and counting processes. The resulting algorithm (Program 1, IC-PROLOG + annotations) is virtually identical to (Program 2, standard PROLOG).

III.2. Iteration and Recursion

Many kinds of computational problem require repetitive algorithmic processes for their solution. Such processes can always be described by using either recursive or iterative procedures. Iteration is usually more efficient than recursion, because the completion of an iterative step—unlike a recursive one—does not need to await the results of future steps. Iteration therefore avoids the run-time burden of managing a stack of latent calls, whereas recursion cannot.

In order to compare iterative and recursive programming styles, suppose a program is required which, given some list x such as (A, B, C, D), produces the reverse list y, which in the latter case would be (D, C, B, A). Program 3 below achieves this using a predicate **reverse**(x, y) to express that y is the reverse of x. Another predicate **append**$(z1, z2, z)$ is used to express that z is the result of appending the list $z2$ to the end of the list $z1$. The general principle of the program is that a non-empty list x of the form $u.x'$ can be reversed by first reversing x' to produce y' and then appending $u.NIL$ to the end of y' to produce y.

Program 3

> ? **reverse**(*A.B.C.D.NIL*, *y*)
> **reverse**(*NIL*, *NIL*)
> **reverse**(*u.x'*, *y*)   **if**   **reverse**(*x'*, *y'*), **append**(*y'*, *u.NIL*, *y*)
> and **append** procedures capable of appending together
> any two concrete lists (e.g., see Program 11, Section III.4.2)

By repeatedly invoking the recursive **reverse** procedure, execution generates a stack of latent **append** calls in the goal, eventually reaching the state

> ? **reverse**(*NIL*, *y4*), **append**(*y4*, *D.NIL*, *y3*),
> **append**(*y3*, *C.NIL*, *y2*),
> **append**(*y2*, *B.NIL*, *y1*),
> **append**(*y1*, *A.NIL*, *y*)

At this point the base procedure for **reverse** now responds, and its invocation yields *y4* := *NIL*. The **append** calls are then solved in turn to produce the output assignment *y* := *D.C.B.A.NIL* as expected.

The list reversal problem can also be solved iteratively by using the more compact, though perhaps more inscrutable, program below.

Program 4

> ? **reverse**(*A.B.C.D.NIL*, *y*)
> **reverse**(*x*, *y*)   **if**   **reverse***(*NIL*, *x*, *y*)
> **reverse***(*y*, *NIL*, *y*)
> **reverse***(*x1*, *u.x2*, *y*)   **if**   **reverse***(*u.x1*, *x2*, *y*)

Here the predicate **reverse***(*z1*, *z2*, *y*) expresses that *y* is the reverse of the list obtained by appending *z2* to the reverse of *z1*. Execution efficiently generates the following iterative computation:

> ? **reverse** (*A.B.C.D.NIL*, *y*)
> ? **reverse***(*NIL*, *A.B.C.D.NIL*, *y*)
> ? **reverse***(*A.NIL*, *B.C.D.NIL*, *y*)
> ? **reverse***(*B.A.NIL*, *C.D.NIL*, *y*)
> ? **reverse***(*C.B.A.NIL*, *D.NIL*, *y*)
> ? **reverse***(*D.C.B.A.NIL*, *NIL*, *y*)
> ?   with answer *y* := *D.C.B.A.NIL*

Here, in each iterative step some new member is effectively deleted from the input list and transferred to the front of another accumulating list of those members already deleted. This latter list is gradually constructed in the first argument position of the calls to **reverse***, and when completed is assigned to *y* by invoking the **reverse*** base procedure.

Program 4 illustrates a typical feature of iterative logic programs, namely the use of special parameters to accommodate information which an equivalent recursive program would encode as a stack of latent calls. For example, after two recursive steps in the execution of Program 3 the goal is

$$? \, \mathbf{reverse}(C.D.NIL, y2), \, \mathbf{append}(y2, B.NIL, y1),$$
$$\mathbf{append}(y1, A.NIL, y \,)$$

in which the two latent **append** calls encode the final solution y as the result of appending $A.NIL$ to the result of appending $B.NIL$ to the reverse $y2$ of $C.D.NIL$. By contrast, the execution of Program 3 encodes essentially the same information in the goal

$$? \, \mathbf{reverse}^*(B.A.NIL, C.D.NIL, y)$$

with the difference that, instead of holding $A.NIL$ and $B.NIL$ explicitly, it holds the result $B.A.NIL$ of appending them, which is in turn going to be appended to the reverse of $C.D.NIL$. (This latter tactic relies upon the *associativity* of the appending operation: in order to prove formally that the two programs compute the same solution for y it is necessary to assume this property.)

In summary, Program 3 uses **reverse** and **append** predicates whose parameters bear conceptually simple relationships to one another, whilst Program 4 uses the **reverse*** predicate whose three parameters have a more complex relationship. The greater efficiency of Program 4 is therefore obtained at the expense of logical clarity.

III.3.   Top-Down and Bottom-Up Behaviour

In a typical sequential algorithm, an initial step manipulates some input data and each subsequent step operates upon results computed by the previous ones. The final step delivers the desired output. This simple paradigm is called 'incremental' problem solving, signifying that the solution is not obtained by a single atomic computational event, but instead must be gradually converged upon through the agency of several interdependent events. The formulation of incremental algorithms presents the logic programmer with the opportunity to compare *top-down* and *bottom-up* programming styles.

III.3.1.   Calculating Factorials

The two styles can be compared using the problem of computing $z = 3!$. Consider first the recursive program below.

Program 5

> ? **fact**(*3*, *z*)
> F1 : **fact**(*0*, *1*)
> F2 : **fact**(*x*, *y*)   **if** *x* > *0*, **fact**(*x* − *1*, *y′*), *y* = *x* ∗ *y′*

We saw in Chapter II that standard execution of this program exhibits the typical features of top-down problem solving: the goal of computing *3*! is reduced to the subgoals of computing *2*! and *3* ∗ *2*!, which are in turn reduced to further subgoals. Each step in this process derives new subgoals with the motivation of solving existing ones, so that execution as a whole is goal-directed. The fact *0*! = *1*, expressed by F1, is not summoned until execution generates a call specifically requesting the value of *0*!.

By contrast, a programmer using a conventional language would probably prefer to write a factorial program whose behaviour was exactly opposite to the above, immediately making use of each available factorial in order to calculate the next higher one, as follows.

> **begin** *x* := *0*; *y* := *1*;
> **while** *x* ≤ *2* **do begin** *x* := *x* + *1*;
>   *y* := *x* ∗ *y*
>   **end**
> **end**

This program would generate a bottom-up computation, computing *1*! from *0*!, then *2*! from *1*! and so on. This method is iterative and more efficient than the recursive top-down method. How, then, can the logic programmer achieve a similar algorithm?

One possibility is to execute Program 5 using a non-standard bottom-up control strategy. Briefly, such a strategy exploits the fact that an assertion

$$F3 : \textbf{fact}(1, 1)$$

is implied by procedures F1 and F2, and is derivable from them by an inference step called bottom-up resolution. A further fact

$$F4 : \textbf{fact}(2, 2)$$

is likewise derivable from F2 and F3. A successful computation generated by this mode of execution consists of a series of assertions followed by □, the final contradiction arising when a derived assertion immediately solves the initial goal. Our example would yield the computation

> F1 : **fact**(*0*, *1*)   (given)
> F3 : **fact**(*1*, *1*)   (derived from F1 and F2)

F4 : **fact**(2, 2)   (derived from F3 and F2)
F5 : **fact**(3, 6)   (derived from F4 and F2)
　　□　　　　　 [derived from F5 and the goal ? **fact**(3, z)].

Clearly this behaviour is just like that of the ALGOL-like program above, and is very efficient.

Unfortunately, bottom-up control strategies are more troublesome to implement than top-down ones, because, for efficiency's sake, one has to incorporate some means of constraining the accumulation of assertions so as to derive just those which contribute toward solving the specific goal of the program: the bottom-up inference step has no inherent goal-directedness and its unconstrained application usually (though not in the factorial example) causes exponential growth in the number of derived assertions. Such means are very difficult to prescribe with any useful degree of generality, which is why standard implementations employ just the top-down mode. In this circumstance the logic programmer desiring bottom-up behaviour must resort to a special kind of program whose style we call 'quasi-bottom-up': although it is executed by the standard top-down strategy, its behaviour *simulates* bottom-up execution. Program 6 below illustrates this style.

Program 6

$$? \, \mathbf{fact}(3, z)$$
$$\mathbf{fact}(x, y) \quad \mathbf{if} \quad \mathbf{fact^*}(0, 1, x, y)$$
$$\mathbf{fact^*}(x, y, x, y)$$
$$\mathbf{fact^*}(u, v, x, y) \quad \mathbf{if} \quad u < x, \, \mathbf{fact^*}(u + 1, (u + 1)*v, x, y)$$

Here, the predicate **fact***(u, v, x, y) expresses the relationship

$$\mathbf{if} \quad u! = v \quad \mathbf{then} \quad x! = y$$

and standard execution produces a very efficient iteration:

$$? \, \mathbf{fact}(3, z)$$
$$? \, \mathbf{fact^*}(0, 1, 3, z)$$
$$\vdots$$
$$? \, \mathbf{fact^*}(1, 1, 3, z)$$
$$\vdots$$
$$? \, \mathbf{fact^*}(2, 2, 3, z)$$
$$\vdots$$
$$? \, \mathbf{fact^*}(3, 6, 3, z)$$
$$? \quad \text{with answer } \underline{z := 6}$$

Observe particularly that the first two argument positions in the successive **fact*** calls contain exactly the same information as held in the assertions forming the bottom-up computation. It is for this reason that we say the new style simulates bottom-up behaviour.

III.3.2. Pathfinding in Graphs

Another instructive example is provided by Kowalski's treatment of pathfinding in graphs. We might wish to search for paths from node A to node E in the directed graph shown in Fig. III.1. A simple program for this task is as follows:

Program 7

$$? \, \mathbf{go}(E)$$
$$\mathbf{go}(A)$$
$$\mathbf{go}(y) \quad \text{if} \quad \mathbf{arc}(x, y), \, \mathbf{go}(x)$$

$\mathbf{arc}(A, B)$	$\mathbf{arc}(B, C)$	$\mathbf{arc}(D, C)$
$\mathbf{arc}(A, C)$	$\mathbf{arc}(B, D)$	$\mathbf{arc}(C, E)$

where $\mathbf{go}(x)$ means that the search process can 'go' to node x, and $\mathbf{arc}(x, y)$ means that an arc exists which points from x to y. Standard execution yields various successful computations, each one corresponding to some path from A to E, for instance

$$? \, \mathbf{go}(E)$$
$$? \, \mathbf{arc}(x, E), \, \mathbf{go}(x)$$
$$? \, \mathbf{go}(C)$$
$$? \, \mathbf{arc}(x, C), \, \mathbf{go}(x)$$
$$? \, \mathbf{go}(A)$$
$$? \qquad \text{with answer } \underline{\textit{yes}}$$

Notice how this path (A, C, E) is explored backward from E to A in the

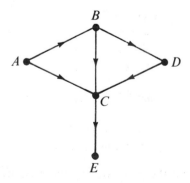

Fig. III.1. A directed graph.

typical top-down manner, using the initial fact **go**(A) only at the end of the computation.

A bottom-up algorithm would instead use the fact **go**(A) immediately and thence proceed forward along the path, finding C next and then E. This effect can be achieved by using a program written in the quasi-bottom-up style.

Program 8

> ? **go***(A, E)
> **go***(x, x)
> **go**∗(x, z)   **if**   **arc**(x, y), **go***(y, z)
> and the same **arc** assertions defining the graph.

The predicate **go***(x, z) means

> **if**   the search can go to x   **then**   it can go to z

and standard execution produces computations like the one below.

> ? **go***(A, E)
> ? **arc**(A, y), **go***(y, E)
> ? **go***(C, E)
> ? **arc**(C, y), **go***(y, E)
> ? **go***(E, E)
> ?   with answer '*yes*'

This clearly simulates the behaviour which would be obtained by executing Program 7 using a bottom-up strategy.

III.3.3. Eigenproblem Using Matrix Iteration

The factorial and pathfinding problems can be solved with acceptable efficiency using either top-down or bottom-up formulations. However, other problems exist for which top-down methods are very inefficient, making the quasi-bottom-up style an essential tool. A good example, slightly disposed toward the more mathematically inclined reader, is provided by the so-called 'eigenproblem': given some $n \times n$ matrix M, compute the scalars ('eigenvalues') e_i and the nonzero vectors ('eigenvectors') X_i satisfying the equation

$$M.X_i = e_i.X_i$$

Although this problem generally has n solutions $(e_1, X_1), \ldots, (e_n, X_n)$ it is often required to find only the 'dominant' eigenvector; this is the eigenvector associated with the largest eigenvalue.

As an example, the eigenproblem for the 2×2 matrix

$$M = \begin{bmatrix} 3 & 2 \\ 3 & 4 \end{bmatrix}$$

has two solutions,

$$e_1 = 6, \qquad X_1 = C. \begin{bmatrix} 1 \\ 1.5 \end{bmatrix}$$

$$e_2 = 1, \qquad X_2 = D. \begin{bmatrix} 1 \\ -1 \end{bmatrix}$$

where C and D are arbitrary constants. The dominant eigenvector is X_1 because $e_1 = 6$ is the largest eigenvalue.

A simple algorithm for determining the dominant eigenvector is available when the structure of M implies that the eigenvectors are linearly independent. Starting with any initial trial vector V, it generates the series $M.V$, $M^2.V$, $M^3.V$ etc., which necessarily converges upon the dominant eigenvector. The algorithm terminates when one of the generated trial vectors $M^k.V$ passes some sort of accuracy test. Program 9 below is a top-down recursive formulation of the algorithm.

Program 9

> ? **trial**(v), **acc**(M, v)
> **trial**($1.1.NIL$)
> **trial**(v)   if   **trial**(v'), **mult**(M, v', v)
> and procedures for **acc** and **mult**

Here, **trial**(v) means that v is a trial vector; **acc**(M, v) means that v is a sufficiently accurate approximation to the dominant eigenvector of M and **mult**(M, v', v) expresses $v = M.v'$. The details of the accuracy test and the matrix multiplication are unimportant here—we just assume that appropriate procedures are supplied for these tasks. The initial trial vector V has been chosen as

$$V = \begin{bmatrix} 1 \\ 1 \end{bmatrix}$$

and is represented by the term $1.1.NIL$ in the first procedure. The matrix M is assumed to be the matrix shown in the example above and we shall suppose that its contents are known to the **acc** and **mult** procedures.

As execution proceeds, V is submitted to the accuracy test

> G1 :   ? **trial**(v), **acc**(M, v)
> G2 :   ?   **acc**(M, $1.1.NIL$)

Assuming it fails the test, execution backtracks to G1 and then continues:

$$G2' : \quad ?\,\textbf{trial}(v'), \textbf{mult}(M, v', v), \textbf{acc}(M, v)$$
$$G3 : \quad ?\,\textbf{mult}(M, 1.1.NIL, v), \textbf{acc}(M, v)$$
$$G4 : \quad ? \qquad\qquad\qquad\qquad \textbf{acc}(M, 5.7.NIL)$$

Thus a matrix multiplication has been performed to generate the next trial $M.V = 5.7.NIL$. If this also fails the accuracy test then execution will backtrack again, and in so doing will *forget* the calculation of $5.7.NIL$; this is because whenever execution backtracks from a failure node, it discards all the knowledge of what has happened (including the bindings) since it met the most recent branch point. After backtracking from the current failure, execution continues:

$$G2'' : \quad ?\,\textbf{trial}(v''), \textbf{mult}(M, v'', v'),$$
$$\textbf{mult}(M, v', v), \textbf{acc}(M, v)$$
$$\vdots$$
$$G6 : \quad ?\,\textbf{acc}(M, 29.43.NIL)$$

In proceeding from G2'' to G6, the multiplication of $1.1.NIL$ by M is performed a second time to produce $5.7.NIL$, which is in turn multiplied by M to produce the next approximation $M^2.V = 29.43.NIL$. These two multiplications will also be forgotten and subsequently recomputed if this latest trial vector fails the accuracy test. This is clearly a very inefficient algorithm, even though the program's logic seems such a straightforward description of the problem. Nevertheless, execution will eventually assign a solution to the goal variable v. We can already see that the approximations computed so far, namely

$$\begin{bmatrix} 1 \\ 1 \end{bmatrix} \quad \begin{bmatrix} 5 \\ 7 \end{bmatrix} \quad \begin{bmatrix} 29 \\ 43 \end{bmatrix}$$

that is,

$$\begin{bmatrix} 1 \\ 1 \end{bmatrix} \quad 5.\begin{bmatrix} 1 \\ 1.4 \end{bmatrix} \quad 29.\begin{bmatrix} 1 \\ 1.483 \end{bmatrix}$$

are converging upon the dominant eigenvector

$$C.\begin{bmatrix} 1 \\ 1.5 \end{bmatrix}$$

The problem can be solved much more efficiently by using a quasi-bottom-up style analogous to the **go*** formulation in Program 8, as follows.

Program 10

> ? **derive**(v, *1.1.NIL*), **acc**(M, v), /
>   **derive**(v, v)
>   **derive**(v, z)   **if**   **mult**(M, z, z'), **derive**(v, z')
>   and other procedures for **acc** and **mult** as before.

The predicate **derive**(v, z) means that the trial vector v is derivable from trial vector z by applying to z zero or more premultiplications by the matrix M. Standard execution now yields an excellent iterative algorithm:

$$? \textbf{derive}(v, \textit{1.1.NIL}), \textbf{acc}(M, v), /$$
$$\vdots$$
$$? \textbf{derive}(v, \textit{5.7.NIL}), \textbf{acc}(M, v), /$$
$$\vdots$$
$$? \textbf{derive}(v, \textit{29.43.NIL}), \textbf{acc}(M, v), /$$
$$\vdots$$

etc.

Following each goal illustrated above, the first **derive** procedure is invoked, which has the effect of submitting the latest approximation to the accuracy test; if it fails, the other **derive** procedure is tried instead, and its effect is to perform one matrix multiplication to obtain the next approximation. Note the use of the cut operator in the goal; this serves to terminate execution as soon as the first accurate solution has been computed, thus preventing further unwanted refinement.

The fundamental difference between the top-down formulations of the factorial problem (Program 5) and the eigenproblem (Program 9) is that they are respectively deterministic and non-deterministic. In the latter case, every activated **trial** call can invoke either of the **trial** procedures, giving rise to a highly branched search tree whose many failure branches contain duplicated chains of (expensive) matrix multiplications. In the former case, execution is deterministic until the solution has been computed.

III.4. Determinism and Non-Determinism

The goal-directed search capability of logic interpreters dispels much of the tedium normally expected of computer programming. It saves the programmer from becoming over-involved in the details of execution. This advantage is made especially apparent by programs written in a non-deterministic style: there the programmer knows that the interpreter will explore various paths without requiring any special guidance from him in the way of control directives. Moreover, non-deterministic programs often exhibit much greater simplicity and elegance than deterministic alternatives for the same problems. This will become clear from the following examples.

III.4.1. Searching a List

Suppose one wishes to search some list L for the least position k, if any, at which a member satisfies a specified property. For example, L may be the list of numbers $(4, 7, -3, 0, -2)$ and the property being searched for may be that of being negative. A simple representation of L would then be the assertion set

$$\mathbf{m}(4, 1, L)$$
$$\mathbf{m}(7, 2, L)$$
$$\mathbf{m}(-3, 3, L)$$
$$\mathbf{m}(0, 4, L)$$
$$\mathbf{m}(-2, 5, L)$$

where $\mathbf{m}(u, i, x)$ means that member u occupies position i in list x. By merely posing the goal

$$? \, \mathbf{m}(u, k, L), u < 0$$

one obtains an extremely simple non-deterministic program whose standard execution will deliver two solutions, $k := 3$ and $k := 5$, in that order. The programmer knows that the first of these is the solution to the original problem because he knows that the interpreter will invoke the $\mathbf{m}$ assertions in their textual order, and this has in turn been arranged to coincide with the position order of members in L. The second solution could, of course, be suppressed by use of the cut operator; thus

$$? \, \mathbf{m}(u, k, L), u < 0, /$$

In any event, the conclusion that the first computed solution gives the least position of a negative member depends here upon the algorithm's control component—that is, upon the assumption of the standard strategy; it does *not* follow from the program logic, which is why that logic is so simple.

The value of this programming style depends partly upon how convenient it is to present members of L in the appropriate order. If there were a great many $\mathbf{m}$ assertions, and these were generated in a disordered fashion by some preceding data preparation process, then it might be preferable to use a deterministic program which was indifferent to their textual order.

Here is one such program:

$$? \textbf{leastpos}(k, 1, 5, L)$$
$$\textbf{leastpos}(k, i, n, x) \quad \textbf{if} \quad \textbf{m}(u, i, x), u < 0, k = i$$
$$\textbf{leastpos}(k, i, n, x) \quad \textbf{if} \quad \textbf{m}(u, i, x), u \geqslant 0,$$
$$\textbf{leastpos}(k, i + 1, n, x)$$

and the same assertions representing L, in *any* order

The predicate $\textbf{leastpos}(k, i, n, x)$ means that k is the least position of a negative member in the sublist of x extending from position i to position n inclusive. The program has just one solution, $k := 3$, and the fact that this is the least position is now logically implied by the procedures. So by simplifying the control requirements—by relaxing all assumptions about textual ordering—and thereby easing the task of data preparation, we have had to make the program more complex logically than it was previously. Both formulations represent essentially the same algorithm and differ little in terms of efficiency.

III.4.2. Peak Detection

Whilst non-deterministic programs can be very easy to write, they cannot always be executed efficiently using the standard control options. A good example of this fact is provided by the problem of deciding whether a series of numbers is unimodal in the sense of ascending to a single maximum and then descending again (i.e., has a single peak). The series $L = (1, 3, 4, 8, 6, 5, 2, 0)$ behaves in this way, the peak's maximum being 8. The simplest way of describing the problem in logic is perhaps the following:

Program 11

$$? \textbf{peak}(1.3.4.8.6.5.2.0.NIL)$$
$$\textbf{peak}(x) \quad \textbf{if} \quad \textbf{append}(x_1, x_2, x), \textbf{up}(x_1), \textbf{down}(x_2)$$
$$\textbf{up}(NIL)$$
$$\textbf{up}(u.NIL)$$
$$\textbf{up}(u.v.y) \quad \textbf{if} \quad u < v, \textbf{up}(v.y)$$
$$\textbf{down}(NIL)$$
$$\textbf{down}(u.NIL)$$
$$\textbf{down}(u.v.y) \quad \textbf{if} \quad u > v, \textbf{down}(v.y)$$
$$\textbf{append}(NIL, x, x)$$
$$\textbf{append}(v.y_1, y_2, v.y) \quad \textbf{if} \quad \textbf{append}(y_1, y_2, y)$$

Here, $\textbf{peak}(x)$ means that x is peaked; $\textbf{append}(x_1, x_2, x)$ means that x is the result of appending x_2 to the end of x_1; $\textbf{up}(x_1)$ means that x_1 is an ascending series, possibly empty, and **down**(x_2) means that x_2 is a descending series, possibly empty.

When the **peak** procedure is invoked, it tries to split the input list into two parts, the first ascending and the second descending; this splitting is carried out by the **append** procedures. Because both **append** procedures usually respond to the **append** calls generated during execution, the algorithm behaves non-deterministically, potentially trying every possible way of splitting the input series. This behaviour has two significant deficiencies. First, each new decomposition is followed by complete inspections of the new choices of x_1 and x_2, say

$$x_1 = (1, 3, 4)$$
$$x_2 = (8, 6, 5, 2, 0)$$

even though an earlier decomposition such as

$$x_1' = (1, 3)$$
$$x_2' = (4, 8, 6, 5, 2, 0)$$

may have already ascertained the correct ordering of certain subseries within x_1 and/or x_2. Second, when the input series does not satisfy the **peak** property, this program does not recognize the fact until it has tried every possible decomposition. This observation brings attention to an important point in logic programming methodology: it is not sufficient to consider only the efficiency of successful computations—one must also try to ensure that execution *fails efficiently* when no solutions exist.

These deficiencies cannot be remedied by any straightforward exploitation of the control strategy, and so if a better algorithm is required then the logic has to be changed. The program below gives a much more efficient and deterministic algorithm, but is not such an obvious way of capturing the problem specification.

Program 12

> ? **peak**$(1.3.4.8.6.5.2.0)$
> **peak**(NIL)
> **peak**$(u.NIL)$
> **peak**$(u.v.y)$ **if** $u < v$, **peak**$(v.y)$
> **peak**$(u.v.y)$ **if** $u > v$, **down**$(v.y)$
> and the same **down** procedures as before

The decomposition of the input series is now implicit in the logic of the **peak** procedures. As execution proceeds, the third procedure is used to search forward through the series, seeking the largest ascending subseries beginning at the start of L. As soon as a descending pair is found, control passes to the fourth procedure, which decides whether the remaining part of the series is descending. There is very little duplication of member comparisons and, for an unsolvable goal, execution terminates as soon as a pair is found to be wrongly ordered. Note that these improvements have not required the introduction of any new predicates, but only more subtle statements about those already used; in fact, the **up** and **append** predicates have been dispensed with.

III.4.3. The Substring Problem

Any non-deterministic program can be transformed into a more deterministic program whose execution simulates the execution of the former one. The transformation does not change the algorithm, but rather aims to describe in the logic of the new program aspects of the algorithm which were realized through the control of the previous program.

This idea is illustrated here by the substring problem: given two character strings x and y, decide whether x is a substring of y. For instance, $x = (A, B, C)$ is a substring of $y = (A, B, \underline{A, B, C,} D)$. Problems of this kind arise in applications such as text editing and bibliographic data retrieval. A simple algorithm is one which generates successive suffixes of y, each time testing whether x is a prefix of the current suffix. In this context, a suffix y' of y is a substring of y which extends up to the end of y, and x is a prefix of y' if it is a substring of y' which starts at the beginning of y'. The algorithm generates from $y = (A, B, A, B, C, D)$ the suffixes

$$(A, B, A, B, C, D)$$
$$(B, A, B, C, D)$$
$$(\underline{A, B, C,} D) \dots (A, B, C) \text{ is a prefix}$$
$$\text{etc.}$$

and so discovers the suffix (A, B, C, D) of which $x = (A, B, C)$ is a prefix, thus solving the problem.

The logic underlying this process can be formulated quite neatly by using the predicates **string**(x, y) and **prefix**(x, y) to mean that x is a substring of y and that x is a prefix of y, respectively. Representing strings by the usual structured terms, one can obtain the algorithm just described by standard execution of the following non-deterministic program:

Program 13

$$? \textbf{string}(A.B.C.NIL, A.B.A.B.C.D.NIL)$$
string1 : **string**(x, y) **if** **prefix**(x, y)
string2 : **string**$(x, v.y')$ **if** **string**(x, y')
prefix1 : **prefix**(NIL, y)
prefix2 : **prefix**$(v.x', v.y')$ **if** **prefix**(x', y')

The resulting behaviour, in terms of applying **prefix** tests to successive suffixes, is shown below, where the first three computations only are illustrated; dots and *NILS*s have been omitted for clarity.

? **string** (*ABC, ABABCD*)	*select first suffix*
? **prefix** (*ABC, ABABCD*)	begin **prefix** test
? **prefix** (*BC, BABCD*)	
? **prefix** (*C, ABCD*)	
■	fails, so backtrack
? **string** (*ABC, ABABCD*)	
? **string** (*ABC, BABCD*)	*select second suffix*
? **prefix** (*ABC, BABCD*)	begin **prefix test**
■	fails, so backtrack
? **string** (*ABC, BABCD*)	
? **string** (*ABC, ABCD*)	*select third suffix*
? **prefix** (*ABC, ABCD*)	begin **prefix** test
? **prefix** (*BC, BCD*)	
? **prefix** (*C, CD*)	
? **prefix** (*NIL, D.NIL *)	
? solved with answer '*yes*'	

Observe how each time a **prefix** test fails, execution backtracks to the most recently activated **string** call. That call previously invoked string1 in order to initiate the (unsuccessful) **prefix** test for the current suffix, but must now be reactivated to invoke string2 instead, thus generating the next suffix. This behaviour occurs every time execution encounters a failure node, of which there are generally many.

When the interpreter backtracks, it effectively reminds itself that the original input string x is (A, B, C) and it also finds out what the current suffix is. Note that this information is not directly available in the goal at the point when failure occurs. For instance, the first computation fails when the goal is

$$? \text{ prefix} (C, ABCD)$$

and this in itself says nothing useful about either x or the current suffix. The information is instead recovered from an earlier goal in the execution's history, accessed via the backtracking mechanism.

It is possible to construct a much more deterministic program which, upon failing a **prefix** test, does not need to backtrack in order to access the information necessary for dealing with the next suffix—it obtains it instead from extra parameters held in the current goal. This is achieved by the use of a new predicate **string***(w, z, x, y'), which is read as

w is a prefix of z **or** x is a substring of y'

This anticipates some stage of execution engaged in deciding whether w is a prefix of z in the course of deciding whether x is a substring of some current suffix $v.y'$; if this **prefix** test fails then the next suffix y' is available in the fourth argument position of **string***, and x is available from the third. For instance, the first failure in the example above arises for the case in which $w = C.NIL$, $z = A.B.C.D.NIL$, $x = A.B.C.NIL$ and $v.y' = A.B.A.B.C.D.NIL$. Here is the new program:

Program 14

$$? \, \text{string}(A.B.C.NIL, A.B.A.B.C.D.NIL)$$

string3 : **string**(NIL, y)

string4 : **string**$(x, v.y')$ **if** **string***$(x, v.y', x, y')$

string*1 : **string***(NIL, z, x, y')

string*2 : **string***(NIL, z, x, y') **if** **string**(x, y')

string*3 : **string***$(v.w, v.z, x, y')$ **if** **string***(w, z, x, y')

string*4 : **string***$(u.w, v.z, x, y')$ **if** $u \neq v$, **string**(x, y')

Here, string3 deals with the case formerly covered by prefixl, whilst string4 instigates both the prefix testing and suffix selection formerly dealt with separately by string1 and string2. Procedures string*1 and string*3 are direct analogues of prefix1 and prefix2, applying the prefix test to the first two parameters of **string*** whilst maintaining a record of x and the next suffix y' in the last two parameters. Procedures string*2 and string*4 contribute the essence of the new program, in that their logic arranges for inspection of the next suffix when the prefix test is concluded for the current one; they deal respectively with the successful and unsuccessful outcomes of that test. In particular, if the test fails then string*4 is invoked and injects x and y' into a new phase of computation processing the next suffix. Here is part of the execution using the new program:

? **string**$(ABC, ABABCD)$
? **string***$(ABC, ABABCD, ABC, BABCD)$ *processing first suffix*
? **string***$(\ BC, \ BABCD, ABC, BABCD)$
? **string***$(\ C, \ \ \ ABCD, ABC, BABCD)$

                                              prefix test now fails

? $C \neq A$, **string**$(ABC, BABCD)$
? **string**$(ABC, BABCD)$
? **string***$(ABC, \ BABCD, ABC, \ ABCD)$ *processing second suffix*
etc.

When the prefix test fails for the first suffix, by virtue of the goal

? **string***$(C, ABCD, ABC, BABCD)$

being unable to invoke string*3 that goal contains sufficient information to generate and initiate inspection of the next suffix. Backtracking is therefore unnecessary upon prefix test failure. The algorithm is unchanged, but is now realized through a different blend of logic and control. Efficiency is not necessarily improved; the tradeoff between the burden of managing back-tracking and the burden of processing more complicated predicates will depend upon the particular interpreter being used. However, the kind of transformation demonstrated here has importance in other directions. Specifically, logic representations of much more sophisticated algorithms for solving the substring problem can be derived more easily from Program 14 than from Program 13. Those algorithms depend crucially upon detailed logical analyses of prefix test failures based upon the sort of information held in the **string*** calls of Program 14.

III.5. Negation

Quite often the programmer meets problems whose most natural formu-lations require the means of expressing 'not'. For instance, one might wish to query a database by asking whether some data item does *not* occur in it. Negation can be expressed straightforwardly in full first-order logic, or even in general clausal form, by using the negation symbol $\neg$. However, this symbol is not available in the more restricted sentences (Horn clauses) used for logic procedures. This deficiency can be remedied in a variety of ways. To illustrate some of them, we shall consider a particular programming problem: given a list x and an element u, insert u somewhere in x if it does not already occur in x, but otherwise delete it from x; whichever is the case, a new list y is generated. The precise details of the insertion and deletion operations are unimportant. What is important is that the program must decide whether or not a condition holds and then take appropriate action. Four different logic formulations of the problem are discussed here.

FORMULATION 1

Let the predicate **newlist**(u, x, y) express that y is the new list obtained from x according to whether or not u occurs in x. Predicates **delete**(u, x, y) and **insert**(u, x, y) respectively express that y results from deleting u from x, and y results from inserting u into x. The test of the occurrence of u in x can be captured by using two more predicates, **inlist**(u, x) and **not-inlist**(u, x), whose meanings are self-evident. Equipped with these, and assuming a typical goal with lists represented by the usual terms, the first formulation is as follows:

Program 15

> ? newlist(D, $A.B.C.NIL$, y)
> newlist(u, x, y)   if   inlist(u, x), delete(u, x, y)
> newlist(u, x, y)   if   not-inlist(u, x), insert(u, x, y)
> inlist(u, $u.x$)
> inlist(u, $v.x$)   if   inlist(u, x)
> not-inlist(u, NIL)
> not-inlist(u, $v.x$)   if $u \neq v$, not-inlist(u, x)
> and procedures for **insert** and **delete**.

This program is perfectly straightforward and will compute some solution like $y := A.B.C.D.NIL$, depending upon just how the insertion is performed. Its main disadvantage is in requiring separate descriptions of the **inlist** and **not-inlist** relations; because they are so closely related there must be considerable redundancy in the program's logical content.

FORMULATION 2

The second approach dispenses with the **not-inlist** procedures by interpreting the *failure* to solve a call **inlist**(u, x) as a cue for performing insertion. It also requires the use of the cut operator.

Program 16

> ? newlist(D, $A.B.C.NIL$, y)
> newlist(u, x, y)   if   inlist(u, x), /, delete(u, x, y)
> newlist(u, x, y)   if   insert(u, x, y)
> and procedures for **inlist**, **insert** and **delete**.

This program is much more concise and also executes much more efficiently, because insertion does not, as in Program 15, depend upon solving a call **not-inlist**(D, $A.B.C.NIL$); it is sufficient instead to fail the **inlist** call in the first procedure and so proceed straight to the second. Otherwise, if the **inlist** call succeeds, the activation of / will excise the untried choice of the second procedure (so preventing insertion) and deletion is then performed.

Although Program 16 is operationally correct, it is nevertheless seriously flawed in its logic, because the second **newlist** procedure is not consistent with the intended meaning of the **newlist** predicate: that procedure declares that y is always obtainable from x by performing an insertion, whereas our specification requires that insertion be conditional upon the non-occurrence of u in x. The reason why this logically incorrect procedure does not produce incorrect run-time results is that its invocation has been carefully constrained by the control information implicit in the textual ordering together with the use of /.

FORMULATION 3

The third method is similar in principle to the first one, but eliminates the need for separate procedure sets describing complementary relations like **inlist** and **not-inlist**. It relies instead upon computing explicit *YES/NO* answers to queries about membership in relations.

Introduce new predicates **inlist***(u, x, YES) and **inlist***(u, x, NO) to express respectively that *u* occurs in *x* and *u* does not occur in *x*. Another predicate **newlist***(u, x, y, z) means that *y* is obtained by either deleting *u* from or inserting *u* into *x* according to whether *z* is *YES* or *NO*. The program can then be written as follows.

Program 17

> ? **newlist**(*D*, *A.B.C.NIL*, *y*)
> **newlist**(*u*, *x*, *y*)   if   **inlist***(*u*, *x*, *z*), **newlist***(*u*, *x*, *y*, *z*)
> **newlist***(*u*, *x*, *y*, *YES*)   if   **delete**(*u*, *x*, *y*)
> **newlist***(*u*, *x*, *y*, *NO*)   if   **insert**(*u*, *x*, *y*)
> **inlist***(*u*, *NIL*, *NO*)
> **inlist***(*u*, *u.x*, *YES*)
> **inlist***(*u*, *v.x*, *z*)   if   *u* ≠ *v*, **inlist***(*u*, *x*, *z*)
> and procedures for **delete** and **insert**

During execution the **inlist*** call computes an answer *YES* or *NO* for the variable *z* and distributes it to the **newlist*** call; this then invokes either a deletion procedure or an insertion procedure as appropriate.

Program 17 is logically correct, efficient, reasonably intelligible and indifferent to the ordering of the principal procedures. It is probably the best choice for use with interpreters offering only the standard control strategy. Despite these advantages, the method becomes unsatisfactory when applied to problems involving a large number of negation tests on different relations, because of the tedium of writing many procedures analogous to those above for **inlist***. Observe also that the method tends to disseminate complications in logical structure throughout the program—for instance, Program 17 has to use the somewhat cumbersome **newlist*** relation in order to cater for the various actions contingent upon the *YES/NO* answers computed by **inlist***.

FORMULATION 4

This final formulation is applicable to implementations which allow quasi-negated calls in programs and which rely upon the so-called "closed-world assumption": the negation of **P** holds if **P** is unprovable. This device is generally known as *negation-as-failure*. Here is the program:

Program 18

> ? **newlist**(D, $A.B.C.NIL$, y)
> **newlist**(u, x, y)   **if**   **inlist**(u, x), **delete**(u, x, y)
> **newlist**(u, x, y)   **if** $\sim$**inlist**(u, x), **insert**(u, x, y)
> and procedures for **inlist**, **delete** and **insert**.

The symbol $\sim$ is read as 'not' but is deliberately different from the strict negation connective $\neg$, because its meaning is not quite the same. The operational effect of $\sim$ is as follows. When the interpreter activates a quasi-negated call of the form $\sim$**P**, it attempts to solve **P**. If this attempt fails then the original call $\sim$**P** is treated as having been solved; thus the failure to prove **P** is taken as proof that $\neg$**P** holds. On the other hand, if the call **P** is solved then the original call $\sim$**P** is treated as having failed.

Applied to our example, execution will eventually activate the call $\sim$**inlist**(D, $A.B.C.NIL$) having entered the second **newlist** procedure. The interpreter therefore tries to solve the call **inlist**(D, $A.B.C.NIL$), fails this task, and so concludes that D does not occur in (A, B, C)—that is, considers the quasi-negated call to have been solved; thus it proceeds to perform the insertion as expected.

The position is a little more complicated in circumstances where a call like $\sim$**P**(x) is activated with x currently unbound. If the ensuing attempt to solve **P** succeeds without binding a term to x then it remains legitimate to fail the call $\sim$**P**(x). However, if instead the call **P**(x) succeeds and makes a binding to x, then this only establishes $(\exists x)$**P**(x), which tells us nothing about the question posed by the quasi-negated call $\sim$**P**(x) whose interpretation is $(\exists x)(\neg$**P**(x)). The interpreter is not justified in either succeeding or failing that call, and so should abort execution and report an operational error. The IC-PROLOG implementation behaves exactly in this manner.

The treatment of negation in early PROLOG implementations also depended upon the closed-world assumption. These systems allowed one to write procedures like

$$\text{proc} : \mathbf{Q}(y) \quad \textbf{if} \quad \textbf{not}(P(x))$$

The call $P(x)$ was passed as a parameter to a built-in procedure set

> not1 : **not**(z)   **if** z, /, **FAIL**
> not2 : **not**(z)

with z taking the role of a metavariable. Again, if the transmitted call $P(x)$ failed (when activated from not1) then the call **not**($P(x)$) would succeed through the subsequent invocation of not2. Alternatively, if $P(x)$ succeeded in not1 then the / would excise the use of not2 and the pseudocall **FAIL** would force a failure exit from not1 as required. Consideration of the binding state of x in the event of $P(x)$ succeeding is unnecessary here, because these systems all interpreted proc as

$$\text{for all } y, \ \mathbf{Q}(y) \quad \textbf{if} \quad \neg(\exists x)\mathbf{P}(x)$$

in contrast to the IC-PROLOG interpretation of

$$\mathbf{Q}(y) \quad \textbf{if} \quad \sim\mathbf{P}(x)$$

as

$$\text{for all } x, y, \ \mathbf{Q}(y) \quad \textbf{if} \quad \neg\mathbf{P}(x)$$

which is equivalent to

$$\text{for all } y, \ \mathbf{Q}(y) \quad \textbf{if} \quad (\exists x)(\neg\mathbf{P}(x))$$

The use of $\sim$ in order to realize negation through failure leads to no inconsistencies in standard (Horn-clause) programs, and adds significantly to the programmer's resources. Although it does not provide quite as much computational power as a logic system supporting strict negation, programmers may nevertheless read $\sim\mathbf{P}(x)$ casually as 'not $\mathbf{P}(x)$' with impunity provided they retain awareness of the device's operational effect. One reason for the diminished power of $\sim$, incidentally, is that whilst it allows for the representation of negated queries, it does not cater for the expression of negative facts. One consequence of this is that even when a call $\sim\mathbf{P}(x)$ succeeds, x remains unbound; thus the computation does not yield particular answers for x. A more general logic system might instead compute $x := 2$, showing that the fact $\neg\mathbf{P}(2)$ was implied by the program's procedures.

Program 18 suffers a run-time inefficiency deserving remedy, in that two attempts are made to solve **inlist**$(D, A.B.C.NIL)$, once in each **newlist** procedure. That is, when it has been tried in the first procedure and has failed, it is tried again in the course of dealing with the second procedure's negated call. Behaviour of this kind is referred to as 'shallow backtracking' and can be reduced by slightly enhancing the syntax of programs with an **if–then–else** construct. Thus in IC-PROLOG one could replace the two **newlist** procedures by the single statement

$$\textbf{newlist}(u, x, y) \quad \textbf{if} \quad \textbf{inlist}(u, x) \quad \textbf{then} \quad \textbf{delete}(u, x, y)$$
$$\textbf{else} \quad \textbf{insert}(u, x, y)$$

This provides some welcome 'syntactic sugar' and also dispenses with explicit negation, being interpreted as

> To solve **newlist**(u, x, y), first attempt to solve **inlist**(u, x);
> if successful then perform deletion; otherwise perform
> insertion.

It also executes more efficiently by only processing the **inlist** call once.

III.6. Parameter Matching

The parameter-matching capability of a logic interpreter can be viewed as a primitive data processor. Although it merely attempts to match data represented by terms, it can be exploited in quite powerful ways.

As a simple example, suppose one wished to decide whether two lists were identical. The most obvious algorithm just compares successive corresponding members of the lists, and can be generated by using the procedures

$$\textbf{equal}(NIL, NIL)$$
$$\textbf{equal}(u.x, u.y) \quad \textbf{if} \quad \textbf{equal}(x, y)$$

Here the incremental process involved in solving a goal like

$$? \, \textbf{equal}(A.B.C.NIL, A.B.C.NIL)$$

has been made explicit through the use of an iterative procedure. However, the same effect can be obtained by using just one procedure instead, namely

$$\textbf{equal}(x, x)$$

Now the programmer relies upon the inherent matching mechanism of the interpreter to perform all the necessary comparisons of members. As well as being simpler, this method is almost certainly more efficient because execution only entails one procedure invocation. Furthermore, this single procedure can be used to compare any pair of terms, whether they represent lists, matrices, trees or much more complicated data structures. Few other programming languages provide such a universal built-in facility for data structure comparison.

In general, parameter matching produces various interrelated assignments of terms to variables. This feature can be used to manipulate the components of a composite data structure in a single step. For example, the procedure

$$\textbf{subtrees}(t(x, y), x, y)$$

can be invoked in order to extract the left and right subtrees x and y from a given binary tree $t(x, y)$ using a goal such as

$$? \, \textbf{subtrees}(t(t(A, B), t(C, D)), x, y)$$

which yields $x := t(A, B)$ and $y := t(C, D)$. On the other hand, a goal like

$$? \, \textbf{subtrees}(z, t(A, B), t(C, D))$$

constructs, from the same procedure, the binary tree $z := t(t(A, B), t(C, D))$. All the concrete data-manipulating operations entailed in the computations are achieved 'behind the scenes' by the interpreter, sparing the programmer the tedium of describing them himself.

Devising programs which commit much of their data processing to single parameter-matching steps is not always possible, and when possible is not necessarily easy or even desirable. Suppose we were presented with the task of attaching an element u to the end of some list x, producing a new list y—a specialized case of list insertion. It is easy enough to compose an appropriate iterative program, say

$$? \text{ attach}(D, A.B.C.NIL, y)$$
$$\text{attach}(u, NIL, u.NIL)$$
$$\text{attach}(u, v.x, v.y) \quad \textbf{if} \quad \text{attach}(u, x, y)$$

which computes $y := A.B.C.D.NIL$. But it is not so easy to find the alternative program

$$? \text{ attach}^*(D, A.B.C.w, w, y)$$
$$\text{attach}^*(z, v, z.NIL, v)$$

which also computes $y := A.B.C.D.NIL$, but does so in one step. The **attach*** program depends upon the somewhat unintuitive device of representing the input list (A, B, C) as the result of deleting any unspecified 'tail' fragment w from the end of $A.B.C.w$, and the final assignment to y emerges from a rather convoluted matching operation. It is probably more efficient than the attach program but is much less intelligible. For other problems, such as that of reversing an arbitrary list, there seem to be no methods of solution which require just one procedure invocation.

III.7. Switches

Many algorithms can be described conveniently by programs which consult and update programmer-defined switches which direct control to particular procedures. Incorporating such mechanisms into logic programs is not necessarily desirable, because programs then tend to be rather inflexible—they are written with perhaps just one control sequence in mind and so have a more limited range of application than logically equivalent programs written with fewer assumptions about run-time behaviour. Nevertheless, if a programmer is not concerned about this then he may favour explicit control-determining devices like switches on the grounds that they make his algorithmic intentions more discernible.

For an example consider again the problem of deciding whether a list x like $(1, 3, 4, 8, 6, 5, 2, 0)$ is peaked, that is, consists of a descending list x_2

appended to an ascending list x_1, allowing both x_1 and x_2 to be empty lists or unit lists as special cases. A sensible algorithm is one whose first phase scans forward through the ascending portion x_1 until discovering the first descending pair, if any, at which point it switches to a second phase which confirms the descending nature of the remaining portion. Program 12 in Section III.4.2 gave this behaviour, using a predicate **peak**(x) to express the desired property of x. A different program is shown below whose logic is based upon the idea of a switch, having two possible states UP and $DOWN$, which directs control to the procedures appropriate to the current phase of the algorithm.

Program 19

> ? **peak***$(1.3.4.8.6.5.2.0.NIL, z)$
> **peak***(NIL, z)
> **peak***$(u.NIL, z)$
> **peak***$(u.v.w, UP\ )$ **if** $u < v$, **peak***$(v.w,\qquad UP)$
> **peak***$(u.v.w, z\quad\ )$ **if** $u > v$, **peak***$(v.w, DOWN)$

Here a predicate of the form **peak***(y, UP) means that y consists of a peaked list y_2 appended to the end of an ascending list y_1, and a predicate **peak***$(y, DOWN)$ means that y is a descending list.

During execution each call to **peak*** after the first carries a constant symbol in its second argument position, which serves as the switch state determining which **peak*** procedures apply to the current phase of the algorithm. Its effect is made clear by the following computation, in which calls to $<$ and $>$, and dots and NILs, have been omitted to ease the presentation.

> ? **peak***$(13486520, z)$
> ? **peak***$(\ 3486520, UP)$ first phase with switch UP
> ? **peak***$(\ \ 486520, UP)$
> ? **peak***$(\ \ \ 86520, UP)$
>
> ? **peak***$(\quad 6520, DOWN)$ second phase with switch $DOWN$
> ? **peak***$(\qquad 520, DOWN)$
> ? **peak***$(\qquad\ 20, DOWN)$
> ? **peak***$(\qquad\ \ 0, DOWN)$
> ?   solved with answer '*yes*'

In the first phase, with the switch in the UP state, only the first iterative **peak*** procedure is used for driving the scanning process forward through the input list. This procedure becomes effectively switched off (no longer invokable) as soon as the switch changes to the $DOWN$ state upon discovery of the first descending pair $(8, 6)$. The second iterative **peak*** procedure is then switched on and is used to complete the scanning process.

Observe that this new formulation dispenses with the **down** procedures necessary for Program 12 and is consequently a rather shorter program. In general, the number of distinct procedure names in a program can be reduced by using more elaborate predicates containing switch variables; theoretically all algorithms can be described by logic programs employing just one procedure name (predicate symbol) provided that one has a sufficiently rich supply of compensating constant symbols to denote the switch states. Also, the use of switches as shown above is probably the closest way of making logic programs mimic the use of GO TO statements as provided, for better or worse, in conventional languages.

III.8. Background

The idea of representing algorithms using separable definitions of their logic and control components plays a central role in the philosophy of logic programming, and is explained in a paper by Kowalski (1979b) entitled

$$\text{algorithm} = \text{logic} + \text{control}$$

This schema is illustrated there using various logic + control combinations for a number of familiar algorithms. This paper also emphasizes how the separation of logic from control simplifies the task of analysing an algorithm's logical competence and run-time efficiency.

Conventionally, a program is thought of as describing an algorithm, allowing us to write

$$\begin{aligned}\text{program} &= \text{description of algorithm} \\ &= \text{description of (logic} + \text{control)}\end{aligned}$$

With logic programming, this schema can be expanded a further step as follows:

$$\begin{aligned}\text{program} = \ &\text{description of logic} \\ &+ \\ &\text{description of control}\end{aligned}$$

Most other programming formalisms are incapable of resolving the composition of programs in this way, only being able to describe (logic + control) as a composite entity. For instance, they typically allow the assigned states of variables to govern the path of execution, yet this in turn determines which assignments take place and in which order. The logical relationships between the variables cannot then be analysed or explained without reference to the state of execution, a circumstance which afflicts current programming practice in a variety of unfortunate ways. The interest in 'structured programming' during the 1970s touched upon this problem but failed to address its fundamental cause. More discussion of this can be found in Chapter VIII.

When provided with a logic interpreter, the programmer is in effect being given a prewritten description of control, so his task is chiefly concerned with composing the remaining description of logic. The former description is not problem specific, whilst the latter one is. It has been one of the major successes of research in logic programming to have shown that, despite the simplicity and non-specificity of the control strategy adopted by standard interpreters, one can nevertheless elicit a rich spectrum of practical algorithms. Previously some critics of logic had held that the absence of explicit control directives in source programs would deprive the programmer of the means of directing execution efficiently, and that this deficit could only be compensated by investing interpreters with very intelligent problem-solving strategies. Such criticism is no longer tenable. Provided that the programmer properly understands his interpreter's behaviour, he can then, broadly speaking, direct execution as efficiently as desired by choosing appropriate input logic. Of course, modern interpreters do provide a number of useful control directives to supplement the built-in strategy, but these are extras which the programmer is not bound to use.

The successful vindication of logic programming arose from careful studies of concrete computational problems undertaken by many researchers. Their work gradually revealed the styles of logic best suited to algorithms performing testing, searching, iteration, recursion, coroutining, parallelism, space saving and many other important mechanisms. The earliest comprehensive collection of such studies is the report 'Logic for Problem Solving' by Kowalski (1974a). Amongst its many examples are ingenious formulations of parsing, sorting and plan-formation problems which illustrate the interplay of logic and control in top-down, bottom-up, deterministic and non-deterministic algorithms.

Comparisons of iterative and recursive styles can be found in papers by Clark (1977) and by Clark and Kowalski (1977). Kowalski's discovery of the quasi-bottom-up style has proved particularly useful; for instance, observing that the 'obvious' definition of Fibonacci numbers inefficiently repeats identical operations when executed top-down, he presents an alternative quasi-bottom-up definition yielding highly efficient behaviour. A similar style was independently discovered by Hogger (1976) which overcame the inefficiencies arising from non-determinism in the top-down recursive definition of the standard linear programming Simplex algorithm; the eigenproblem of Section III.3.3 is based upon the same treatment.

The conversion to deterministic form of the non-deterministic 'quadratic' program for the substring problem (Program 13 in Section III.4.3) was first reported by Hogger (1978b), who then (1979b) showed it to be an important first step in the logical derivation of the more difficult linear and sublinear algorithms developed respectively by Knuth, Morris and Pratt (1976) and by Boyer and Moore (1977).

The use of argument positions to accommodate explicit *YES/NO* answers was first proposed by Clark (1977), to whom is owed the list-membership procedures given in Section III.5 for the third formulation of the negation problem. Clark (1978) also undertook the metatheoretical analysis necessary for justifying the use of quasi-negation ($\sim$). The semantics and implementation of $\sim$ in IC-PROLOG are described by Clark and McCabe (1980), and the general negation problem and its interaction with other classical PROLOG control features are surveyed in a paper by Dahl (1980).

Several subtle ways of exploiting parameter matching were presented by Tärnlund to a Logic Programming Workshop held at Imperial College in 1976. Some of these relied upon clever uses of the 'difference list' data structure representation used in the **attach*** program in Section III.6; other examples of its usefulness appear in a paper by Clark and Tärnlund (1977).

In this chapter it has been possible to survey only a small sample of logic programming styles. Many more can be found in the report 'Logic Information Processing' by Tärnlund (1975b); the book *Logic for Problem Solving* by Kowalski (1979a); the paper 'Algorithm = Logic + Control' by Kowalski (1979b), from which the pathfinding Programs 7 and 8 presented here were adapted, and in the doctoral theses by Hogger (1979a) and Clark (1979). Programmers who have worked extensively with PROLOG implementations will have already discovered many other techniques not described in the literature.

IV DATA STRUCTURES

Definitions of programming languages often treat data structures and procedures as distinct kinds of computational resource. This supposed distinction is apparent in the familiar slogan

$$\text{program} = \text{algorithm} + \text{data structure}$$

that is,

$$= \text{method of processing} + \text{object processed}$$

It also underlies certain programming methods which, in pursuit of flexibility, encourage one to define procedures and their associated concrete data structures separately. It is particularly apparent in the usual presentations of conventional languages like FORTRAN and BASIC, and is arguably useful for teaching basic computational concepts to novice programmers.

If we substitute 'logic + control' for 'algorithm' in the schema above and make a slight rearrangement, then we obtain

$$\text{program} = (\text{logic} + \text{data structure}) + \text{control}$$

Now, in the logic programming context, logic procedures can themselves be employed as data structures, so dispelling any supposed difference between these entities. Terms, of course, also serve as data structures. So whatever kinds of data structures are used, they are necessarily subsumed within the logic component. Moreover, logic programs provide a more or less null description of control, because this is the province of the interpreter. By combining all these considerations, the schema applied to logic programming therefore contracts to

$$\text{program} = \text{logic}$$

and is consistent with our applying the term 'program' to a set of logic statements.

Since the essential ingredients (terms and procedures) of data structures have already been presented, this chapter does not need to introduce any new entities. Instead it concentrates upon the various ways of using terms and procedures in order to achieve particular kinds of data processing.

IV.1. Representation and Access

The most primitive data items in logic programming are constants, such as *10* and *NIL*, which have no internal structure. We use them for all sorts of purposes: as numerals, items in strings, switches and sometimes as names for other data items, to mention but a few. More often, though, programs deal with structured data items, which are organized collections of primitive items. The two principal ways of representing structured data are the *term representation* and the *assertional representation*, although there are other ways besides these. They each have various merits and demerits in relation to programming style and ease of implementation.

IV.1.1. Terms and Assertions

In the term representation, structured data is formed by using function symbols to collect components into groups. A list $(10, 20, 30)$ could be represented by the term *10.20.30.NIL* in which each dot functor groups the element to its left with the tail fragment to its right. Both constants and structured terms can be viewed as essentially passive objects available for manipulation by procedures.

Structured terms of this kind will probably appear rather alien to those programmers only familiar with languages like FORTRAN, BASIC and ALGOL, which rely almost exclusively upon arrays for representing structured data. The various kinds of tree-structured records definable in COBOL, PL/1 and PASCAL bear a little more resemblance to logic terms, but the greatest similarity is probably manifested in LISP; in fact, the use of structured terms can be loosely thought of as the 'LISP-like' mode of logic programming.

A major benefit of using terms to represent data is the degree of compactness and elegance they can confer upon the procedures employed to process them. A classic example is the appending of two lists to produce a third one. If one is using an ALGOL-like language dependent upon array representations, the individual members of the two given lists must be accessed and copied to appropriate positions of the third one, all of which demands the customary paraphernalia of iterative subscript generation, for instance, checking list lengths, defining loop bounds, preventing array overflow and so on. Whereas in logic one may simply write

$$\textbf{append}(NIL, y, y)$$
$$\textbf{append}(u.x, y, u.z) \quad \textbf{if} \quad \textbf{append}(x, y, z)$$

which is perfectly adequate to solve a call like **append**$(A.B.NIL, C.D.NIL, z)$ to produce $z := A.B.C.D.NIL$.

On the other hand, a potential disadvantage of structured terms is that their use can result in serious run-time inefficiencies, due mostly to the computational effort required to access their components, and partly to the burden they place upon the unification process. The problem of accessing components efficiently can be largely overcome by resorting to the assertional representation, which for the list $(10, 20, 30)$ could be as follows:

List Representation 1

$$\textbf{m}(10, 1, L)$$
$$\textbf{m}(20, 2, L)$$
$$\textbf{m}(30, 3, L)$$
$$\textbf{length}(L, 3)$$

Here a constant L has been used to name the data structure, and the last assertion states that the length of list L is 3.

This style sometimes introduces its own problems, in that it can force one to program at a 'lower' (more machine-oriented) level in order to compose the necessary accessing procedures: the programmer can become embroiled in considerations of bounds, subscripts, pointers, loop control, space saving and the like. In short, if one wants better access to data, one must work for it. It would be mistaken, however, to adopt the view that terms and assertions have opposite qualities regarding style and efficiency; much depends upon the particular programming problem under consideration.

IV.1.2. Direct and Indirect Access

Suppose that a list L has been represented in some way, and that we then wish to answer the query

$$?\,\textbf{m}(u, 2, L)$$

which asks which member occupies the second position. The determination of u is achieved by *direct access* if it requires no more than one computational step; otherwise it is achieved by *indirect access* (or 'computed' access). In general we expect direct access to be the more efficient case.

The mode of access depends upon the way the data is represented. If List Representation 1 above is used then the query can be answered by direct access, because its **m** call is immediately solvable by invoking the second **m** assertion, in other words, by performing one computation step. This is a consequence of making the data representation state the list's components explicitly.

The same list L could instead be represented by a set of statements defining the components implicitly, as follows:

List Representation 2

$$\mathbf{m}(u, i, L) \quad \mathbf{if} \quad \mathbf{length}(L, n),$$
$$1 \leqslant i, i \leqslant n, u = i * 10$$
$$\mathbf{length}(L, 3)$$

Solving the query does not now entail a direct lookup on a series of passive assertions; instead, this new representation behaves in a dynamic, procedural manner, instigating a computation of several steps in order to access the second member of L. Although this indirect access is slower, a proper comparison of the relative utilities of the two representations would also have to consider other factors, such as the amount of memory available for storing L; the second method is clearly more compact than the first when L is large and has a regular internal structure.

When structured terms are used, programming style becomes disposed toward the use of indirect accessing procedures which incrementally assemble or disassemble the terms in order to process their components. This is illustrated by the use of

List Representation 3

$$\mathbf{list}(L, 10.20.30.NIL)$$

which simply asserts that L is the list $(10, 20, 30)$.

In order to solve the query $\mathbf{m}(u, 2, L)$ we must now provide some accessing procedures such as

$$\mathbf{m}(u, 1, x) \quad \mathbf{if} \quad \mathbf{list}(x, u.x')$$
$$\mathbf{m}(u, i, x) \quad \mathbf{if} \quad \mathbf{list}(x, v.x'), \mathbf{m}(u, i-1, x')$$

whose invocation will, in general, incrementally decompose the term denoting L until it finds the required component.

Procedure sets representing structured data possess the interesting and occasionally useful property of being capable of generating alternative representations. For instance, List Representation 2 logically implies List Representation 1 and could be instructed, using appropriate control directives, to produce the latter as output. In this context, List Representation 2 would behave like an ordinary procedure set generating output data. This capacity of logic statements to function both as conventional procedures and as data structure representations shows that any supposed distinction between procedures and data is essentially a pragmatic one, applying to the use of those resources rather than to their intrinsic attributes.

IV.2. Structured Term Representations

IV.2.1. Some Common Data Types

All structured terms can be viewed as trees. For instance, a term of the form $f(t_1, t_2, \ldots t_n)$ can be viewed as the tree shown in Fig. IV.1a. For this reason, term representations are often eminently suitable for data structures which fall naturally into the tree data type. Thus the tree depicted in Fig. IV.1b, each of whose nodes bear some label, is directly representable

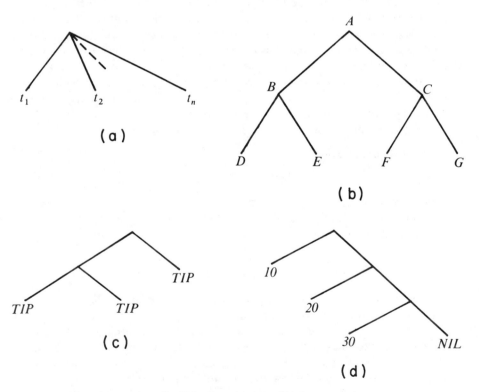

Fig. IV.1. Tree structure of terms.

by the term $t(t(D, B, E), A, t(F, C, G))$, where each subterm $t(u, x, v)$ depicts a tree with root node labeled x and two immediate descendant subtrees u and v. Likewise the tree in Fig. IV.1c is directly representable by a term $f(f(TIP,TIP),TIP)$.

When we use a term like $10.20.30.NIL$ to represent $(10, 20, 30)$, that term in standard prefix notation is $.(10,.(20,.(30,NIL)))$ and so has the tree structure shown in Fig. IV.1.d. Note in particular that the higher an element's position in the list, the deeper its position in the tree. The significance of this lies in the fact that algorithms which require that components of a term representation be accessed almost always have to decompose the term top-down, so that the deeper the components, the more effort is needed to access them. Thus if we want a list-processing program whose strategy entails making many random accesses to the list's members, then a term representation is likely to be a bad choice.

In principle terms can also be used to represent multidimensional arrays. For example, the term

$$10.20.30.NIL; \; 40.50.60.NIL; \; 15.20.25.NIL; \; NIL$$

could represent the matrix

$$\begin{bmatrix} 10 & 20 & 30 \\ 40 & 50 & 60 \\ 15 & 20 & 26 \end{bmatrix}$$

by treating each row as a list of elements and using the infix functor ; to bind the rows into a list terminating with an empty row NIL. This sort of representation is likely to be practical only for matrix-processing algorithms which process elements sequentially within their rows and also process the rows sequentially within the matrix.

IV.2.2. Consecutivity Programs

In order to illustrate further the impact of data structure representation upon programming style, we reconsider here the consecutivity problem; specifically, the problem is to determine which member t immediately follows C in the list $L = (A, B, C, D, E)$, and is posed by the goal

$$? \; \mathbf{consec}(C, t, A.B.C.D.E.NIL)$$

Now the most direct way of expressing the notion of consecutivity is probably as follows:

$$\mathbf{consec}(u, v, y) \quad \text{if} \quad \mathbf{m}(u, i, y), \mathbf{m}(v, i+1, y)$$

which says that u and v are consecutive in y if their positions differ by 1. If this statement is to be used as a procedure in the consecutivity program, then it will be necessary to devise further procedures which deal with the two **m** calls. Observe that the first of these, when activated, will seek the position i of C in L, whilst the second will seek the member v in L having the (now known) position $i+1$; thus the two **m** calls have different input/output characteristics. It is fairly easy to find a simple procedure set which is reasonably neutral, in terms of efficiency, with respect to these two input/output modes. It makes use of the predicate **occupies**(u, i, j, z), which means that member u occupies position $i - j + 1$ in the tail fragment $(z_j, \ldots z_n)$ of list z. Here is the resulting program.

Program 20

$$? \, \mathbf{consec}(C, t, A.B.C.D.E.NIL)$$
$$\mathbf{consec}(u, v, y) \quad \mathbf{if} \quad \mathbf{m}(u, i, y), \, \mathbf{m}(v, i+1, y)$$
$$\mathbf{m}(u, i, y) \quad \mathbf{if} \quad \mathbf{occupies}(u, i, 1, y)$$
$$\text{occ1} \; : \mathbf{occupies}(u, i, i, u.x)$$
$$\text{occ2}: \mathbf{occupies}(u, i, j, w.x) \quad \mathbf{if} \quad \mathbf{occupies}(u, i, j+1, x)$$

Procedures occ1 and occ2 generate a typical iteration whose index j controls search through the list L up to the point where the desired member is found. Although they accomplish this very efficiently, the program's execution as a whole is unfortunately inefficient, for the following reason. In order to compute the position of C in L, the first call to **m** has to decompose L, using occ2, into successive tail fragments $A.B.C.D.E.NIL$, $B.C.D.E.NIL$ and $C.D.E.NIL$; this is acceptable in itself as it just amounts to a linear search for C through L. However, the second call to **m**, which seeks the 4th member of L, has to generate those same fragments all over again. This is the penalty of posing the notion of consecutivity in terms of two independently processed **m** calls each of which suffers the burden of performing indirect access upon a structured term representation of the list L.

One way of obtaining better run-time behaviour without sacrificing the **consec** procedure used by Program 20 is to dispense with all the other procedures and simply rely upon a special **m** procedure built into the interpreter. This would represent the term $A.B.C.D.E.NIL$ by using an internal array, and the solution of the program's call $\mathbf{m}(v, 4, A.B.C.D.E.NIL)$ would then be accomplished in one step using direct access to the array's 4th cell. Built-in direct access procedures for list processing are worthwhile facilities because list processing is so ubiquitous in computational problem solving. However, logic admits so many other kinds of terms that it is impractical to build in direct access procedures for all of them, and so the general problem of accessing terms still remains.

Another way of improving efficiency is to alter the definition of consecutivity, for example by using the one shown in earlier chapters:

$$\mathbf{consec}(u, v, u.v.x)$$
$$\mathbf{consec}(u, v, w.y) \quad \textbf{if} \quad \mathbf{consec}(u, v, y)$$

These procedures effectively coalesce the separate **m** calls of Program 20 and consequently decompose the input list once instead of twice. They are highly efficient but less intuitive than the **consec** procedure of Program 20.

IV.2.3. Palindrome Programs

A palindrome is a list which reads forward the same as it reads backward—that is, is its own reverse. The problem of deciding whether a given list is a palindrome presents a number of choices of algorithm and programming style. Suppose the given list is (A, B, C, B, A). One way of posing the problem is to interpret the specification just given at face value; thus

$$? \mathbf{palin}(A.B.C.B.A.NIL)$$
$$\mathbf{palin}(x) \quad \textbf{if} \quad \mathbf{reverse}(x, x)$$
$$\text{and any procedures for } \mathbf{reverse}$$

The choice of reversal procedures strongly determines the efficiency of this approach. In Section III.2 of the last chapter we looked at two possibilities. The first one was to use

$$\mathbf{reverse}(NIL, NIL)$$
$$\mathbf{reverse}(u.x', y) \quad \textbf{if} \quad \mathbf{append}(y', u.NIL, y),$$
$$\mathbf{reverse}(x', y')$$

These procedures, when invoked in the present context, will try to show that $u.x' = A.B.C.B.A.NIL$ is the reverse of $y = A.B.C.B.A.NIL$ by (i) deleting the first member $u = A$ from $u.x'$ to leave $x' = B.C.B.A.NIL$, (ii) confirming that $u = A$ is the last member of y and then deleting it to leave $y' = A.B.C.B.NIL$ and finally (iii) showing that the reverse of x' is y'.

The second of these three tasks is undertaken by the **append** call and is the major source of inefficiency: no **append** procedures can be devised which solve that call in one step—instead, they invariably have to decompose y incrementally and simultaneously construct y' incrementally. Worse still, each invocation of the iterative **reverse** procedure instigates the decomposition by **append** of fragments which were identically decomposed by preceding invocations; consequently the execution contains much redundancy. The overall consequence is that the time taken by this algorithm is at least quadratically dependent upon the length of the input list. This poor behaviour can be traced fundamentally to the impossibility of gaining direct access to the last member of a term constructed from dot and *NIL*.

Another possibility is to use the following reversal procedures:

$$\textbf{reverse}(x, y) \quad \textbf{if} \quad \textbf{reverse*}(NIL, x, y)$$
$$\textbf{reverse*}(y, NIL, y)$$
$$\textbf{reverse*}(x_1, u.x_2, y) \quad \textbf{if} \quad \textbf{reverse*}(u.x_1, x_2, y)$$

As seen in Chapter III, these behave much more efficiently, even though their logic is harder to understand. Their use here makes the resulting algorithm only linearly dependent in time upon the length of the input list.

A more radical improvement still can be achieved by altering the initial specification; namely, we now say that a list is a palindrome if its first half is the reverse of its second half. This means that it is not necessary to reverse the whole list, as the previous methods did. The program below exploits this idea and also manages to dispense with explicit reversal procedures.

Program 21

$$? \, \textbf{palin}(A.B.C.B.A.NIL)$$
$$\textbf{palin}(x) \quad \textbf{if} \quad \textbf{palin*}(x, NIL)$$
$$\textbf{palin*}(z, z)$$
$$\textbf{palin*}(u.z, z)$$
$$\textbf{palin*}(u.z', z) \quad \textbf{if} \quad \textbf{palin*}(z', u.z)$$

Here a predicate **palin***(z_1, z_2) means that a palindrome results from appending z_1 to the reverse of z_2. The resulting execution is very pretty (exercise: execute the program manually). This algorithm is about twice as fast as that above using **reverse***. Such inefficiencies as remain arise chiefly from the burden incurred in unifying various structured terms. This burden is outside the control of the programmer, and will be determined by the interpreter's particular way of processing terms. Of course, the effort entailed in run-time unification may be much reduced if the interpreter can perform an intelligent pre-execution analysis of the input program and so discern ways of implementing the programmer's intentions efficiently. This possibility, which belongs to the general topic of compile-time optimization, is particularly attractive in allowing one to write relatively high-level term-based programs, knowing that their concrete implementations will be arranged so as to avoid significant overheads in data access and unification. Program 21, for instance, might be implemented using just two linear arrays, corresponding to the two arguments of **palin***. Then the third **palin*** procedure would be effectively compiled into a set of machine-level operations which rapidly transferred an element from the first array to the second.

If one's interpreter is unable to perform any significant optimization, then in order to improve upon Program 21 it is necessary to abandon the structured term representation. Instead, one can resort to an assertional representation of the input list and compose procedures exhibiting an ALGOL-like behaviour, that is, involving low-level control over loops and subscripts. An illustration of this is given in Section IV.3.

IV.2.4. Type Checking

When large data structures are assembled by some method subject to error (for example, by manual input), it can be profitable to perform some sort of check before carrying out the principal processing upon them. Although the check could entail many kinds of tests on the data, the most fundamental of them is the *type check*, which tests whether the data conforms structurally to its intended data type.

As an example, suppose we wished to input a tree z of the kind depicted in Fig. IV.1c and then process it in some way. If a type check were inserted between the inputting and processing stages then the goal might be formulated as follows:

$$? \, \textbf{input}(z), \, \underline{\textbf{tree}(z)}, \, \textbf{process}(z, z'), \, \textbf{output}(z')$$

Here the underlined call **tree**(z) is intended to check whether the data input for z conforms to the type 'tree'. If this type check fails then execution will be saved from generating a possibly more expensive and less comprehensible failure in the **process**(z, z') call. The check could be carried out using the procedures

$$\textbf{tree}(z) \quad \textbf{if} \quad z = TIP$$
$$\textbf{tree}(z) \quad \textbf{if} \quad z = t(z_1, z_2), \, \textbf{tree}(z_1), \, \textbf{tree}(z_2)$$

Type checking can be an expensive run-time overhead, and so it is worthwhile to detect errors as early as possible. In the example above, the **input**(z) call might be implemented as an invitation to the user to enter data from an input device. If the data structure fed in is large and susceptible to several errors then it is very inefficient to input all of it before proceeding to the type check; it is better to continue inputting only for as long as no errors have occurred. In view of this, a substantial advantage is gained if the interpreter's control strategy includes the capability of *coroutining*. IC-

PROLOG, for instance, supports a 'producer–consumer' coroutining strategy which can be instructed to make the **input**(z) call produce more data only when the processing of the **tree**(z) call is ready to consume more in order to continue type checking. The actual behaviour might be as follows. The **tree**(z) call makes an initial request for some data from the **input**(z) call, which is consequently activated and invites the user to begin data entry; he types in, perhaps, $z := t(x, y)$, at which point control reverts to the type check call and develops it a few steps; thus

$$? \, \textbf{tree}(z)$$
$$? \, \textbf{tree}(t(x, y))$$
$$? \, t(x, y) = t(z_1, z_2), \, \textbf{tree}(z_1), \, \textbf{tree}(z_2)$$
$$? \, \textbf{tree}(x), \, \textbf{tree}(y)$$

At this point, type checking cannot proceed further with concrete data until more has been provided as input, so control reverts again to the input process and prompts the user, who now enters, say, $x := t(TIP, TIP)$ and so fills in a further component of the data structure. This is in turn type checked, and finally the user is prompted to fill in the last component, say $y := TIP$, and then this also is checked. In this way, an entire data structure $z := t(t(TIP, TIP), TIP)$ has been input in stages punctuated by type checking, so that an error in any stage will be detected before later stages are dealt with. Finally, observe the capability of logic programs of processing *partly determined data* in the form of terms containing unbound variables. We have seen above that the partly determined structure $t(x, y)$ could be passed to the type checking procedures and partly processed before either x or y were known concretely. This kind of behaviour has no direct analogues in many conventional languages.

IV.3. Assertional Representations

Assertional representations of data exploit the fact that logic procedures can themselves serve as descriptions of data structure components. They can be used to describe all the data types, for instance lists, matrices and trees, that could otherwise be represented by terms; the general characteristic of these data types is that they have a regular structure. Programs which process assertional representations of these kinds of data often have to resort to rather low-level accessing procedures which regulate the use of subscripts, pointers and the like. In addition, assertional representations are also extremely useful for describing very irregular collections of data such as databases, whose descriptions using terms would be inordinately cumbersome.

IV.3.1. General Principles

When we describe some relation by stating a rule capable of generating the relation's members, the relation is said to have been defined *intensionally*. Thus the procedure

$$\mathbf{m}(u, i, L) \quad \textbf{if} \quad 1 \leqslant i, i \leqslant 3, u = i * 10$$

serves as an intensional definition of the **m** relation; the definition has to be *applied* in order to determine the constituents of **m**. By contrast, a set of assertions

$$\mathbf{m}(10, 1, L)$$
$$\mathbf{m}(20, 2, L)$$
$$\mathbf{m}(30, 3, L)$$

constitutes an *extensional* definition of **m**, in that it explicitly declares the entire contents of **m**, making it unnecessary to apply a rule in order to determine those contents. The simplest kind of assertional representation is just an extensional definition.

Observe that each of the assertions in the example above quotes a name L, which serves there as the name of the data structure being represented. This device is only needed when one is dealing with several data structures at a time, as a means of distinguishing them.

It is often the case that several relations are needed in order to describe a particular data structure, so that the name will be quoted in the assertion set for each one. Thus in the case of representing a list we would typically accompany the **m** assertions by another assertion

$$\textbf{length}(L, 3)$$

which defines the length of L. Note that conventional programmers do much the same thing; they store the list in an array L and also store its length in some variable n in readiness for operations needing to know n, such as

$$\textbf{for} \quad i = 1 \textbf{ to } n \quad \textbf{do process } L(i)$$

A great many relations may be needed when describing a real-world database. For a simple illustration consider a database used for managing a hotel's reservations. Each room will have some identifier, chosen perhaps from $1, 2, 3, \ldots$etc.; a capacity, perhaps single (S) or double (D); a floor level; a shower option and a set of date ranges for which it is already reserved. The state of the hotel at any time is a somewhat irregular data structure whose assertional representation could be like that shown below.

level(*1, GROUND*)	**capacity**(*1, D*)	**shower**(*1, NO*)
level(*2, GROUND*)	**capacity**(*2, S*)	**shower**(*2, YES*)
level(*3, FIRST*)	**capacity**(*3, D*)	**shower**(*3, YES*)
level(*4, FIRST*)	**capacity**(*4, D*)	**shower**(*4, YES*)
level(*5, SECOND*)	**capacity**(*5, S*)	**shower**(*5, NO*)

$$\text{\textbf{reserved}}(1, NOV19, NOV22)$$
$$\text{\textbf{reserved}}(2, DEC14, DEC14)$$
$$\text{\textbf{reserved}}(2, FEB04, MAR03)$$
$$\text{\textbf{reserved}}(4, DEC14, DEC15)$$

This database might be typically interrogated by queries like

$$? \text{ \textbf{capacity}}(r,D), \text{ \textbf{shower}}(r,YES), \text{ \textbf{available}}(r,DEC13,DEC16)$$

that is, which room r is double, has a shower and is available from December 13 to 16? It would be supported by various procedures capable of searching or updating the database in response to queries or amendments. If we were dealing with a reservation agency's database then the assertions would also have to include the names of the various hotels subscribing to it.

IV.3.2. Type Checking

Type checks may occasionally have to be applied to assertional representations in order to assess their structural well-formedness. For example, inadvertent corruption of the assertions representing our list L might mutate them to the following state

m(*10, −1, L*)	**length**(*L, 2*)
m(*20, 2, L*)	**length**(*L, 4*)
m(*30, 2, L*)	

which no longer conforms to the assumed list data type. Thus a program to process L might usefully make a type checking call **list**(L) first, using procedures which checked that L had a non-negative, unique length n and a unique member in every integer position i in the range 1 to n. These procedures could be as follows:

> **list**(x)   **if**   **length**(x, n), $n \geqslant 0$, $\sim$**other-length**(x, n),
> $$\text{\textbf{members}}(x, 1, n)$$
> **members**(x, i, n)   **if** $i > n$
> **members**(x, i, n)   **if** $i \leqslant n$, **m**(u, i, x), $\sim$**other-member**(u, i, x),
> $$\text{\textbf{members}}(x, i + 1, n)$$
> **other-length**(x, n)   **if**   **length**(x, n'), $n \neq n'$
> **other-member**(u, i, x)   **if**   **m**(u', i, x), $u \neq u'$

Serious database programs may also have to perform checks on the well-formedness of the data, especially in the course of updating it. The rules governing the well-formedness are called *integrity constraints*; conventional type checking is just a simple example of the more general process of testing whether a collection of data satisfies its integrity constraints. In terms of our earlier hotel reservation example, one possible constraint could be the following statement which, if always satisfied by the data, guards against the double-booking of a room:

$$d_2 < d_3 \quad \textbf{if} \quad \textbf{reserved}(r, d_1, d_2), \textbf{reserved}(r, d_3, d_4), d_1 \leqslant d_3$$

Statements like this can be incorporated in logic database systems and invoked in special ways in order to detect inconsistency or incompleteness in the data, or to prevent those conditions from arising.

IV.3.3. Indexing

A typical logic interpreter will store an input program's procedures in memory using some kind of *indexing* scheme. The scheme is applied at compile time and effectively classifies the procedures according to both their names and the structural and lexical content of their formal parameters; it then establishes pointers to the whereabouts in memory of each class of procedures discriminated by this classification. The class-pointer information is assembled in an efficiently accessible form in one or more index tables, also stored in memory, which will be consulted at run time in order to gain fast access to the stored procedures. More specifically, when a call is activated, the interpreter compares its name and actual parameters with the table entries and so determines a pointer to that area of memory containing potentially responding procedures; this is clearly more efficient than performing a blind search through a disordered collection of stored procedures. The precise scheme used for mapping procedure headings into memory references will depend upon the interpreter, which may combine default arrangements with special indexing advice supplied by the programmer.

Indexing is especially important for the efficient implementation of assertional representations of data. Applying the above ideas to our assertional representation of the list L discussed earlier, we can construct a primary index table for the **m** relation containing an entry pointing to the memory area allocated to all the **m** procedures which have L as their third parameter. Amongst these, every **m** procedure whose second parameter is a positive integer can be allocated to an appropriate region within that area, and accessed by using a secondary index table classifying the second parameter.

When a call like $\textbf{m}(u, 2, L)$ is activated during execution, the interpreter compares the index table entries with the symbols **m**, 2 and L—which thus serve as retrieval keys—in order to find a memory reference locating the potentially responding procedures; in our example, the single assertion **m**(*20*, *2*, *L*) will be thus located. A slightly more sophisticated scheme could apply if the interpreter could act upon compile-time advice about the data type of the **m** assertion set. For then the secondary index table could simply associate any **m** assertion having second parameter *i* with the *i*th slot of the memory area, which in turn would store nothing more than the first parameter of the assertion—in other words, just the value of the *i*th member of *L*. This scheme would clearly emulate a compiled conventional program accessing the value of *L*(*2*) by using the subscript *2* as an offset from the base address of *L* in memory.

The availability of indexing schemes is an essential precondition for the view that assertional representations make the components of data structures easily accessible. Such schemes encourage us, for instance, to pose the consecutivity problem of Section IV.2.2 in the following style:

$$? \, \textbf{consec}(C, t, L)$$
$$\textbf{consec}(u, v, y) \quad \textbf{if} \quad \textbf{m}(u, i, y), \, \textbf{m}(v, i+1, y)$$
$$\textbf{m}(A, 1, L) \qquad \textbf{m}(B, 2, L) \qquad \textbf{m}(C, 3, L)$$
$$\textbf{m}(D, 4, L) \qquad \textbf{m}(E, 5, L)$$

A good interpreter will be able to implement the **m** assertions as a linear array representation of *L*, as described above, and access the members directly using indexed look-up.

IV.3.4. Arrays and Subscripts

Lists, matrices and other array-structured data sets are especially suited to assertional representations. In particular, indexed storage and access of assertions ensures efficient implementation of algorithms governed by the control of subscripts. The palindrome problem of Section IV.2.3 is reconsidered here in order to see how the logic programmer can express a subscript-controlled iteration scanning through the elements of a linear array. The input data comprises the list $L = (A, B, C, B, A)$ having a length $n = 5$, and is represented in the usual way by using **m** and **length** assertions.

The algorithm used is as follows. In each iterative step two subscripts *i* and *j*, initially set to *1* and *n*, respectively, select two members *L*(*i*) and *L*(*j*) which, in a palindrome, ought to be identical. The iteration gradually works inward from the two ends of *L* by simultaneously incrementing *i* and decrementing *j*. This process terminates when *i* and *j* 'cross over'; that is when $i > j$. This algorithm is not much different from that produced from the term-based Program 21 but is more efficiently implementable because the members of L can be accessed and compared more directly. It can be summarized in conventional notation by

$$n := \text{length of list } x; \; i := 1; j := n;$$
$$\textbf{while} \quad i \leqslant j \quad \textbf{do}$$
$$\textbf{begin} \quad \textbf{if} \quad x(i) = x(j) \quad \textbf{then} \quad \textbf{begin} \quad i := i+1;$$
$$j := j-1;$$
$$\textbf{end}$$
$$\textbf{else } FAIL;$$
$$\textbf{end}; \; SUCCEED$$

In order to capture this in logic, we choose a name, say **palin****, to denote the **while** ... **do** iteration. Specifically, **palin****(x, i, j) means that $(x(i), \ldots, x(j))$ is a palindrome, and x, i and j are the arguments of **palin**** because they are the variables consulted in each iterative step. The initial values 1 and n of i and j are injected by an initial call to **palin**** after looking up the length n of L. Here is the entire program.

Program 22

$$? \, \textbf{palin}(L)$$
$$\textbf{palin}(x) \quad \textbf{if} \quad \textbf{length}(x, n), \textbf{palin**}(x, 1, n)$$
$$\textbf{palin**}(x, i, j) \quad \textbf{if} \quad i > j$$
$$\textbf{palin**}(x, i, j) \quad \textbf{if} \quad i \leqslant j, \textbf{m}(u, i, x),$$
$$\textbf{m}(u, j, x),$$
$$\textbf{palin**}(x, i+1, j-1)$$
$$\textbf{m}(A, 1, L) \qquad \textbf{m}(B, 2, L) \qquad \textbf{m}(C, 3, L)$$
$$\textbf{m}(B, 4, L) \qquad \textbf{m}(A, 5, L) \qquad \textbf{length}(L, 5)$$

Each circuit around the loop starts by invoking the first **palin**** procedure to test the termination condition; if this fails then the other **palin**** procedure is used to test the next selected pair of members. Logically, this other procedure must also include the test $i \leqslant j$, which adds a little inefficiency to the execution. However, this can be eliminated by using the **if–then–else** syntax mentioned in Chapter III in connection with Program 18, replacing the two **palin**** procedures by a single conditional statement

$$\textbf{palin**}(x, i, j) \quad \textbf{if} \quad i \leqslant j \quad \textbf{then} \quad \textbf{m}(u, i, x), \textbf{m}(u, j, x),$$
$$\textbf{palin**}(x, i+1, j-1)$$
$$\textbf{else} \quad \textbf{exit}$$

The style of Program 22 can clearly be extended to deal with iterations through multidimensional arrays.

IV.4. Processing Data in Assertional Form

In general we require data structure representations to be suitable for both input and output. Neither the concept nor the implementation of this requirement raises any difficulties in connection with structured term representations, whose input/output properties have already been discussed in Chapter II. However, the manipulation of data in assertional form is not so straightforward and requires special programming techniques.

IV.4.1. Names as Output Data

The goal of Program 22 queries the properties of an object with a given name L. Because of their input–output non-determinism, logic procedures can also be used to discover and output the names of objects satisfying given properties.

As an example, suppose a database has been set up containing many lists in assertional form, and that it is required to find all lists x, y and z such that z is the vector sum of x and y. The vector sum $z = x \oplus y$ is defined such that each ith member of z is the sum of the ith members of x and y, it being assumed that x, y and z have equal lengths. The program below performs this task straightforwardly.

Program 23

$$? \; \textbf{sum}(x, y, z)$$

$\textbf{sum}(x, y, z)$ **if** $\textbf{length}(x, n)$, $\textbf{length}(y, n)$, $\textbf{length}(z, n)$,

$\qquad\qquad\qquad \textbf{sum}^*(x, y, z, 1, n)$

$\textbf{sum}^*(x, y, z, i, n)$ **if** $i > n$

$\textbf{sum}^*(x, y, z, i, n)$ **if** $i \leqslant n$, $\textbf{m}(u, i, x)$, $\textbf{m}(v, i, y)$, $\textbf{m}(w, i, z)$,

$\qquad\qquad\qquad \textbf{plus}(u, v, w)$, $\textbf{sum}^*(x, y, z, i+1, n)$

$\qquad\qquad\qquad$ and the **length** and **m** assertions defining

$\qquad\qquad\qquad$ all the lists in the database

When invoked, the **sum** procedure will select certain lists x, y and z of equal lengths and then invoke the **sum*** procedures to test whether these lists stand in the desired vector sum relation. Successful computations will bind various list names to the goal variables x, y and z. One can say that the program delivers the lists as output in the limited sense that it reports their names. In the same sense, specific names quoted in the goal could be viewed as supplying lists as input to the program.

IV.4.2. Assertions as Output Data: PROLOG's Method

A quite different concept of output arises when one considers the possibility of causing execution to generate new assertions representing data. Those assertions initially given in the program can then be viewed as input data, whilst those brought into existence by execution constitute output data. There are several ways of generating assertions as output, all of which require special adaptations of the standard interpreter.

The method used in classical (i.e., Marseille) PROLOG relies on the programmer writing calls of the form **assert**(t), where t is a structured term. Any such term has the same syntax as an assertion, and so the call can be read as the directive 'assert that t holds', that is, 'add the assertion t to the program'. When activated, the call is solved directly by a built-in procedure which adds the assertion t to the other program statements. For instance, suppose t is the term $m(20, 2, C)$; then the **assert**(t) directive interprets the functor m of t as a procedure name **m** and the arguments 20, 2 and C of t as the formal parameters of **m**. So the result of solving a call **assert**($m(20, 2, C)$) is the addition to the program of the assertion **m**($20, 2, C$).

The use of **assert** can be illustrated by the following problem: given assertional representations of lists A and B, generate the assertional representation of the list $C = A \oplus B$. This can be solved by Program 24 below, which is adapted from Program 23 by simply placing **assert**( ) directives around two of the existing calls.

Program 24

> ? **sum**(A, B, C)
> **sum**(x, y, z) **if**   **length**(x, n), **length**(y, n),
>   **assert**($length(z, n)$),
>   **sum***$(x, y, z, 1, n)$
> **sum***(x, y, z, i, n) **if** $i > n$
> **sum***(x, y, z, i, n) **if** $i \leqslant n$, **m**(u, i, x), **m**(v, i, y),
>   **plus**(u, v, w), **assert**($m(w, i, z)$),
>   **sum***$(x, y, z, i+1, n)$
> and the **length** and **m** assertions defining A and B

If the input lists are, say, $A = (3, 12, 23)$ and $B = (7, 8, 7)$, then execution will generate the assertions

$$\mathbf{m}(10, 1, C) \qquad \mathbf{m}(30, 3, C)$$
$$\mathbf{m}(20, 2, C) \qquad \mathbf{length}(C, 3)$$

representing $C = A \oplus B$.

Because the terms in activated **assert** calls can be constructed arbitrarily by the data distributions of earlier steps in the execution, the **assert** mechanism enables programs to extend themselves to any extent desired by the programmer. Moreover, as soon as an assertion has been generated it can be invoked by subsequent calls and so influence the remaining course of execution. Later on we will examine an example of this behaviour.

Unless instructed otherwise, the interpreter probably ought—for consistency in implementation philosophy—to retract (delete) assertions when it backtracks through the steps which produced them, just as it retracts bindings of variables when it backtracks. At the least, they should generally be retracted when the interpreter backtracks through an unsuccessful computation. Some implementations provide a range of directives which give the programmer complete control over the run-time creation and deletion of assertions.

The **assert** directive is a powerful one and can be easily implemented, but has the drawback that, whilst the operational effect of an **assert** call may be clear enough when considered in isolation, the logical significance of the execution as a whole can become obscured. The facility is really too powerful if applied without restraint. In general it clouds one's perception of the relationship between the input program and the 'solutions' computed from it. Its critics argue that its unrestrained use causes a departure from pure logic programming toward a formalism having rather different semantics. Nevertheless, it is sometimes possible to tread a delicate path around this criticism by explaining the execution of a non-standard (**assert**-containing) program P in terms of the normal execution of some closely related standard program Q. A justification of P then relies upon arguing that any 'solution' computed by P is necessarily a logically correct solution of Q, and that execution of P is therefore just a convenient way of realizing execution of Q.

To illustrate this, suppose that P is our example Program 24. If we remove from P all the **assert( )** directives, but leave their arguments intact in the program, and add to P all the assertions created by the original **assert** calls, the result is a standard program Q as follows.

Program 25

$$? \mathbf{sum}(A, B, C)$$
$$\mathbf{sum}(x, y, z) \quad \text{if} \quad \mathbf{length}(x, n), \mathbf{length}(y, n), \mathbf{length}(z, n),$$
$$\mathbf{sum}^*(x, y, z, 1, n)$$
$$\mathbf{sum}^*(x, y, z, i, n) \quad \text{if} \quad i > n$$
$$\mathbf{sum}^*(x, y, z, i, n) \quad \text{if} \quad i \leqslant n, \mathbf{m}(u, i, x), \mathbf{m}(v, i, y),$$
$$\mathbf{plus}(u, v, w), \mathbf{m}(w, i, z),$$
$$\mathbf{sum}^*(x, y, z, i+1, n)$$

and the **length** and **m** assertions representing
A, B <u>and C</u>

This is essentially the earlier Program 23, but with a more specific goal. It then turns out that if the (non-standard) execution of P 'solves' $sum(A, B, C)$ then so does the (standard) execution of Q. Therefore P just serves as a convenient version of Q to be used when the assertions representing C constitute output rather than input.

A program P which subsequently invokes the assertions which it creates using **assert** calls can be very difficult to justify in this way. The difficulty is worsened if P also contains '**retract**' calls, which specify the run-time deletion of assertions and are also provided in PROLOG. There may then appear to be no standard program Q which can be both directly and intelligibly related to P and whose execution can explain that of P. Even greater difficulties arise in trying to justify programs which use these directives and also contain negated calls solved using non-provability, because the dynamic self-modification of the program alters what is non-provable from it. In fact, the general problem with the semantics of classical PROLOG comes about not so much from the effects of non-standard features in isolation, but rather from their potential interactions.

Although **assert** can be used as a 'brute force' assertion generator, it can be used in restricted ways which preserve the logical semantics. For instance, the generation of a correctly implied assertion upon successful procedure exit is achievable by constructions like

$$\mathbf{p}(x) \quad \mathbf{if} \quad \dots \mathbf{assert}(p(x))$$

Equivalently, a correctly implied assertion following the solution of a particular call, say $\mathbf{p}(x)$, is achievable by constructions like

$$\mathbf{q} \quad \mathbf{if} \quad \dots, \mathbf{p}(x), \mathbf{assert}(p(x)), \dots$$

Standard PROLOG enables mechanisms of this sort to be packaged up in the form of metalevel procedures. For example, the procedure

$$\mathbf{lemma}(z) \quad \mathbf{if} \quad z, \mathbf{assert}(z)$$

constructs a correctly implied assertion from any solvable call input through the metavariable z. Using this the former procedure can be shortened to

$$\mathbf{q} \quad \mathbf{if} \quad \dots, \mathbf{lemma}(p(x)), \dots$$

This brings us to the next section's discussion of lemma generation, which avoids the semantic dangers of unrestricted **assert**.

IV.4.3. Assertions as Output Data: Lemma Generation

This new method of generating assertions exploits the fact that after any call has been solved it can be added as an assertion to the executing program without altering the program's logical content. For instance, suppose the input program contains a call $m(w, i, z)$ which is eventually activated in the normal way; by this time, i and z may have been assigned values 2 and C. If the activated call $m(w, 2, C)$ is solved, assigning, say, 20 to w, then this establishes that $m(20, 2, C)$ is implied by the program's procedures. Thus the assertion $m(20, 2, C)$ is merely a statement about the problem domain which is implied by the statements already in the program. Adding it to the program therefore in no way extends or diminishes what the program says about the problem, and consequently cannot affect what is computable from it.

Adding proven assertions at run time can increase efficiency, because some of the subsequent calls may then become directly solvable by invoking the new assertions, rather than (as would otherwise be necessary) by invoking the procedures which were used to establish them. When such assertions are invoked, they function as lemmas, that is, as intermediate theorems developed during the proof process. We therefore refer to the method as *lemma generation*.

As an example, consider the problem of printing first a list C and then its reverse, where C is to be computed as the vector sum of $A = (3, 12, 23)$ and $B = (7, 8, 7)$. We begin by looking at a standard program for the task, shown below.

Program 26

> $?$ **length**(C, n), **print***$(C, 1, n)$, **print****$(C, 1, n)$
> **print***(z, i, j) **if** $i > j$
> **print***(z, i, j) **if** $i \leqslant j$, $m(w, i, z)$, **print**(w),
> $\qquad\qquad\qquad$ **print***$(z, i+1, j)$
> **print****(z, i, j) **if** $i > j$
> **print****(z, i, j) **if** $i \leqslant j$, $m(w, j, z)$, **print**(w),
> $\qquad\qquad\qquad$ **print****$(z, i, j-1)$
> **length**(C, n) **if** **length**(A, n), **length**(B, n)
> $m(w, i, C)$ **if** $m(u, i, A)$, $m(v, i, B)$, **plus**(u, v, w)
> and **length** and m assertions representing A and B

Here it is supposed that a call **print**(w) transmits its parameter to a printer by invoking a built-in procedure. The **print*** and **print**** procedures just drive iterations respectively forward and backward through a list in order to print its members in natural or reverse order. The last two procedures shown in the program provide for the determination of the length and members of C by indirect access. Thus the iteration generated in solving the eventual call **print***$(C, 1, 3)$ computes each ith member of C by adding the ith members of A and B. The second iteration, generated in solving

print**$(C, 1, 3)$, has to do the same, which is clearly inefficient. A sensible programmer would arrange to preserve the members of C as soon as they were computed during the first iteration, so that they could be accessed directly during the second.

To produce this behaviour by lemma generation we can employ a simple annotation scheme whereby any call whose solution is required to generate a corresponding assertion is labeled by the symbol $\triangle$. (The symbol points *upward* because lemma generation is characteristic of bottom-*up* problem solving; the addition of $\triangle$ to the standard strategy yields a mixed top-down/bottom-up mode of behaviour.)

Applying this scheme to the example, the iterative **print*** procedure is modified by simply inserting a $\triangle$ symbol; it then reads as follows:

$$\textbf{print}^*(z, i, j) \quad \text{if} \quad i \leqslant j, \ \triangle\textbf{m}(w, i, z), \ \textbf{print}(w),$$
$$\textbf{print}^*(z, i+1, j).$$

The rest of the program remains unchanged. The result is that when **print***$(C, 1, 3)$ is being solved, each activated labeled call $\triangle\textbf{m}(w, i, C)$ for $i = 1, 2$ and 3 creates an assertion as soon as w has been successfully computed. So this phase of execution adds to the program the assertions

$$\textbf{m}(10, 1, C)$$
$$\textbf{m}(10, 2, C)$$
$$\textbf{m}(30, 3, C)$$

When the goal's remaining call **print****$(C, 1, 3)$ is being solved, the **m** calls which it generates to look up the members of C can be solved directly by using these new assertions, rather than using the original **m** procedure. In order to ensure that this is what actually happens, some convention is needed to govern the invocation precedence over input procedures and generated assertions. A simple rule could be that calls always try firstly to invoke the 'youngest' procedures, that is, those which have become available most recently during execution. This clearly deals with the present example satisfactorily, but the rule might need to be more elaborate in other circumstances.

In the normal course of events, the interpreter would eventually backtrack after the first solution of **print****$(C, 1, 3)$ in order to seek alternative solutions, and so would find that the original **m** procedure was so far untried at each branch node where an **m** assertion had been already selected. In order to suppress an inefficient and unwanted second solution of **print****$(C, 1, 3)$ we can excise those branch nodes using the cut operator in the goal as follows:

$$? \ \textbf{length}(C, n), \ \textbf{print}^*(C, 1, n), \ \textbf{print}^{**}(C, 1, n), \ /$$

Implementations which generate assertions during execution, by whatever method, must also be capable of run-time determination of how to store the assertions and make them subsequently accessible. This may mean that the software normally used for arranging indexing at compile time must be made available at run time as well, adding some overhead to the execution process.

The modified Program 26 suffers a minor defect of style in the placing of $\triangle$ within the **print*** procedure set, because the latter cannot then be invoked without generating assertions and so reducing its flexibility. A neater approach, giving a more modular structure, is to employ a new procedure set whose purpose is solely to produce a set of assertions without making any assumptions about their future use. This new procedure set, which can also be called a list-generator module, could be as follows:

> **generate**(z) **if** $\triangle$**length**(z, n), **members**$(z, 1, n)$
> **members**(z, i, j) **if** $i > j$
> **members**(z, i, j) **if** $i \leqslant j$, $\triangle$**m**(w, i, z), **members**$(z, i+1, j)$

The program's goal is then written as

> ? **generate**(C), **length**(C, n), **print***$(C, 1, n)$, **print****$(C, 1, n)$, /

so that the first call generates a complete assertional representation of the list C. The rest of the program is then exactly as first given in Program 26, that is, with no $\triangle$ symbols. Once the list C has been generated by computing its length and members from the data given for lists A and B, the two printing tasks can both proceed by directly accessing the members of C from the generated assertions. The result is an excellent algorithm and a well-styled program having a pure semantics.

IV.4.4. Names for Assertional Data Structures

Program 26 computed and printed a specific vector sum $C = A \oplus B$. This assumption was built into the **length** and **m** procedures. More generally, we may require a program whose goal can quote any vector sum to be computed and printed, which raises the question of how we can generalize those two procedures. Intuitively their new forms would be as follows:

> **length**$(? , n)$ **if**   **length**(x, n), **length**(y, n)
> **m**$(w, i, ?)$ **if**   **m**(u, i, x), **m**(v, i, y), **plus**(u, v, w)

in which the argument positions marked ? must somehow accommodate a name for the intended vector sum $x \oplus y$, where x and y can be any lists transmitted by the invoking calls. These positions cannot be merely filled in with some arbitrary third variable, say z, because the procedures would not then be logically correct statements about lists. Moreover, they must incorporate references to both x and y in order that the chosen lists can be made known to the procedures.

One way of achieving the desired outcome is to employ a structured term $sum(x, y)$ to serve as the name for the list $x \oplus y$ and substitute this in each of the ? positions. The program's goal can then quote any specific lists using structured names for them, such as $sum(A, B)$ or $sum(A, sum(A, B))$. A complete program for computing and printing $A \oplus B$ using generalized procedures and exploiting lemma generation would then have the following structure.

Program 27

> $? z = sum(A, B)$, **generate**(z), **length**(z, n),
> $\qquad\qquad$ **print***$(z, 1, n)$, **print****$(z, 1, n)$, /
> **generate**(z) **if** $\triangle$**length**(z, n), **members**$(z, 1, n)$
> **members**(z, i, j) **if** $i > j$
> **members**(z, i, j) **if** $i \leqslant j$, $\triangle$**m**(w, i, z), **members**$(z, i+1, j)$
> **length**$(sum(x, y), n)$ **if**   **length**(x, n), **length**(y, n)
> **m**$(w, i, sum(x, y))$ **if**   **m**(u, i, x), **m**(v, i, y), **plus**(u, v, w)
> and the **print*** and **print**** procedures of Program 26
> and the **length** and **m** assertions representing A and B

Note the usefulness of the goal's first identity call in saving us the tedium of quoting the name $sum(A, B)$ in various other places in the goal.

This program gives good run-time behaviour, first invoking the list-generator module as described in the previous section in order to generate the assertional representation of the list $A \oplus B$, each of whose assertions will bear the name $sum(A, B)$. The data is then accessed directly in the subsequent printing tasks. If we want to process other vector sums, it is only necessary to change the name quoted in the goal's first call and supply appropriate **length** and **m** assertions for the chosen input lists.

This naming method can become tedious when dealing with highly composite names. For instance, suppose the input data consisted of lists $A1$, $A2$, $B1$ and $B2$, and that it were required to compute and print the list $(A1 \oplus A2) \oplus (B1 \oplus B2)$. The corresponding name $sum(sum(A1, A2), sum(B1, B2))$ is cumbersome to write, and could impose significant overheads upon run-time storage and unification. An alternative programming style can be used which dispenses with structured names and improves the program's intelligibility. This style entails a modification of the generalized **length** and **m** procedures shown in Program 27, so that they become

> **length**(z, n) **if**   **sum**(x, y, z), **length**(x, n), **length**(y, n)
> **m**(w, i, z) **if**   **sum**(x, y, z), **m**(u, i, x), **m**(v, i, y), **plus**(u, v, w)

where the predicate **sum**(x, y, z) means $z = x \oplus y$. The desired output list can be given a simple name, say C, and quoted in the goal as follows:

$?$ **generate**(C), **length**(C, n), **print***$(C, 1, n)$, **print****$(C, 1, n)$, $/$

It then only remains to inform the program that $C = (A1 \oplus A2) \oplus (B1 \oplus B2)$, which can be easily stated by adding three assertions:

$$\begin{aligned} &\text{\textbf{sum}}(A1, A2, A3) \\ &\text{\textbf{sum}}(B1, B2, B3) \\ &\text{\textbf{sum}}(A3, B3, C) \end{aligned}$$

Here $A3$ and $B3$ respectively name the intermediate sums $A1 \oplus A2$ and $B1 \oplus B2$. Apart from these changes, the program's procedures are exactly as in Program 27, and the database now contains assertional representations of $A1$, $A2$, $B1$ and $B2$. During execution, the list generator is invoked in order to generate list C and consequently asks for, via the **length** and **m** procedures, the contents of lists $A3$ and $B3$. As these are not directly available from the database, further recursive calls are made to the **length** and **m** procedures in order to look up the contents of the constituents $A1$ and $A2$ of $A3$ and $B1$ and $B2$ of $B3$. As soon as these input lists have been accessed from the database, the various addition processes can be undertaken and hence the contents of C will be computed, generated in assertional form and finally printed. Execution is quite efficient, and the choice of input and output can be easily altered in the program.

IV.4.5. The Eigenproblem Revisited

The naming methods discussed previously are adequate for problems involving only a known finite number of assertional data structures. Slightly more elaborate methods are required in programs whose executions generate sequences of data structures the sequence lengths of which are initially unknown. These circumstances usually arise in matrix iteration programs in which termination has to await satisfaction of some sort of convergence criterion.

The eigenproblem described in Chapter III is just such an example. The algorithm used there is given an initial vector V and a fixed matrix M, and generates a sequence of further vectors $M.V$, $M^2.V$, $M^3.V$, $\ldots$ etc. until one of them satisfies an accuracy criterion; that vector is then the desired solution.

If each vector in the sequence is to be represented in assertional form (rather than by a structured term, as in the program shown in Chapter III), then it must be given a name which distinguishes it from the other vectors.

This means that the algorithm generates a sequence of names as well as vectors. For efficiency's sake it is important that these names do not expand as the sequence develops. Thus it would not be practical, for instance, to use names like $mult(M, V)$, $mult(M, mult(M, V))$, ... etc. for the vectors $M.V$, $M^2.V$, ... etc., since the storage and processing of them would diminish efficiency.

One way of achieving a satisfactory naming scheme is to incorporate in each name a count of the number of multiplications by M which are necessary in order to generate the named vector from the initial vector V. Thus we could use

$$vector(M, V, 0) \qquad \text{to name } V$$
$$vector(M, V, 1) \qquad \text{to name } M.V$$
$$vector(M, V, 2) \qquad \text{to name } M^2.V$$
$$\text{etc.}$$

These structured terms provide an indefinite sequence of distinct names of equal sizes. The eigenproblem program originally suggested in Program 10 can then be reorganized as follows.

Program 28

> ? **derive**$(v, vector(M, V, 0))$, **acc**(M, v)
>   **derive**(v, v)
>   **derive**(v, z) **if**   **mult**(M, z, z'), **derive**(v, z')
>   **mult**(M, z, z') **if** $z = vector(M, V, k)$,
> $z' = vector(M, V, k+1)$,
>   **generate**(z')

together with

(a) **acc** procedures encoding the accuracy test;

(b) **length** and **m** assertions representing the input vector V, using the name $vector(M, V, 0)$;

(c) some suitable data structure representation of the matrix M;

(d) **length** and **m** procedures capable of computing for any $k \geqslant 0$, the length and members of $vector(M, V, k+1)$ obtained by multiplying $vector(M, V, k)$ by M; it is in these procedures that the details of the matrix multiplication operation are encoded, and their logic will involve looking up the components of M from the representation given in (c);

(e) the list-generator module used in Program 27, which uses lemma generation in order to create assertional representations of each new vector in readiness for the next iterative step

This is how the program works. The first call to **derive** will assign $v := vector(M, V, 0)$, and the ensuing **acc** call will apply the accuracy test to the input vector. Assuming the test fails, backtracking occurs and the second **derive** procedure is invoked, whereupon the **mult** call uses the current name $vector(M, V, 0)$ in order to construct the next name $vector(M, V, 1)$. The **mult** procedure's **generate** call will create the assertional representation of the new vector having this name. The next time the **acc** call is activated, the test is applied to $v := vector(M, V, 1)$. The entire process of constructing the next name, creating the corresponding vector and submitting it to the accuracy test is performed repeatedly until convergence is attained.

This behavior is efficient in time, but will not utilize memory efficiently unless arrangements are made to ensure that each new vector overwrites its predecessor. The necessity for destructive assignment arises chiefly in algorithms producing indefinite sequences of data structures. A certain amount of automatic space saving is undertaken by most implementations, some of which can also respond to appropriate directives from the programmer. The general problem of run-time memory conservation encounters a number of theoretical and practical difficulties, and has not yet been fully resolved. Different implementations employ their own idiosyncratic controls over memory allocation. Thus the programmer who wishes to derive the most benefit from a particular data representation must understand his implementation well and program accordingly.

Finally, it should be noted in the present example that it is not really necessary to include the constants V and M in the vectors' names. The latter can, in fact, be simplified drastically to just the symbols $0, 1, 2, \ldots$ etc., thus making the program more readable and a little more efficient. The first few statements shown in Program 28 could then be simplified and condensed as follows:

> ? **derive**$(v, 0)$, **acc**(M, v)
> **derive**(v, v)
> **derive**(v, k) **if**   **generate**$(k+1)$, **derive**$(v, k+1)$
> and the previous constituents (a), ... (e)
> adapted to the simplified names.

Thus the (b) constituent provides the input data in the form

$$
\begin{array}{l}
\mathbf{m}(1, 1, 0) \\
\mathbf{m}(1, 2, 0) \qquad \text{representing } V = \begin{bmatrix} 1 \\ 1 \end{bmatrix} \\
\mathbf{length}(0, 2)
\end{array}
$$

and the iteration generates the vector representations

$\mathbf{m}(5, 1, 1)$	$\mathbf{m}(29, 1, 2)$
$\mathbf{m}(7, 2, 1)$	$\mathbf{m}(43, 2, 2)$
$\mathbf{length}(1, 2)$	$\mathbf{length}(2, 2)$ ... etc.

The need for more elaborate names incorporating other symbols like M and V only arises in programs which have to distinguish between several distinct input vectors or several distinct matrices.

IV.5. Background

The first comparative study of data structures for logic programs appears in the report by Kowalski (1974a). Interesting examples are given there of parsing, sorting and plan-formation problems, using both terms and assertions for data representation.

Data representations are also investigated in Kowalski's paper (1979b) on logic algorithms. This includes a novel example in which each individual component of a data structure is represented by an implication rather than a simple assertion, producing a more subtle way of defining a relation quasi-extensionally. That paper also introduces some simple program annotations which specify the controlled mixing of top-down and bottom-up execution strategies and which can be used to elicit the lemma generation mechanism described earlier in this chapter.

The palindrome programs presented here have been selected from a more comprehensive study of logic data structures included in the thesis by Hogger (1979a). The task of logically transforming a term-based program to an assertion-based one (for instance, transforming Program 21 to Program 22) has been illustrated both there and in (Hogger, 1981). Examples of term styles for processing lists, trees and other structures have also been amply demonstrated by Clark (1979) and by Clark and Tärnlund (1977).

A detailed account of how implementations typically represent terms internally is given by Warren (1977a) and indexing schemes for storing and accessing assertions (and other statements) are outlined in the paper by Clark and McCabe (1980). Both topics are dealt with by Warren *et al.* (1977) in their comparison of PROLOG with LISP. References to work on the special topic of logic databases can be found in Chapter VIII.

V PROGRAM VERIFICATION

Whether one is using logic or any other programming formalism, it is desirable to have some practical means of deciding whether any particular program is correct. Loosely, a program is correct if its execution produces correct solutions to the intended problem. The correctness of computed solutions is relative to some specification of the problem asserted independently of the program. It is also assumed, of course, that the program's interpreter is itself correctly executed on the machine.

In the logic programming context, verification encompasses a number of considerations. Perhaps the most important of these is the question of whether computed solutions are correct. Another is the question of whether all correct solutions to the problem are in fact computable from the program. Verification is the process of proving that programs do or do not satisfy requirements of this sort. Such an undertaking would not be necessary if all logic programs in practical use could be regarded as specifications in their own right. It is certainly arguable that some programs do consist of statements which would be generally considered as self-evidently correct. But more often it is the case that, in order to construct an efficient, non-trivial program, one has to compose program statements whose correctness is not obvious from mere inspection.

As might be expected, the material in this chapter is rather more theoretical than in the preceding ones. It includes a number of formal definitions of the more important program properties and outlines one approach to practical verification.

V.1. Computed and Specified Relations

In order to formalize notions such as correctness it is first necessary to have precise ways of characterizing what a program computes and what a specification specifies. This in turn requires some stipulations about the class of programs considered and some suitable terminology for discussing their features.

V.1.1. Notation and Terminology

For the purposes of verification it is convenient to require that the program of interest be structured in such a way that its goal G contains just one call, and so takes the form

$$G : \quad ? \, g(t)$$

where t is some n-tuple of terms. The entire procedure set used by the program is denoted by P, and includes any built-in procedures to which the program may refer. The entire program can then be denoted by the pair (P, G).

A specification for a program is any set of definitions, not necessarily written in logic, which specifies precisely the contents of every relation mentioned in the program. In particular it will specify the contents of the relation named in the goal G; henceforth this is called the *principal specified relation* and denoted generally by the symbol **R***. For example, if the program's goal is

$$G : \quad ? \, \mathbf{subset}(w : A : \emptyset, \, A : B : C : \emptyset)$$

then the principal specified relation bears the name **subset**, so we may write **R*** = **subset**. In general the symbol S is used to denote a specification. A specification for a program having the goal just shown will determine exactly which 2-tuples belong to **subset** and which ones do not, and be treated as the authoritative definition of **subset** from the programmer's point of view. In particular, S will determine which 2-tuples are correct solutions to the goal G.

Suppose any predicate **subset**(x, y) is intended to express that set x is a subset of y, and suppose also that sets are represented by using the functor : and the constant $\emptyset$, where $\emptyset$ denotes the empty set and a term like $v : z$ denotes the set formed from the union of $\{v\}$ with some other set z, where v is any element. Then the goal above asks which elements w make $\{w, A\}$ a subset of $\{A, B, C\}$. Observe that this is a *limited* query about **subset**, in that G focuses only upon certain 2-tuples in the relation. More formally we say that, in this example, the goal G *spans* some subrelation of **R***, specifically the subrelation

$$\{(A : A : \emptyset, \, A : B : C : \emptyset),$$
$$(B : A : \emptyset, \, A : B : C : \emptyset),$$
$$(C : A : \emptyset, \, A : B : C : \emptyset)\}$$

Other 2-tuples in $\mathbf{R}^*$ such as $(B:\varnothing, B:D:\varnothing)$ are clearly not queried by G and so do not lie within its span.

Other programs may have goals which span the entirety of $\mathbf{R}^*$. One way of arranging this is to pose a *most general goal* G^* whose parameters are all distinct variables, such as

$$G^* : \quad ?\,\mathbf{subset}(x, y)$$

This is not the only way. For instance, if $\mathbf{R}^*$ is some other relation, say $\mathbf{R}^* = \{(A, B), (C, B)\}$, and the goal is

$$G : \quad ?\,\mathbf{R}^*(x, B)$$

then G spans $\mathbf{R}^*$ entirely but is not most general.

The span of any goal

$$G : \quad ?\,\mathbf{R}^*(t)$$

is the set of solutions to that goal according to the specification S, each one being some substitution instance $t\Theta$ of t. Formally, then, the span of G with respect to S is the set

$$\{t\Theta \mid t\Theta \in \mathbf{R}^*\}$$

where S specifies $\mathbf{R}^*$. Note that if the span is empty, then, according to S, G should have no solutions. In general, of course, solutions will exist; each solution $t\Theta$ is called a *specified solution* of G in order to emphasize that it is a solution *according to* S. Whether or not it is also a solution computed by the program is another question, and it is just such questions that verification is intended to answer.

V.1.2. The Computed Relation

The *computed relation* of a program (P, G) is the set of all solutions to G which are computable from the program using the given procedure set P. The relation is generally denoted by $\mathbf{R}$, and the solutions in it are referred to as *computed solutions*.

Suppose the program admits several successful computations. Each one of these yields some output assignment Θ of terms to the variables of the initial goal n-tuple t, and so establishes that $t\Theta$ solves G *according to* P. If $t\Theta$ is variable-free then it belongs to $\mathbf{R}$; otherwise it stands generically for all its variable-free substitution instances, and each of these belongs to $\mathbf{R}$. Note that if $\mathbf{R}$ is empty then the program is unsolvable.

It will be recalled from Chapters I and II that a fundamental feature of logic programming is that a solution $t\Theta$ to the goal

$$G : \quad ?\,\mathbf{R^*}(t)$$

is computable using P if and only if $P \vDash \mathbf{R^*}(t\Theta)$, assuming a resolution execution. This enables us to define the computed relation $\mathbf{R}$ formally as follows.

Definition 1

$$\mathbf{R} = \{t\Theta \,|\, P \vDash \mathbf{R^*}(t\Theta)\}$$

where P is the procedure set and $?\,\mathbf{R^*}(t)$ is the goal.

A concrete example will help to clarify these ideas. Suppose the entire program is the one below.

Program 29

$$G : \quad ?\,\mathbf{subset}(w:A:\varnothing, A:B:C:\varnothing)$$
$$\mathbf{subset}(x, y) \quad \mathbf{if} \quad \mathbf{empty}(x)$$
$$\mathbf{subset}(v:x', y) \quad \mathbf{if} \quad v \in y, \mathbf{subset}(x', y)$$
$$v \in v:z$$
$$v \in u:z \quad \mathbf{if} \quad v \in z$$

Here $\mathbf{empty}(x)$ holds when x is an empty set (not having the form $v:x'$). The procedure sets for **subset**, $\in$ and **empty** (assumed built-in) jointly constitute P. The programmer intends this program to explore the subset relation in connection with certain sets. The intended contents of $\mathbf{R^*} = \mathbf{subset}$ are determined by some independent specification S. The program determines three successful computations which assign A, B and C to the initial goal variable w. Therefore each ith one of these computations contributes to the computed relation $\mathbf{R}$ a computed solution $(w:A:\varnothing, A:B:C:\varnothing)\Theta_i$, where Θ_i is either $\{w := A\}$ or $\{w := B\}$ or $\{w := C\}$. Therefore the contents of $\mathbf{R}$ are as follows:

$$\mathbf{R} = \{(A:A:\varnothing, A:B:C:\varnothing),$$
$$(B:A:\varnothing, A:B:C:\varnothing),$$
$$(C:A:\varnothing, A:B:C:\varnothing)\}.$$

Observe that for each $t\Theta$ in this $\mathbf{R}$, the goal

$$?\,\mathbf{subset}(t\Theta)$$

is solvable using P in accordance with Definition 1. This is because $?\,\mathbf{subset}(t\Theta)$ is solvable using P if and only if $?\,\mathbf{subset}(t)$ is solvable with output assignment Θ; this is just a consequence of the input–output non-determinism of the logic procedures in P.

In the example just shown, the computed relation **R** turns out to be the span of G with respect to S as given in the previous section. Informally, this just means that the program computes exactly what the assumed specification says it should—that is, the specified solutions and computed solutions coincide.

V.2. Correctness of Programs: Definitions

The overall correctness of a logic program entails two requirements. First, any solution computed from the program should be correct according to the specification; this property is referred to as *partial correctness*. Second, any solution attributed by the specification to the goal should be computable from the program; this property is referred to as *completeness*. If both properties hold then the program is said to be *totally correct*. In order to present precise definitions of these terms it is convenient to assume that the specification S is itself written in logic. This assumption makes it possible to express the principal specified relation **R*** as follows.

Definition 2

$$\mathbf{R}^* = \{T \mid S \vDash \mathbf{R}^*(T)\}$$

where T is any n-tuple (a specified solution) and the program's goal is
G :   ? $\mathbf{R}^*(t)$.

In addition we can now also define the span of G (the set of correct solutions to G) with respect to S using

Definition 3.   Span of G with respect to (w.r.t.) S = $\{t\Theta \mid S \vDash \mathbf{R}^*(t\Theta)\}$.

Then the three Definitions 1, 2 and 3 describe computed and specified solutions in terms of what P or S logically imply. The value of this arrangement will become apparent later on.

V.2.1. Partial Correctness

A program (P, G) is partially correct with respect to a specification S if and only if it satisfies the following requirement: for all Θ, if $t\Theta$ is a computed solution then it must be a specified solution. The definition below states this in three equivalent ways.

Definition 4.   Partial correctness of (P, G :   ? $\mathbf{R}^*(t)$) w.r.t. S.

(a)   for all Θ, $t\Theta \in \mathbf{R}^*$ **if** $t\Theta \in \mathbf{R}$
(b) $\mathbf{R} \subseteq$ (span of G w.r.t. S)
(c)   for all Θ, S $\models \mathbf{R}^*(t\Theta)$ **if**   P $\models \mathbf{R}^*(t\Theta)$

Consider Program 29 as an example. It was shown that three distinct solutions are computable from it, each having the form $t\Theta$, where $t = (w:A:\varnothing, A:B:C:\varnothing)$ and Θ is some assignment to w. In order for Program 29 to be partially correct, each $t\Theta$ must have the form (*set-1*, *set-2*) where *set-1* is a subset of *set-2* according to whatever specification of the **subset** relation is provided by S. For instance, for the case $\Theta = \{w := B\}$ we have a computed solution $t\Theta = (B:A:\varnothing, A:B:C:\varnothing)$. Now $\{B, A\}$ is a subset of $\{A, B, C\}$ and so the specification S will presumably specify that $(B:A:\varnothing, A:B:C:\varnothing)$ belongs to **subset**—in which case $t\Theta$ is also one of the specified (i.e., correct) solutions to the goal. The same is true for the other two computed solutions, and therefore Program 29 is partially correct.

This concept of partial correctness for logic programs is similar in spirit to that used in conventional program proving. In both contexts, partial correctness does not in itself require that any solution actually be computed from the execution, but only requires that *if* one is computed then it will satisfy the input–output relation described by the specification.

Observe also that all unsolvable programs are partially correct according to Definition 4. This may seem rather strange upon first consideration. It means, for instance, that even though the program's procedures may be nonsensical statements about the problem domain and incapable of delivering any solutions to the goal, the program is nonetheless partially correct. This apparent terminological anomaly is made acceptable by conceding that an unsolvable program is certainly *not incorrect*—a program which computes no solutions clearly cannot compute any incorrect ones. To say that a logic program is partially correct is only to say that it computes no solutions which would violate the specification.

It is important that our definitions should be sufficiently flexible to allow unsolvable programs to be correct, because such programs form a valuable part of the programmer's repertoire. For example, one might set up an input data list L represented by some set P of **m** assertions in the usual way, and require a demonstration that some element A does not occur in any position i of L. The simplest method is to pose the goal

$$G :   ? \mathbf{m}(A, i, L)$$

and observe that no solution is computed from an execution of (P, G).

Although that program is unsolvable it nevertheless performs exactly as required and so cannot be reasonably denied the title 'partially correct'.

V.2.2. Completeness

A program (P, G) is complete with respect to a specification S if and only if it satisfies the following requirement: for all Θ, if $t\Theta$ is a specified solution then it must also be a computed solution. The definition below states this in three equivalent ways

Definition 5.   Completeness of $(P, G : \quad ?\, R^*(t))$ w.r.t. S.

(a)   for all Θ, $t\Theta \in R$ **if** $t\Theta \in R^*$

(b)   (span of G w.r.t. S) $\subseteq R$

(c)   for all Θ, $P \vDash R^*(t\Theta)$ **if** $S \vDash R^*(t\Theta)$

An alternative way of saying that (P, G) is complete is to say that P is complete for G or, more compactly, that P is G-*complete*. This just means that the procedures in P are sufficient for computing all solutions in the span of G. If P is not G-complete then this means that P does not contain enough information about the specified relation **R*** to make all correct solutions of G computable. Consider Program 29 again. There, P is certainly G-complete because each of the three specified solutions to G is computable from P. Now suppose that the second $\in$ procedure is slightly modified to

$$v \in A:z \quad \textbf{if} \quad v \in z$$

producing a new procedure set P'. It then turns out that P' is not G-complete, because the third correct solution $(C:A:\varnothing, A:B:C:\varnothing)$ to G is no longer computable. The modification of the $\in$ procedure specializes it so as to deal only with sets of the form $A:z$, thus losing information about the membership of other sets and hence about the **subset** relation. On the other hand, P' is complete for certain other goals, such as

$$G' : \quad ?\,\textbf{subset}(w:A:\varnothing, A:B:\varnothing)$$

Some procedure sets are complete for whatever goal G is posed. The procedure set P of Program 29 is such an example. No matter what call to **subset** is posed in the goal, all that goal's specified solutions will be computable using P. When P has this property we simply say that it is *complete*. The formal definition is as follows.

Definition 6.   Completeness of P w.r.t. S.

Procedure set P is complete with respect to specification S if and only if

$$\text{for all } T,\ P \vDash R^*(T) \quad \textbf{if} \quad S \vDash R^*(T)$$

Observe that this definition only needs to refer to n-tuples by the general symbol T—that is, does not constrain them to have the form $t\Theta$ where t is the goal n-tuple. This is because a complete procedure set can deal with all possible goal n-tuples, and hence with all possible choices of input and output arguments.

Finally, note that when a procedure set P is complete it is necessarily G^*-complete; that is, it is complete for the most general goal

$$G^* : \quad ? R^*(t)$$

in which t is an n-tuple of distinct variables. The span of this goal is the entire specified relation R^*, and a complete procedure set P contains enough information about R^* to make all its contents computable solutions to G^*. This means, for example, that if we pose the goal

$$G^* : \quad ? \textbf{subset}(x, y)$$

and solve it using the complete procedure set in Program 29, then we should obtain the entire infinitude of pairs of sets satisfying the **subset** relation as the computed output.

V.2.3. Total Correctness

A program (P, G) is totally correct with respect to a specification S if and only if it is both partially correct and complete. The definition below states this in three equivalent ways.

Definition 7.   Total correctness of (P, G : $? R^*(t)$) w.r.t. S.

- (a)   for all Θ, $t\Theta \in R$ **if and only if** $t\Theta \in R^*$
- (b)   (span of G w.r.t. S) = R
- (c)   for all Θ, $P \vDash R^*(t\Theta)$ **if and only if** $S \vDash R^*(t\Theta)$

Less formally, a program is totally correct with respect to S when the solutions computed by it are exactly those specified by S. Program 29 is an example of a totally correct program. If a program is not totally correct then either it computes some incorrect solutions or it fails to compute some correct ones; the first case implies that the procedures make incorrect statements about the problem domain, whilst the second implies that they are not sufficiently informative about it. The first case is the more serious one in normal circumstances, although the second one can also be serious when programs contain negated calls relying upon the negation-as-failure method.

V.3. Correctness of Programs: Sufficient Criteria

The formal definitions 4, 5 and 7 establish criteria for the correctness of a program in terms of what is computable from it, without imposing any requirements upon its individual procedures. In view of this, consider the following program.

Program 30

$$
\begin{array}{ll}
\text{G} : & ? \, \mathbf{times}(4, 6, z) \\
\text{P1} : & \mathbf{times}(x, 3, x) \\
\text{P2} : & \mathbf{times}(w, 2, 24) \\
\text{P3} : & \mathbf{times}(x, 6, z) \quad \text{if} \quad \mathbf{times}(x, 3, w), \mathbf{times}(w, 2, z)
\end{array}
$$

Here a predicate $\mathbf{times}(x, y, z)$ is intended in the usual way to express the arithmetic multiplication $z = x * y$. Assume that some specification S is available which formally assigns this intended meaning to $\mathbf{times}(x, y, z)$.

The goal G asks for the value z of $4 * 6$. According to S there will be exactly one specified solution, $z := 24$. The program computes exactly one solution and this is indeed $z := 24$. Therefore the program is totally correct.

Now consider the individual procedures. P3 states that in order to compute $z = x * 6$, one can multiply x by 3 and then double the result w to produce z. This makes perfect sense arithmetically. On the other hand, P1 states that multiplying x by 3 always gives x, whilst P2 states that doubling a number always gives 24. These two statements are nonsensical. Despite this, their invocations in the context shown produce errors which happen to be mutually compensating, so that no overall error arises.

Suppose next that the goal is changed to

$$
\text{G}' : \quad ? \, \mathbf{times}(5, 2, z)
$$

The specification will dictate that G' has one solution $z := 10$. However, the program computes only $z := 24$ (using P2), and is therefore neither partially correct nor complete. Intuitively it is unsatisfactory that a previously correct program should become an incorrect one by merely posing a different query and leaving the facts asserted about the problem domain unaltered.

Consider next the program below, whose goal is asking which members in a list L are negative.

Program 31

$$G :   ? \, \mathbf{m}(u, i, L), \, u < 0$$
$$P1 :   \mathbf{m}(10, 1, L)$$
$$P2 :   \mathbf{m}(30, 3, L)$$

Suppose the specification S states that L is the list $(10, 20, 30, 40)$. It might do this by, for instance, posing the statement

$$\mathbf{m}(u, i, L) \quad \textbf{if and only if} \quad (u = 10, i = 1) \vee (u = 20, i = 2) \vee$$
$$(u = 30, i = 3) \vee (u = 40, i = 4)$$

Then according to S the goal G has no specified solutions, since the members of L are all non-negative. Furthermore the program computes no solutions, and so must be totally correct. On the other hand, we can see that its procedures incompletely describe L because they omit mention of its 2nd and 4th members. Intuitively it is unsatisfactory that the execution should reach its (correct) conclusion despite not having inspected all members of L.

These simple examples indicate that the minimal correctness criteria established earlier should be strengthened by further conditions imposed upon the procedures. In fact two such conditions suffice for eliminating the kinds of anomaly just discussed. We describe them as 'sufficient criteria' in view of the fact that they are sufficient, but not necessary, to ensure total correctness.

Sufficient Criterion 1.   Partial correctness of (P, G) w.r.t. S.

   if $S \vDash P$ **then**   (P, G) is partially correct w.r.t. S.

In other words, if the procedures are implied by the specification then the program will be partially correct irrespective of which goal is chosen.

Proof.   Suppose $S \vDash P$ holds, and let $t\Theta$ be any computed solution to the goal $? \, R^*(t)$. Then $P \vDash R^*(t\Theta)$. Since logical implication is transitive it follows that

$$\text{for all } \Theta, \quad \textbf{if} \quad S \vDash P \quad \text{and} \quad P \vDash R^*(t\Theta)$$
$$\textbf{then} \quad S \vDash R^*(t\Theta)$$

which can be reorganized in the equivalent form

$$(\text{for all } \Theta, \, S \vDash R^*(t\Theta) \quad \textbf{if} \quad P \vDash R^*(t\Theta)) \quad \textbf{if} \quad S \vDash P$$

This just says that, if $S \vDash P$ holds, then so does the condition for partial correctness given by Definition 4.

This stronger requirement $S \vDash P$ would then preclude the nonsensical procedures P1 and P2 in Program 30, because neither is implied by S. That program, of course, also shows that $S \vDash P$ is not a necessary condition for partial correctness, that is, is not itself implied by that property.

Sufficient Criterion 2.   Completeness of (P, G) w.r.t. S.

> **if**   P is complete w.r.t. S
> **then**   P is G-complete w.r.t. S

In other words, if P is complete in the sense of Definition 6 (that is, P describes the entire contents of the specified relation **R***) then P is certainly sufficient for computing those solutions requested by any specific goal G.

Proof.   Suppose that P is complete w.r.t. S, so that

$$\text{for all } T, \; P \vDash \mathbf{R}^*(T) \quad \text{if} \quad S \vDash \mathbf{R}^*(T)$$

For any computed solution $T = t\Theta$ of the goal G :   ? $\mathbf{R}^*(t)$ it follows from the above that

$$P \vDash \mathbf{R}^*(t\Theta) \quad \text{if} \quad S \vDash \mathbf{R}^*(t\Theta)$$

But this conclusion would hold for any Θ — so prefixing it with 'for all Θ' produces the condition (Definition 5) for the G-completeness of P w.r.t. S.

The stronger requirement that P should be complete would preclude the omissions in Program 31; procedures would have to be present describing the members in positions *2* and *4* of the list *L*. Then the goal would (correctly) fail only after inspecting all the list's members. Note that Program 31 shows that the completeness of P is not a necessary condition for the completeness of (P, G).

Sufficient Criterion 3.   Total correctness of (P, G) w.r.t. S.

> (P, G) is totally correct w.r.t. S
> **if** $S \vDash P$ and P is complete

Proof. $S \vDash P$ implies partial correctness (Sufficient Criterion 1); P is complete implies (P, G) is complete (Sufficient Criterion 2); together they imply total correctness (Definition 7).

Observe that this criterion is *goal-independent*; it simply requires that P say nothing false about the problem domain and completely describe the specified relation. When satisfied by any given P, it fixes the total correctness of an entire class of programs (P, G) covering all possible choices of G having the form ? $\mathbf{R}^*(t)$.

As well as ensuring total correctness, the requirements posed in the sufficient criterion make sense both intuitively and methodologically. There can never be any good reason for writing programs like Program 30 which employ incorrect statements. However, there may sometimes be some justification for not making P complete. For instance, one might be content to compute only certain solutions, and so omit procedures capable of finding other solutions in order to reduce execution costs. This is more economical that the alternative of writing a complete procedure set and inserting cut operators to excise unwanted solutions, because it conserves memory as well as execution time. On the other hand, the use of an incomplete procedure set can complicate one's interpretation of an execution yielding no solutions, and likewise of an execution relying upon negation-as-failure. On the whole it is best to use complete procedure sets unless there are compelling reasons for doing otherwise.

Just as partial correctness may be established by showing $S \vDash P$, it is possible in some circumstances to demonstrate the completeness of P by showing $P \vDash S$, since the latter implies the completeness condition (Definition 6). In practice, though, this is rarely possible: logic procedure sets usually have less information content than the specifications to which they conform, even though they may be complete. We can illustrate this by a trivial example. Suppose $\mathbf{R^*}$ is the relation $\{(A, B), (C, B)\}$ and is specified in S by the sentence

$$S1 : \quad \mathbf{R^*}(x, y) \quad \textbf{if and only if} \quad (x = A, y = B) \vee$$
$$(x = C, y = B)$$

Assume that the only other component of S is some complete definition of the identity relation $(=)$. Then the following procedure set P

$$\mathbf{R^*}(x, y) \quad \textbf{if} \quad x = A, y = B$$
$$\mathbf{R^*}(x, y) \quad \textbf{if} \quad x = C, y = B$$
$$A = A$$
$$B = B$$
$$C = C$$

is complete, because every pair (x, y) in $\mathbf{R^*}$ can be computed from it. Yet P does not imply the statements in S. This 'weakness' of P arises from the fact that although P implies the 'if' part of S1

$$\mathbf{R^*}(x, y) \quad \textbf{if} \quad (x = A, y = B) \vee (x = C, y = B)$$

it does not imply the 'only if' part

$$(x = A, y = B) \vee (x = C, y = B) \quad \textbf{if} \quad \mathbf{R^*}(x, y)$$

and therefore cannot imply S1. Likewise, many identity relationships (like $D = D$) specified by S cannot be inferred from P. In general, much information in S will be absent from P because it is not employed for computational purposes; P can compute the entirety of $\mathbf{R^*}$ without needing to know or imply that it is doing so. The completeness of P has to be established by other means, outlined in Section V.7.

V.4. Solvability

A program (P, G) is *solvable* when at least one solution is computable from it; that is, when its computation space contains at least one successful computation. The property can be defined formally as follows.

Definition 8.   Solvability of (P, G :   ? **R***(t)).

> (P, G) is solvable
> **if and only if**   for some Θ, P $\vDash$ **R***($t\Theta$)

Solvability is a property purely of the program, making no reference to any specification. Although it is not customarily incorporated into the requirements for total correctness, it can sometimes be useful to investigate it along with the rest of the verification process.

In order to establish the solvability of Program 29, for example, it would be necessary to show that

> for some Θ, P $\vDash$ **subset**($w : A : \varnothing, A : B : C : \varnothing)\Theta$

that is,

> P $\vDash$ ($\exists w$)**subset**($w : A : \varnothing, A : B : C : \varnothing$)

One way of achieving this, of course, would be to execute the program! However, for reasons explained later (Section V.5), solvable programs do not necessarily produce solutions when executed, and so this approach is not generally reliable. In any case, execution always attempts to determine the actual values of the goal variables rather than being merely content to prove that such values exist. The former task requires the greater effort in most circumstances. This is particularly true of programs containing recursive or iterative procedures: whereas execution must actually carry out all the steps induced by these procedures, other proof methods have been devised for demonstrating solvability which infer the outcomes of such computations without having to generate them. These methods typically need to augment the knowledge encoded by P with first-order induction axioms, and are then sufficiently informed to be capable of inferring, for instance, that an iteration necessarily converges upon a solution after some finite number of steps. Proofs of this kind are called 'non-constructive existence proofs' since, unlike resolution proofs, they do not need to construct the solutions whose existence they establish.

Solvability can sometimes be established more easily by analyzing a specification S for the program. Suppose first that the program (P, G) is already known to be complete. Then (P, G) is solvable if (but not only if)

> for some Θ, S $\vDash$ **R***($t\Theta$)

This follows trivially from Definitions 5 and 8. Its practical significance is that $\mathbf{R}*(t\Theta)$ may be much easier to prove from a straightforward descriptive specification than from a set of computationally oriented procedures. It also has the advantage of confirming that a computable solution $t\Theta$ not only exists but is also correct according to S.

Similarly, an analysis of S may be the easiest way of proving *unsolvability*. Suppose (P, G) is already known to be partially correct. Then (P, G) is unsolvable if (but not only if)

$$\text{for all } \Theta, \ S \vDash \neg \mathbf{R}*(t\Theta)$$

It may be easier to show this than using P to show that

$$\text{for all } \Theta, \quad \textbf{not } (P \vDash \mathbf{R}*(t\Theta))$$

which is the strict definition of unsolvability. These uses of S, like all others, rely upon the assumption that S is self-consistent.

V.5. Correctness of Algorithms: Definitions

In this section we examine the correctness properties of *logic algorithms*. A logic algorithm is the result of prescribing some control strategy C for controlling the execution of some logic program (P, G), and can itself be denoted by the triplet (P, G, C). Since (P, G, C) also contains all the information necessary for determining every run-time detail of the algorithm, it can simultaneously be regarded as denoting an *execution*. So here we shall use the terms algorithm and execution interchangeably.

In any real implementation the primary constituent of C is usually the standard control strategy, which governs the selection of calls and responding procedures, and promotes a depth-first search through the program's computation space. In previous chapters we have also seen that this basic strategy can be variously enhanced or restricted by other control mechanisms such as lemma generation, negation-as-failure, cut operators and so on. In order to simplify the presentation of the more important issues in algorithm verification, these modifications will not be considered further, and so our analysis will be confined mainly to algorithms controlled by the standard strategy.

V.5.1. Producibility

The purpose of execution is to generate computations. In what follows, any computation is denoted generally by the symbol Γ (gamma). Assuming that

C is the standard strategy for top-down execution, Γ will consist of a sequence of goals beginning with the program's initial goal G.

A computation can be classified as either *producible* or *unproducible* under a particular control C. These terms are defined as follows.

Definition 9.   Producibility of Γ from (P, G) under C. A computation Γ is producible from a program (P, G) under control C if and only if the execution (P, G, C) generates every goal in Γ after some finite number of steps (i.e., after some finite time from the commencement of execution); otherwise it is unproducible under C.

This definition applies to any top-down control strategy as well as to the standard (depth-first) one.

The notion of producibility can be usefully applied to computed solutions as well as to computations, according to the following definition.

Definition 10.   Producibility of T from (P, G) under C. A computed solution T is producible from a program (P, G) under control C if and only if it is the solution computed by some producible computation under C (i.e., is computable after some finite time); otherwise it is unproducible.

The purpose of these definitions is to make a clear distinction between what is *logically computable* according to the program and what is *actually computable* (producible) when it is executed in a particular way. It will be shown presently that not all computable solutions are necessarily producible, even with the standard strategy; whether they are or not depends partly upon the control and partly upon the structure of the program's total computation space. This will become clearer in the next section, which examines some specific examples.

V.5.2. Comparison of Three Algorithms

The program shown below is a highly contrived example which is sufficient to illustrate all the algorithm properties of immediate interest. No attempt is made to assign any practical significance to the program.

Program 32

$$
\begin{aligned}
&\text{G} : \quad ?\,\mathbf{g}(y) \\
&\text{P1} : \quad \mathbf{g}(y) \quad \text{if} \quad \mathbf{p}(y),\, \mathbf{q}(y) \\
&\text{P2} : \quad \mathbf{p}(A) \\
&\text{P3} : \quad \mathbf{q}(A) \\
&\text{P4} : \quad \mathbf{q}(f(x)) \quad \text{if} \quad \mathbf{q}(f(f(x)))
\end{aligned}
$$

Procedures P1–P4 make up the total procedure set P. Suppose now that the program is executed using the standard strategy together with the textual ordering shown—these two aspects of the control constitute the total control C1. The resulting algorithm (P, G, C1) generates exactly one computation Γ_1 as follows.

$$\Gamma_1 : \quad ? \, \mathbf{g}(y)$$
$$? \, \mathbf{p}(y), \, \mathbf{q}(y$$
$$? \, \mathbf{q}(A)$$
$$? \qquad \text{solution } \underline{y := A}$$

This computation is finite, producible, successful and yields the solution $y := A$. This solution is a computed solution because $P \vDash \mathbf{g}(A)$ and is also a producible solution because execution actually produces it after a finite number of steps. The algorithm is perfectly innocuous and comparable to the many programming examples already illustrated.

Consider next the effect of reversing the textual order of the two calls in procedure P1. This does not alter the program's logical content, and so (P, G) remains unaltered. However, it does alter the control: it is equivalent to leaving P1 unaltered textually and choosing a computation rule which selects the last call in the goal instead of the first. Whichever way one views it, the new total control C2 differs from C1. The resulting algorithm (P, G, C2) generates two computations as shown below.

$$\Gamma_{2a} : \quad ? \, \mathbf{g}(y) \qquad\qquad \Gamma_{2b} : \quad ? \, \mathbf{g}(y)$$
$$? \, \mathbf{q}(y), \, \mathbf{p}(y) \qquad\qquad\qquad ? \, \mathbf{q}(y), \, \mathbf{p}(y)$$
$$? \, \mathbf{p}(A) \qquad\qquad\qquad\qquad ? \, \mathbf{q}(f(f(x))), \, \mathbf{p}(f(x))$$
$$? \qquad \text{solution } \underline{y := A} \qquad\quad ? \, \mathbf{q}(f(f(f(x)))), \, \mathbf{p}(f(x))$$
$$\qquad\qquad\qquad\qquad\qquad\qquad\qquad \text{etc. to infinity.}$$

The computation Γ_{2a} is finite, producible, successful and yields the solution $y := A$, and is the first one generated. The next one, Γ_{2b} is infinite and thus, although itself producible, yields no associated producible solution.

Finally, consider a third algorithm obtained by making two textual alterations to Program 32: the first reverses the two calls in P1 (like the second algorithm) and the second reverses the order of procedures P3 and P4. Thus we again use the same program (P, G) but employ a new total control C3. The algorithm (P, G, C3) begins by developing Γ_{2b}; since this is infinite and since the standard strategy is depth-first, execution will be preoccupied with Γ_{2b} in perpetuity and so make Γ_{2a} unproducible.

These differing behaviours can be understood most easily by considering the total computation space determined by (P, G) under the assumption of top-down execution. This space consists of just the three computations Γ_1, Γ_{2a} and Γ_{2b}. We saw in Chapter II that different computation rules for call selection corresponded to different subspaces of the total space. This is clearly shown by the three algorithms above. The first selects the subspace $\{\Gamma_1\}$ by incorporating the standard left-to-right computation rule in the control C1 of Program 32. The other two both select $\{\Gamma_{2a}, \Gamma_{2b}\}$ by effectively incorporating a right-to-left computation rule in the controls C2 and C3 of Program 32. Every selected subspace covers the entire solution set $\{y := A\}$.

Changing the textual order of procedures is equivalent to choosing a different search rule for procedure selection. Again, it was seen in Chapter II that different search rules correspond to different orders in which computations are generated from the selected subspace. The search rule used in C1 is only offered one computation Γ_1 to generate, whilst the same search rule in C2 is offered two, and generates them in the order shown. However, reversing the textual order of P3 and P4 is equivalent to reversing the standard first-to-last search rule, and so C3 explores the same subspace as did C2 but in the reverse order.

In conclusion, the main points to be observed are the following: (i) the existence or otherwise of infinite computations depends only upon the logic expressed in (P, G); (ii) the total control determines whether or not existing infinite computations are contained in the selected subspace; (iii) the total control determines whether or not infinite computations in the subspace are generated before some or all of the finite ones; (iv) a logically computable solution is not necessarily producible under a particular control—it will only be produced if, after some finite time, execution selects and completes the computation associated with the solution.

In view of (iv) above, it should now be clear why, as stated in Section V.4, execution is not always a sufficient test of solvability—it will fail to find any solutions if it first becomes engaged in exploring some infinite region of the computation space.

The possibility of logically computable solutions being unproducible arises whenever the control strategy used is *unfair*, that is, does not divide its attention equally between all the available computations. A sequential, depth-first strategy is inevitably unfair by virtue of its commitment to develop the current computation to its conclusion before developing any others.

By contrast, a sequential, breadth-first strategy, which develops all computations one step at a time in rotation and thus generates them in an almost parallel fashion, is virtually *fair* and so normally produces all finite computations (and hence all computed solutions) in a finite time. An exception to this can occur when the search encounters an infinite number of computations: for then it is possible for a partially developed successful computation to remain uncompleted in perpetuity whilst the interpreter is preoccupied with applying the current extension step to all the remaining infinitude. This sort of computation space typically arises from programs invoking built-in procedures which behave as though implemented by infinitely many assertions.

Computable solutions can be rendered unproducible even when (P, G) determines a *finite computation space* (one containing a finite number of computations and containing no infinite ones). This can occur when the control C is capable of excising computations during execution, for instance in response to cut operators or to procedure-deletion directives. In effect this is equivalent to controlling execution by a *non-exhaustive* search strategy—that is, one which does not exhaustively explore all the possibilities logically determined by (P, G).

V.5.3. Termination

Termination is a simple concept when applied to a program written in a conventional deterministic language: such a program offers just one possible computation (once the input data, if any, have been decided) and its execution terminates if and only if that computation is finite.

The concept is potentially more complicated when applied to logic algorithms offering several computations. For then, depending on the chosen definition, termination of (P, G, C) could require, for example, (i) that all successful computations be producible, or (ii) that computations of all kinds be producible and finite in number. Requirement (i) is weaker than (ii) in saying only that all computable solutions must be produced in finite time, even though execution may thereafter continue indefinitely, either by becoming trapped in an infinite computation or by having to explore an infinitude of unsuccessful computations. Requirement (ii) is stronger in demanding that the entire execution process must halt after a finite time.

Intuitively, (ii) seems the more desirable requirement, provided that we accept that it will not be satisfied by certain kinds of program which are nevertheless of practical value. These are programs which behave as though intended to run indefinitely, such as operating systems and real-time process controllers. For instance, one might wish to execute the following program which monitors the state x of some process at time steps $t = 0, 1, 2, \ldots$ etc.

Program 33

> ? **monitor**(0)
> **monitor**(t)   **if**   **state**(x, t), **display**(x, t),
> $\qquad\qquad\qquad\qquad\qquad$ **monitor**($t+1$)
> and appropriate **display** procedures,
> and **state** calls being solved directly via
> some interface with the process hardware

The time steps here are determined by the monitor program, and we assume that each **state** call returns a unique value for x for each value of t. In this event the program will be deterministic, and its single computation is an infinite one. Therefore execution never yields a solution to the initial goal and never halts. The desired output is instead a sequence of (x, t) values, which are themselves only computed solutions of the **state** calls.

Approximately similar behaviour can be obtained using a different programming style, as in the program below.

Program 34

> ? **state**(x, t), **display**(x, t)
> and **display** procedures,
> and **state** calls solved as before

Here we assume that the process, rather than the monitor, reports the time steps t as well as the states x. This program is non-deterministic because the process behaves as though implemented by infinitely many **state** assertions, one for each time step. Successive (x, t) pairs are now output by repeated backtracking, thus invoking each of the (implicit) **state** assertions in turn. The computation subspace now consists of an infinitude of successful computations but contains no infinite computations. Execution is again non-terminating.

Notwithstanding exceptional programs of this sort, we shall adopt, somewhat arbitrarily, the requirement (ii) above for termination, formalizing it as follows.

Definition 11.   Termination of (P, G, C). An execution (P, G, C) terminates if and only if it yields a finite number of computations and all of these are of finite length.

This definition determines that the algorithms obtained by executing Programs 33 and 34 under the standard strategy are both non-terminating. In relation to Program 32 discussed in the previous section, it determines that (P, G, C1) terminates whilst both (P, G, C2) and (P, G, C3) do not.

V.5.4. Correctness Definitions

In conventional program proving it has been customary to incorporate a termination requirement into definitions of total correctness. In dealing with logic algorithms we shall not follow suit in this respect, but shall instead focus only upon the correctness and completeness of the generated solution set. The termination of algorithms, like the solvability of programs, is viewed as an important property deserving investigation but not inclusion within the necessary correctness criteria.

Informally, a logic algorithm (P, G, C) is defined to be *totally correct* with respect to a specification S if and only if it is both *partially correct* and *complete*. It is partially correct if and only if all its producible solutions are specified solutions, and is complete if and only if all the specified solutions are producible solutions. In other words, a totally correct algorithm produces, in a finite time, exactly those solutions which S attributes to G.

In order to state these requirements formally in a logical notation, it is convenient to employ propositions of the form

$$A \vdash_c B$$

to express that B is provable from A using resolution controlled by the strategy C. In particular, the proposition

$$P \vdash_c R^*(t\Theta)$$

means that the solution $t\Theta$ of the assumed goal G : ? $R^*(t)$ is producible under C. The necessary correctness criteria for logic algorithms can now be summarized as follows.

Definition 12.   Partial correctness of (P, G, C) w.r.t. S.

for all Θ, $S \vDash R^*(t\Theta)$ if $P \vdash_c R^*(t\Theta)$

Definition 13.   Completeness of (P, G, C) w.r.t. S.

for all Θ, $P \vdash_c R^*(t\Theta)$ if $S \vDash R^*(t\Theta)$

Definition 14:   Total correctness of (P, G, C) w.r.t. S.

for all Θ, $S \vDash R^*(t\Theta)$ if and only if $P \vdash_c R^*(t\Theta)$

These definitions bear a pleasing structural similarity to those given previously for program correctness (Definitions 4, 5 and 7), as a consequence of employing the dual notions of (logical) computability and (actual) producibility to distinguish the output of programs from the output of algorithms.

V.6. Correctness of Algorithms: Sufficient Criteria

The verification of logic algorithms can be simplified by the use of sufficient criteria. As in our similar earlier treatment of program verification, these criteria are not only logically stronger requirements than the necessary ones, but also prescribe methodologically sensible properties for algorithms. They can be summarized as follows.

Sufficient Criterion 4.   Partial correctness of (P, G, C) w.r.t. S.

(P, G, C) is partially correct   if   (P, G) is partially correct

This criterion should be obvious enough: if (P, G) is partially correct then every computed solution $t\Theta$ is a specified solution and, provided that C is founded upon a correct inference system such as resolution, every producible solution $t\Theta$ is a computed solution; the result then follows directly.

Sufficient Criterion 5.   Completeness of (P, G, C) w.r.t. S.

(P, G, C) is complete   **if** (P, G) is complete and determines
a finite computation space, and
C is exhaustive

This is also straightforward: if the computation space is finite and C explores all computations in any selected subspace, then all computed solutions are producible; then if (P, G) is complete, all specified solutions are computed solutions and hence are producible, which establishes the result. The control C will be exhaustive if it is the standard strategy and is unmodified by cut operators and other such directives.

Sufficient Criterion 6.   Total correctness of (P, G, C) w.r.t. S.

(P, G, C) is totally correct   **if** (P, G) is totally correct and
determines a finite computation
space, and C is exhaustive

This follows directly from the previous two criteria and Definition 14. By virtue of the Sufficient Criterion 3 given earlier for the total correctness of (P, G), one can state an even stronger condition for the total correctness of (P, G, C) as follows.

Sufficient Criterion 7.   Total correctness of (P, G, C) w.r.t. S.

(P, G, C) is totally correct   **if**   S implies P and P is complete,
and (P, G) determines a finite
computation space, and C is
exhaustive

In the next section an outline is given of a verification of Program 29 (the **subset** program) and of its execution under the standard strategy, using this last criterion.

V.7. An Example of Verification

The application of the verification theory is now demonstrated in outline for Program 29, and shows that the rather theoretical ideas discussed previously can be used to verify programs in a reasonably straightforward manner. It is useful to restate the program's statements and give them some labels for easy reference.

Program 29

$$
\begin{array}{ll}
\text{G}: & ?\,\textbf{subset}(w:A:\varnothing,\ A:B:C:\varnothing) \\
\text{P1}: & \textbf{subset}(x, y) \quad \textbf{if} \quad \textbf{empty}(x) \\
\text{P2}: & \textbf{subset}(v:x',y) \quad \textbf{if} \quad v \in y,\ \textbf{subset}(x', y) \\
\text{P3}: & v \in v:z \\
\text{P4}: & v \in u:z \quad \textbf{if} \quad v \in z \\
& \text{and built-in procedure(s) for } \textbf{empty}
\end{array}
$$

We will show that this program and any execution of it under the standard strategy are both totally correct with respect to a given specification.

V.7.1. Choosing Criteria

In order to verify the program it is necessary to decide whether to employ the necessary criteria or the sufficient criteria. In general, two considerations favour the latter choice. The first of these is that the sufficient criteria test three program properties, namely

  (i)   P is implied by the specification S;
  (ii) P is complete w.r.t. S;
  (iii) (P, G) determines a finite computation space;

which one would expect to be true of a well-styled program. It is sensible to attempt first to prove the properties believed most likely to hold. Second, the sufficient criteria are easier to articulate and to investigate than the necessary ones. In what follows, the first two properties above are established in order to confirm that (P, G) is totally correct. Afterward, the third property is established and so guarantees that standard execution will produce, in finite time, exactly those correct instances of w which make $\{w, A\}$ a subset of $\{A, B, C\}$.

V.7.2. Choice of Specification

The chosen specification S consists of a set of sentences written in general first-order logic, the principal ones being shown below. The first sentence states the standard definition of **subset**; the second defines set membership for the chosen representation of sets (structured terms) and the third defines the empty set. The specification also (implicitly) includes a complete description of the identity ($=$) relation.

Specification for Program 29

S1 :   **subset**(x, y) **iff** $(\forall u)(u \in y$ if $u \in x)$
S2 : $u \in x$ **iff** $(\exists v \exists x')(x = v:x', (u = v \lor u \in x'))$
S3 :   **empty**(x) **iff** $\neg (\exists v \exists x')(x = v:x')$
        and a complete description of the $=$ relation

In these sentences the symbol **iff** just abbreviates **if and only if**.

V.7.3. Definiens Transformation

In the specification above, each sentence has been deliberately structured in the form

definiand   **iff**   definiens

where the *definiand* (the object being defined) is a single predicate **r( )** naming some specified relation **r**, and the *definiens* (the defining property of the object) is any formula. This standard specification style has the following motivation. Suppose it can be shown that the specification S implies a sentence having the form **D   iff   D′** where **D** is a definiens for a specified relation **r**. Then it follows that **D′** is another, equivalent definiens for **r**. More formally, we are saying that

> **if** $S \vDash r(\ ) \text{ iff } D$ **and** $S \vDash D \text{ iff } D'$
> **then** $S \vDash r(\ ) \text{ iff } D'$

The replacement of **D** by **D′** in the definition of **r** is called a *definiens transformation*. By applying such transformations successively one obtains a *proof* in which each step produces a new definition of **r** implied by S. The proof will have the following appearance:

> **r( )**   **iff**   **D₁**   (given initially in S)
> **r( )**   **iff**   **D₂**   (using $S \vDash D_1 \text{ iff } D_2$)
> **r( )**   **iff**   **D₃**   (using $S \vDash D_2 \text{ iff } D_3$)
> etc.

The purpose of pursuing such a proof is to arrive at some nth definition

$$r(\ ) \quad \text{iff} \quad D_n$$

in which D_n is some disjunction $B_1 \lor B_2 \lor \ldots \lor B_m$ where each disjunct B_i has the syntax of a procedure body. When this is so, it follows immediately that S implies the following set of m *derived procedures*:

$$\mathbf{r}(\ ) \quad \mathbf{if} \quad \mathbf{B}_1$$
$$\mathbf{r}(\ ) \quad \mathbf{if} \quad \mathbf{B}_2$$
$$\vdots$$
$$\mathbf{r}(\ ) \quad \mathbf{if} \quad \mathbf{B}_m$$

In the course of performing a verification based upon the sufficient criteria, a proof of this kind is pursued for every relation named in the program other than those implemented by built-in procedures. So in the present example two proofs will be necessary, one for **subset** and one for $\in$. The proofs are 'steered' toward deriving exactly those procedures appearing in the program. If this is accomplished successfully then the program (P, G) is thereby proven to be totally correct. Its partial correctness is directly established by the fact that every procedure has been shown to be implied by S. Its completeness is established by the fact that each definiens transformation preserves equivalence—this ensures that every tuple described by any definiens continues to be described by the next one.

V.7.4. Deriving the Procedures

The use of definiens transformation to derive the **subset** procedures P1 and P2 is outlined below. For presentation's sake, only the definiens $\mathbf{D}_i$ is shown in each step, rather than the entire sentence **subset** (x, y) **iff** $\mathbf{D}_i$.

Proof of the **subset** *procedures*

$\mathbf{D}_1$: $(\forall u)(u \in y \quad \mathbf{if} \quad u \in x)$

$\mathbf{D}_2$: $(\forall u)(u \in y \quad \mathbf{if} \quad (\exists v \exists x')(x = v:x', (u = v \lor u \in x')))$

$\mathbf{D}_3$: $\neg(\exists v \exists x')(x = v:x') \lor$
$\qquad (\exists v \exists x')(x = v:x', (\forall u)(u \in y \quad \mathbf{if} \quad u = v \lor u \in x'))$

$\mathbf{D}_4$: $\mathbf{empty}(x) \lor (\exists v \exists x')(x = v:x', (\forall u)(u \in y \quad \mathbf{if} \quad u = v),$
$\qquad\qquad\qquad\qquad\qquad\qquad (\forall u)(u \in y \quad \mathbf{if} \quad u \in x'))$

$\mathbf{D}_5$: $\mathbf{empty}(x) \lor (\exists v \exists x')(x = v:x', v \in y, \mathbf{subset}(x', y))$

At this stage each disjunct in the definiens $(\mathbf{D}_5)$ has become a conjunction of predicates and is therefore a well-formed procedure body. Note that it does not matter if any of these disjuncts are prefixed by existential quantifiers, because any derived sentence

$$\mathbf{A} \quad \mathbf{if} \quad (\exists z)\mathbf{B}(z) \qquad \text{where } z \text{ does not occur in } \mathbf{A}$$

is equivalent to the sentence

$$(\forall z)(\mathbf{A} \quad \mathbf{if} \quad \mathbf{B}(z))$$

which is in the standard procedure form. Thus from $\mathbf{D}_5$ we can now infer two sentences corresponding to the two disjuncts as follows:

P1 : **subset**(x, y) **if** **empty**(x)
 subset(x, y) **if** $x = v : x'$, $v \in y$, **subset**(x', y)

The second of these can be simplified by using elementary properties of $=$ in order to obtain

P2 : **subset**$(v : x', y)$ **if** $v \in y$, **subset**(x', y)

Both **subset** procedures of Program 29 have now been derived. The steps in the proof can be explained informally in the following manner.

Step 1. $\mathbf{D}_1$ is transformed to $\mathbf{D}_2$ by replacing the subformula $u \in x$ by its definiens according to S2.

Step 2. $\mathbf{D}_2$ is transformed to $\mathbf{D}_3$ by exploiting a generalization of the rule

A **if** $(\exists z)(\mathbf{B}(z), \mathbf{C}(z))$ is logically equivalent to
 $\neg(\exists z)\mathbf{B}(z) \vee (\exists z)(\mathbf{B}(z), \mathbf{A}$ **if** $\mathbf{C}(z))$

Step 3. $\mathbf{D}_3$ is transformed to $\mathbf{D}_4$ by exploiting the rule

A **if** $\mathbf{B} \vee \mathbf{C}$ is logically equivalent to
 $(\mathbf{A}$ **if** $\mathbf{B}), (\mathbf{A}$ **if** $\mathbf{C})$

to split its subformula $(\forall u)$ (etc.) into two conjuncts.

Step 4. Finally, the first of the latter conjuncts is simplified to the equivalent $v \in y$, and the second is replaced by its definiand **subset**(x', y) according to S1, giving $\mathbf{D}_5$.

The sequence $(\mathbf{D}_1, \ldots \mathbf{D}_5)$ depicts only the principal 'stepping stones' of the proof. In general, each step entails some arbitrary amount of inner manipulation, either of the current definiens alone (e.g., to derive $\mathbf{D}_4$ from $\mathbf{D}_3$) or of both it and some sentence selected from S (e.g., to derive $\mathbf{D}_5$ from $\mathbf{D}_4$). All such manipulations exploit various inference rules for first-order logic. In order to perform manual verification successfully and efficiently, one must be considerably proficient in the use of such rules. No attempt is made here to provide a comprehensive collection of useful inference rules for program verification. Instead, the interested reader is referred (in Section V.9) to standard texts on mathematical logic and to research papers describing the rules found to be most useful in practice.

The next task in the present example is to verify the $\in$ procedures P3 and P4. The proof begins with the definiens of $u \in x$ supplied by S2, namely

$$\mathbf{D}_1 : (\exists v \exists x')(x = v : x', (u = v \vee u \in x'))$$

The first step uses the rule

$$\mathbf{A}, (\mathbf{B} \vee \mathbf{C}) \quad \text{is logically equivalent to} \quad (\mathbf{A}, \mathbf{B}) \vee (\mathbf{A}, \mathbf{C})$$

in order to transform $\mathbf{D}_1$ to

$$\mathbf{D}_2 : \quad (\exists v \exists x')((x = v:x', u = v) \vee (x = v:x', u \in x'))$$

from which we can infer two procedures,

$$u \in x \quad \text{if} \quad x = v:x', u = v$$
$$u \in x \quad \text{if} \quad x = v:x', u \in x'$$

Because of the assumed properties of the identity ($=$) relation, these procedures simplify to

$$v \in v:x'$$
$$u \in v:x' \quad \text{if} \quad u \in x'$$

which, apart from an inconsequential renaming of z by x', are exactly the procedures P3 and P4 of Program 29 as desired.

This concludes the verification of (P, G): it is now proven to be totally correct with respect to the given specification. Moreover, it will remain totally correct for any other goal because our analysis, using the sufficient criteria, took no account of G.

V.7.5. Proving Termination

The termination of (P, G, C) for Program 29 is established here by an informal argument. Consider any computation Γ logically determined by the program. It begins by activating a call of the form **subset**($s1, s2$) where $s2$ is a variable-free term. Suppose that P1 is invoked; in this case the next activated call is to **empty**, and we assume that the built-in procedure always processes such a call in finite time. Alternatively, suppose P2 is invoked; in this case the next activated call has the form $t \in s2$.

Consider how this $\in$ call is processed. If $s2$ is not some structured term $v:x'$ then the call fails in finite time because neither P3 nor P4 respond to it. Otherwise $s2$ is some variable-free term $r:s2'$. If P3 is invoked then the $\in$ call is immediately solved. Alternatively, if P4 is invoked then the next activated call is $t \in s2'$, whose second argument $s2'$ is *smaller* than $s2$; repeated invocation of P4 to process an $\in$ call clearly cannot be repeated indefinitely because the second arguments in the recursive $\in$ calls cannot reduce in size indefinitely. This establishes that any $\in$ call must succeed or fail in finite time.

Now focus attention again on the former call $t \in s2$. If it fails, then so does Γ. If it succeeds, then the next activated call has the form **subset**($s1, s2'$), where *s2'* is *smaller* than *s2*. Using the same reasoning as above, recursion on P2 could not continue indefinitely. Since we have argued that all calls to **empty**, $\in$ and **subset** are processed in finite time, it follows that Γ must be finite. This conclusion holds for all Γ and so the program's total computation space is finite: execution of Program 29 under the standard strategy, or any exhaustive strategy, therefore terminates. The termination proof can be easily established more formally by using structural induction.

V.8. Limitations on Verification

Verification in the manner just shown may not always be successful. In the first place, the program or algorithm under consideration might not meet the sufficient criteria, for instance if the procedure set were incomplete or not wholly implied by the specification. In this case one could only hope to show correctness by employing the necessary criteria, which would entail taking careful account of the particular goal and the particular control strategy.

More fundamental obstacles to verification are posed by the various limitative theorems which have been long established for formal logical systems. For example, the semi-decidability of the validity question in first-order logic (see Chapter I) means that no infallible procedure exists which is capable of deciding whether or not any given program is partially correct, complete or totally correct. Thus a theoretical limitation is immediately placed upon the scope of program verifiers. For the same fundamental reason it is impossible to construct procedures which fully decide other properties such as program solvability and the self-consistency of specifications.

Likewise it is not possible to devise an infallible test of termination for logic algorithms. Theorem-proving investigations based upon characterizations of the finiteness of computation spaces may, depending on how the properties of interest are formulated, be restricted in scope by the decidability limitations of either first-order or second-order logic. An equivalent confirmation lies in the argument that every logic algorithm can be represented by some Turing machine, and it is well-known that the termination question (or 'halting problem') for such algorithms is only semi-decidable.

These theoretical obstacles need not, of course, deter us from attempting to construct automated or semi-automated tools for verifying logic programs: for the great majority of practical programs it is perfectly feasible to decide their correctness (or incorrectness) by systematic and efficient analytical methods. Apart from this it is also important to recognize that the correctness criteria presented here can be viewed as conditions governing the *synthesis* of necessarily correct programs. The use of proven synthesizers based upon these criteria effectively eliminates all incorrect programs from our consideration, and the decidability limitations which potentially afflict the logical analysis of arbitrarily constructed programs are thus largely circumvented. Program synthesis is considered in more detail in Chapter VI.

V.9. Background

The first formulations of verification criteria are due to Clark and Tärnlund (1977). They regarded verification as just one topic within a general first-order theory of programs and data. This theory is elaborated and reorganized in Clark's thesis (1979), and is described there as the 'theory of the program computed relation'; here we shall refer to it as the 'PCR theory' for short.

The 'program computed relation', denoted here by $\tilde{R}$, is defined by

$$\tilde{R} = \{T \mid P \vDash R^*(T)\}$$

where P is the procedure set and G :   ? $R^*(t)$ is the goal. Then $\tilde{R}$ is just the set of all solutions computable from P, covering all possible choices of the goal n-tuple t. It is therefore goal independent. [What we have called the 'computed relation' R in this chapter is just that subset of $\tilde{R}$ which is computable for a given goal G; this distinction between the relations analysed reflects the fact that Clark treats P as 'the program' and any goal G as a 'use' of P, in preference to treating (P, G) as 'the program'.]

The basis of the Clark–Tärnlund analysis is the treatment of the procedures of P as first-order axioms describing $\tilde{R}$; these are taken to be the principal constituents of an axiom set A from which a *theory of* $\tilde{R}$ can be evolved for the purpose of determining various properties of $\tilde{R}$ and hence of the program. This PCR theory consists of A and all the sentences (theorems) provable from it using only first-order deduction. Depending upon the properties being investigated, it may be necessary to include axioms in A which make the theory stronger than if A consisted of P alone; these axioms typically encode various induction rules.

Verification using the PCR theory can be established by proving theorems from A such as

$$s : \text{for all } T,\ R^*(T) \quad \textbf{iff} \quad D(T)$$

where $D(T)$ is some self-evidently correct definiens for $R^*(T)$. In effect, one is deriving the desired specification from the program's statements.

Clark (1979) has also cast logic program verification in the style of conventional program proving by incorporating input and output predicates into the verification conditions. For instance the total correctness criterion can be cast in the PCR theory as the requirement that some sentence of the form

$$s' : \quad \text{for all } T_1, \quad \textbf{if} \quad I(T_1)$$
$$\textbf{then} \quad \text{for all } T_2, \mathbf{R}^*(T_1, T_2) \quad \textbf{iff} \quad \mathbf{O}(T_1, T_2)$$

be provable from A. In this formulation, T_1 and T_2 denote some selections of the arguments of $\mathbf{R}^*$. $I(T_1)$ is some predicate describing the assumed input arguments T_1, whilst $\mathbf{O}(T_1, T_2)$ is a predicate describing the desired relationship between the output T_2 and the input T_1; the sentence s' just requires that the program's solutions to an $\mathbf{R}^*$ call exactly satisfy the input–output predicate $\mathbf{O}$ whenever $\mathbf{I}$ is satisfied by the input.

The PCR theory can also be used for proving other logic program properties, for example solvability and equivalence to other programs. The approach taken by Clark to these ends is directly analogous to that customarily taken in the analysis of programs in other languages, relying particularly upon various species of well-founded induction. Verification by procedure derivation was investigated shortly after the PCR theory, and appears to give a simpler method of proving partial correctness. The possibility of formulating much of the PCR theory in first-order logic itself is important to mechanized metalevel processing.

The literature of logic program verification contains some potential confusions for anyone who is unaware of certain changes in definitions which have occurred during its history. The Clark–Tärnlund approach adopted the standard concept of partial correctness, but also chose 'termination' as the additional requirement for total correctness in an attempt to imitate the concepts of conventional program proving. The completeness requirement of logic programs was not explicitly dealt with in this formulation. In order to investigate total correctness using PCR theory, it was then necessary to define termination in such a way that it could be proved using first-order deduction. This was achieved by defining it as the property which in this book has been called solvability—that is, the existence of at least one successfully terminating computation. An exactly similar approach had been taken some years earlier by Chang and Lee (1973) in their use of clausal-form logic for verifying conventional programs.

Solvability does not, of course, have any bearing upon the usual concept of termination, which refers to the completion of the entire execution process in a finite time, except in the special case in which the execution is also deterministic (offering exactly one computation). Fundamentally it is the possibility of non-determinism which makes it impossible to force logic program verification into an exact correspondence with conventional program proving. This is because (a) the potential plurality of solutions suggests a completeness requirement, (b) the independence of logic from control suggests a distinction between program verification and algorithm verification, and (c) the potential plurality of computations and the diversity of possible control strategies both complicate the definition and analysis of termination. Very little research has yet been undertaken to develop systematic methods for proving the termination of logic algorithms.

Verification using procedure derivation was developed independently by Clark (1977), by Clark and Sickel (1977) and by Hogger (1977, 1978a). Clark has referred to it as 'consequence verification' in order to emphasize its goal of showing that the procedures are a logical consequence of (implied by) the specification. More recent formulations are given by Clark (1979) and by Hogger (1981, 1982a). Viewed as a tool for either verification or synthesis, logic procedure derivation differs from the analysis of conventional programs in that (a) it avoids the onerous task of axiomatizing heterogeneous and strongly interdependent machine-oriented programming constructs; (b) it confines attention to the logical properties of algorithms, ignoring all their control features, and (c) it is goal independent and therefore neutral with respect to the intended input–output use of the derived procedures. Its conceptual basis is also simple and intuitive.

Despite these advantages, practical difficulties still arise: often, the specification and the target procedures will not share close logical proximity, in the sense that the necessary derivations will pose challenging exercises in theorem proving. This is likeliest when the program's logic exploits very subtle properties of the problem domain, as it might do in many mathematical and scientific applications. The difficulty of proving these properties is not much affected by the choice of programming formalism.

On the other hand a great many practical programs, especially those used in commerical data processing, deal only with comparatively trivial properties of the specified relations. It is in these sorts of application that significant advantages should follow from the use of logic, not only because of the clarity which it can bestow upon the programs themselves, but also because, even when those programs are very large, their verifications using procedure derivation should entail just a correspondingly large number of trivial proofs. It ought to be feasible to develop programmed derivation systems for such programs, perhaps guided by an interacting user. An implementation of this kind has been described by Balogh (1981), which uses deductions of the kind proposed by Hoare (1969). Other implementations have been proposed by Hansson and Tärnlund (1979) and by Hansson and Johansson (1980), both based upon natural deduction systems; good introductions to natural deduction have been provided by Quine (1959) and Manna (1974).

Finally, logic procedure derivation has also been applied by Clark and van Emden (1981) to conventional program proving. They show how to derive logic procedures representing the logical content of flowchart programs, and the latter are then verified by showing that these procedures conform to given specifications. They then establish a number of interesting relationships between their approach and various conventional verification methods.

VI FORMAL PROGRAM SYNTHESIS

This chapter considers the composition and modification of logic programs. Truly systematic methods of program development cannot yet be prescribed, given the absence both of any simple theory capable of characterizing efficient algorithms and of any practical technique for discovering them. It is nonetheless possible and useful to outline a logical framework for program derivation upon which mechanizable rules of operation might be superimposed as and when our knowledge of programs and algorithms improves. In presenting this framework we make use of the concepts of logical specification and procedure derivation as described in Chapter V, and also assume that the reader has some proficiency in first-order logical inference.

VI.1. Program Correctness

An important consideration when developing any program is the question of whether and how one intends to ensure its correctness. Any decision about this must influence the style and spirit in which the program's logic is conceived and articulated in the programming language. Specifically, it will determine the role played by the specification to which the finished program is desired to conform.

It is probably fair to say that the 'typical' programmer prefers to develop a program in an intuitive and experimental manner, relying primarily upon a mental impression of some preconceived algorithm to direct the composition of the program's statements. It is only afterward that a precise specification might be invoked for the purpose of assessing the program's correctness. This *analytic* approach consists approximately of experiment-then-analysis, perhaps iterated several times to incorporate corrections and refinements.

It gives priority to the task of outlining a known effective algorithm, with any logical defects in its description being eliminated later on by analyzing the program's relationship to the specification. This may not be the most productive or reliable way of programming, yet is nevertheless what most programmers tend to do when not constrained by an imposed methodology.

A different approach can be taken which is *synthetic* rather than analytic in the way it deals with the correctness question. The program steps are derived logically from the specification. This ensures their logical correctness, although any choices between alternative steps in the derivation will be governed by judgements about run-time behaviour. The priority here is to obtain an initial version of the program which necessarily delivers the right solutions, whilst improvements in efficiency can be made later on by correctness-preserving modifications. The specification now plays an active, motivating role throughout the creative process, making each newly created step fulfil some logically necessary requirement and so keeping the overall goal at the forefront of the programmer's mind. Current programming methodology broadly favours this kind of approach, imposing disciplines designed to maintain logical integrity right from the start.

VI.2. Synthesis of Logic Programs

There are a number of reasons why the synthetic approach is especially favourable to the development of logic programs. First, the verification technique described in Chapter V as 'procedure derivation' immediately provides a synthesis tool capable of ensuring that programs conform to their specifications: the derivation process effectively creates the program text. Second, the separation of logic from control means that this tool can be applied without committing the programmer to decide all behavioural details in advance: although the synthesis of each program segment may anticipate some particular behaviour, the latter is not irrevocably fixed by the segment itself because of the various control options which can be exercised independently of the segment's logic. Third, by writing specifications and programs in the common language of logic and relating them through the simple concept of logical implication, the programmer can see directly how the assumptions inherent in the specification contribute to the computational solution of the problem. In effect the synthesis consists of selecting computationally useful facts from the total knowledge base implied by the specification. By expressing these facts as logic program statements and applying the procedural interpretation to them, the programmer can examine their operational contribution to the algorithm under various

modes of control as well as reading them purely declaratively in order to
see what they say about the problem.

These merits of logic are not matched by conventional formalisms. In
the first place, many of the standard verification techniques cannot be trivially
inverted so as to become synthetic tools for generating algorithmic constructs
realizing given logical objectives. Moreover, the synthesis of a conventional
program cannot defer decisions about run-time behaviour. In particular,
the use of ordered sequences of destructive assignments creates strong
logical and operational dependences between program segments, making
them difficult to develop and analyze individually and less flexible in their
eventual application. Finally, the semantic disparity between declarative,
logic-based specifications and the operational constructs of machine-oriented
languages appreciably diminishes the programmer's perceptions of their
interrelationship, dependent as it is upon a large and heterogeneous collection of correspondences linking the two kinds of formalism.

In the subsequent illustrations of logic program synthesis, then, we
adopt procedure derivation as the standard technique: given a complete,
self-consistent and self-evidently correct specification written entirely in
first-order logic, each procedure of the program is derived from it by using
logical inference. The control of the inference process is guided by consideration of the algorithmic utility of the steps taken, this being assessed
informally.

VI.3. Synthesis Using Procedure Derivation

Our treatment of practical verification in Section V.7 of the previous chapter
introduced the idea of deriving from the specification S a single sentence
implying a set of procedures for a particular relation. For example, from a
specification describing sets and subsets we derived the sentence

$$\mathbf{subset}(x, y) \quad \textbf{iff} \quad \mathbf{empty}(x) \vee$$
$$(\exists v \exists x')(x = v : x', v \in y, \mathbf{subset}(x', y))$$

which implies the two procedures

$$\mathbf{subset}(x, y) \quad \textbf{if} \quad \mathbf{empty}(x)$$
$$\mathbf{subset}(x, y) \quad \textbf{if} \quad x = v : x', v \in y, \mathbf{subset}(x', y)$$

for the **subset** relation.

The first sentence above contains on the right of **iff** a disjunction of two
cases for which **subset**(x, y) holds, each disjunct contributing toward the
body of a derived **subset** procedure. Sentences of this kind can become very

cumbersome when many cases need to be dealt with. A more compact approach is that which instead derives each procedure individually from S, that is, which deals with just one case at a time.

It is convenient to combine this arrangement with another new feature which we call *goal-directed derivation*; this is a means of deriving a procedure by processing an initial goal consisting of a call to the relation of interest. For example, consider a derivation consisting of the following sequence of goals:

$$G_1 : \quad ? \, \text{subset}(x, y)$$
$$\vdots$$
$$G_n : \quad ? \, \text{empty}(x)$$

Also suppose that, for each $t \geqslant 1$, we have $S, G_t \vDash G_{t+1}$; in other words, each derived goal is implied jointly by S and the preceding goal. When this is so, it follows that the procedure

$$\text{subset}(x, y) \quad \text{if} \quad \text{empty}(x)$$

is implied by S; the procedure's heading is the call in G_1 and its body is the set of calls in G_n.

More generally, the goal-directed derivation of a procedure for some relation r begins with a goal

$$G_1 : \quad ? \, r(\ )$$

and ends with some goal

$$G_n : \quad ? \, r_1(\ ), r_2(\ ), \ldots, r_k(\ )$$

The entire derivation establishes that, assuming S holds, a call $r(\ )$ can be solved by solving the conjunction of calls $r_1(\ ), \ldots r_k(\ )$, and this, of course, is exactly what is stated by the inferred procedure '

$$r(\ ) \quad \text{if} \quad r_1(\ ), \ldots, r_k(\ )$$

This conclusion can be argued more formally by observing that, provided each goal is implied jointly by S and its predecessor, the implication $S, G_1 \vDash G_n$ holds because of the transitivity of $\vDash$. Since each goal is some negated formula, the implication can be rewritten as

$$S, \neg \text{heading} \vDash \neg \text{body}$$

and the rearrangement of this in the form

$$S \vDash (\text{heading} \quad \text{if} \quad \text{body})$$

then follows as a consequence of a metatheorem of logic known as the Deduction Theorem.

Observe that the sequence $(G_1, \ldots, G_n)$ resembles a typical top-down computation from a logic program, except that goals intermediate between G_1 and G_n are not limited to conjunctions of predicates. For instance, the second goal in the sequence might be

$$G_2 : \quad ? (\forall u)(u \in y \quad \text{if} \quad u \in x)$$

The spirit in which the goals are developed is also similar to that of program execution. Execution of a program (P, G_1) generates each new goal G_{t+1} so as to satisfy $P, G_t \vDash G_{t+1}$ as a consequence of using resolution. Procedure derivation just uses S instead of a procedure set P to provide the knowledge selected in each step, and generally requires inference rules more elaborate than resolution in order to deal with the more arbitrary syntax of the goals.

The advantage of casting procedure derivation in this quasi-computational format consists not only in the greater compactness arising from the pursuit of one procedure at a time, but also in revealing exactly how the specification contributes toward solving the problem initially posed by the goal $? r( )$. This overall objective of the synthesis is sustained in the programmer's mind by the action required of him at each step, which entails applying some fact selected from S to the current goal G_t in a computationally motivated way. Note that in principle he could pursue the derivation to a point where it actually solved the original goal, as though he were executing a 'program' whose 'procedure set' was S; but in practice the derivation is normally terminated at some earlier point at which a useful procedure can be inferred. So whereas program execution pursues a solution, procedure derivation seeks a *way* (a procedure) of pursuing a solution.

VI.4. An Example Using Resolution

Resolution alone can sometimes serve as a practical inference system for deriving programs from specifications. This is demonstrated by the following example, which deals with the problem of finding those pairs (u, v) of members in a set z which satisfy $p(u, v)$, where $\mathbf{p}$ names some binary relation of interest. For instance, if $z = \{1, 2, 3\}$ and $\mathbf{p}$ is the 'greater than' ($>$) relation, then the solutions are $(2, 1)$, $(3, 1)$ and $(3, 2)$.

The desired relationship between u, v and z can be described using the predicate find(u, v, z). The relations relevant to the problem can then be specified by the following **iff** definitions:

$$\mathbf{find}(u, v, z) \quad \text{iff} \quad u \in z, \ v \in z, \ \mathbf{p}(u, v)$$
$$u \in z \quad \text{iff} \quad (\exists w \exists z')(z = w : z', (u = w \lor u \in z'))$$

and a complete definition of $=$.

The intention of using resolution for the synthesis makes it convenient to extract from these sentences a number of trivially implied consequences, each of which has the structure of a standard logic procedure:

S1 :   **find**(u, v, z) **if** $u \in z$, $v \in z$, $\mathbf{p}(u, v)$
S2 : $u \in z$ **if**   **find**(u, v, z)
S3 : $v \in z$ **if**   **find**(u, v, z)
S4 : $\mathbf{p}(u, v)$ **if**   **find**(u, v, z)
S5 : $u \in u{:}z'$
S6 : $u \in w{:}z'$ **if** $u \in z'$

Sentences S1–S4 are just the separate implications contained in the **iff** definition of **find**, whilst S5 and S6 are the standard $\in$ procedures and are implied by the **iff** definition of $\in$. The entire set $\{S1, \ldots, S6\}$ can now serve as the specification set S for the synthesis of a **find** program. The **p** relation is left unspecified—any definition of **p**, such as a set of **p** assertions, can be added later to the program as an arbitrary data structure.

Before proceeding further, it is worth noting that this specification could be used directly for computing solutions to **find** problems. For example, suppose **p** is chosen to be the (built-in) relation $>$ and that the goal is $?$ **find**$(u, v, 1{:}2{:}3{:}\varnothing)$; then all the solutions can be computed by using just $\{S1, S5, S6\}$ as the procedure set (with tolerable efficiency). We shall nevertheless proceed to derive a different procedure set and compare the two afterward.

The synthesis begins by posing the most general goal

$$G_1 :   ? \, \mathbf{find}(u, v, z)$$

so that no restrictions are placed upon the class of **find** problems solvable by the derived procedures. By applying top-down resolution it is possible to obtain the following derivation, in which activated calls have been underlined:

G_1 : $? \, \underline{\mathbf{find}(u, v, z)}$
G_2 : $? \, \underline{u \in z}$, $v \in z$, $\mathbf{p}(u, v)$
G_3 : $? \, \underline{v \in u{:}z'}$, $\mathbf{p}(u, v)$ (assigning $z := u{:}z'$)
G_4 : $? \, \mathbf{p}(u, u)$ (assigning $v := u$)

Here, G_2 is obtained by invoking S1, G_3 by invoking S5 and G_4 by invoking S5. No obvious purpose would be served by continuing this derivation by invoking S4 in response to G_4, since that would introduce a **find** call referring to some arbitrary set unrelated to the set z currently under consideration. Therefore at this point we infer the first **find** procedure

$$(\mathbf{find}(u, v, z)   \text{ if }   \mathbf{p}(u, u))\Theta$$

where Θ is the set of accumulated bindings $\{z := u:z', v := u\}$, thus obtaining

$$\text{P1} : \quad \mathbf{find}(u, u, u:z') \quad \text{if} \quad \mathbf{p}(u, u)$$

This procedure tries to solve any call $\mathbf{find}(u, v, z)$ by choosing both u and v as the set's first member and then trying to show that $\mathbf{p}(u, u)$ holds.

There are clearly other ways of choosing u and v from the set z, and these can be revealed by backtracking through the derivation just pursued, seeking steps affording alternative untried choices. Thus if we backtrack to G_3 we find that S6 could be invoked instead of S5, so generating a new goal

$$G_4' : \quad ? v \in z', \mathbf{p}(u, v) \qquad (\text{assigning } w := u)$$

From this point either S5 or S6 could be invoked in response to the $\in$ call, but this would introduce references to the components of z'; we resist this possibility in the present synthesis, and stop the derivation at G_4' in order to infer another **find** procedure

$$\text{P2} : \quad \mathbf{find}(u, v, u:z') \quad \text{if} \quad v \in z', \mathbf{p}(u, v)$$

This chooses u as the first member of z, chooses v from the remainder z' and then tries to show that $\mathbf{p}(u, v)$ holds.

Likewise we can backtrack to G_2 and thence proceed as follows:

$$
\begin{aligned}
G_2 &: \quad ? \underline{u \in z}, v \in z, \mathbf{p}(u, v) \\
G_3' &: \quad ? u \in z', \underline{v \in w:z'}, \mathbf{p}(u, v) \qquad (\text{assigning } z := w:z') \\
G_4'' &: \quad ? u \in z', \mathbf{p}(u, v) \qquad (\text{assigning } w := v)
\end{aligned}
$$

Here, G_3' is obtained by invoking S6 and G_4'' by invoking S5. The procedure inferred at this point is

$$\text{P3} : \quad \mathbf{find}(u, v, v:z') \quad \text{if} \quad u \in z', \mathbf{p}(u, v)$$

which is similar to P2 but interchanges the way u and v are selected from z.

Finally it is possible to backtrack to G_3' and then invoke S6 in response to the second $\in$ call, producing

$$
\begin{aligned}
G_4''' &: \quad ? \underline{u \in z'}, v \in z', \mathbf{p}(u, v) \\
G_5 &: \quad ? \mathbf{find}(u, v, z'), \underline{v \in z'}, \mathbf{p}(u, v) \qquad (\text{invoking S2}) \\
G_6 &: \quad ? \mathbf{find}(u, v, z'), \mathbf{find}(u, v, z'), \underline{\mathbf{p}(u, v)} \qquad (\text{invoking S3}) \\
G_7 &: \quad ? \mathbf{find}(u, v, z'), \mathbf{find}(u, v, z'), \mathbf{find}(u, v, z') \qquad (\text{invoking S4}) \\
G_8 &: \quad ? \mathbf{find}(u, v, z') \qquad (\text{merging identical calls})
\end{aligned}
$$

In the above we have again refrained from invoking either S5 or S6 in response to the ϵ calls, in order to avoid decomposition of z'. This derivation deals with the case in which both u and v are sought in the remainder z', as expressed by the procedure inferred at this point:

$$P4 : \quad \textbf{find}(u, v, w : z') \quad \textbf{if} \quad \textbf{find}(u, v, z')$$

The derived set $\{P1, \ldots, P4\}$ exhausts all ways of choosing u and v from the primary components w and z' of the set $z = w : z'$. Combined with S5, S6 and data describing the **p** relation, it provides a complete procedure set for investigating any **find** problem. For instance, if the **p** data were chosen to be the assertions

$$\textbf{p}(2, 1)$$
$$\textbf{p}(1, 3)$$
$$\textbf{p}(x, x)$$

then the goal $? \textbf{find}(u, v, 1 : 2 : 3 : \emptyset)$ would be solved completely with the (u, v) solutions $(1, 1)$, $(1, 3)$, $(2, 1)$, $(2, 2)$ and $(3, 3)$.

The synthesis just illustrated can be viewed as a constrained exploration of the total tree of top-down derivations determined by G_1 and S. Each distinct path in the tree from the initial goal G_1 to some final goal on the search frontier yields some derived procedure; this is depicted in Fig. VI.1. The exploration was constrained in two ways: (a) the frontier was allowed to proceed only a certain way down the tree, and (b) no step was taken which either decomposed the primary components of z, or produced a goal identical to an earlier one or introduced any sets unrelated to z. More positively, the strategy used was one which confined the analysis of the problem posed by the goal to an examination of all ways of choosing u and v from the primary components of z; consequently not all paths in the total tree are shown in Fig. VI.1, since not all were explored. Different constraints would result in different procedure sets and would be motivated by different computational intuitions.

The completeness of $\{P1, \ldots, P4\}$ for the **find** relation can be argued informally on the grounds that whenever S5 was invoked in response to an ϵ call, S6 was also invoked for the call in due course.

The procedures $\{P1, \ldots, P4\}$ give much the same behaviour as would the alternative ones $\{S1, S5, S6\}$, but can be more easily adapted to take advantage of any special properties which the chosen **p** relation might be known to possess. As an example, suppose **p** is known to be irreflexive, that is, contains no pairs (u, u); then P1 can be deleted from the program, improving the efficiency of execution by eliminating futile searches for pairs

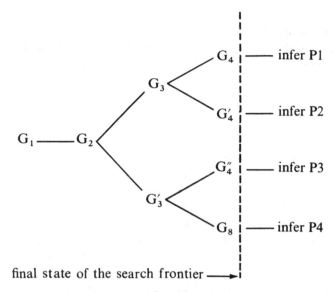

Fig. VI.1.   Procedures inferred from the derivation tree.

(u, u). Similarly, if **p** is known to be symmetric, that is, contains (v, u) whenever it contains (u, v), then either P2 or P3 (but not both) can be advantageously deleted from the program. By contrast, there is no simple way of adapting either the logic or the control of $\{S1, S5, S6\}$, which secures the same improvements. Thus the synthesis can be viewed as a correctness-preserving transformation of $\{S1, S5, S6\}$ into $\{P1, \ldots, P4\}$, which results in more flexible provisions for improving run-time behaviour.

VI.5. An Example Using Non-Resolution Inference

In principle, resolution is a sufficient tool for deriving logic procedures from specifications. This is because any sentence of standard logic which might appear in our initial specification can be converted by various systematic methods into a (virtually) equivalent set of sentences in clausal form. Depending upon the original sentence, the clausal-form version may or may not consist wholly of Horn clauses. If it does then the ensuing synthesis can employ just the simple top-down Horn-clause mode of resolution shown in the previous example. Otherwise (if non-Horn clauses are present) one can use general resolution instead.

In practice this sort of approach is almost always unsatisfactory, chiefly because the standard conversion of a specification into clausal form typically results in a substantial reduction in both compactness and intelligibility. It is also difficult to assign any straightforward computational interpretation to general resolution which is capable of bringing a goal-directed, problem-solving flavour to the derivation process. Consequently it is usually preferable not to convert the initial specification into clausal form, but instead to derive the desired procedures directly from it using whatever inference rules seem most convenient. The penalty of this is in the fact that these rules are generally more complicated and less uniform than resolution.

This section demonstrates the use of non-resolution inference by applying it to the task of program transformation. An initial program is given which deals with a particular data representation, and the purpose of the transformation is to modify the program so that it can deal with a different one.

VI.5.1. The Initial Program

The program's task is to test whether a given list L is ordered with respect to some ordering relation $<$. For instance, the list $L = (3, 5, 7, 9)$ is ordered with respect to the usual 'less than' relation $<$ over the integers. Program 35 below shows the initial version. Its procedures have been designed specifically for lists represented by the usual structured terms constructed from dot and NIL.

Program 35

$$? \ \textbf{ord}(3.5.7.9.NIL)$$

P1 : $\textbf{ord}(x)$ if $\textbf{length}(x, n), n \leqslant 1$

P2 : $\textbf{ord}(x)$ if $\textbf{append*}(u, x', x),$
                          $\textbf{append*}(v, x'', x'), u < v, \textbf{ord}(x')$

P3 : $\textbf{length}(NIL, 0)$

P4 : $\textbf{length}(w.NIL, 1)$

P5 : $\textbf{append*}(w, z', w.z')$

Here, $\textbf{ord}(x)$ means that list x is ordered, $\textbf{length}(x, n)$ means that list x has length n and $\textbf{append*}(u, x', x)$ means that list x results from appending list x' to the unit list (u).

The execution consists mostly of iterative cycles driven by P2, each of which extracts, using the two **append*** calls, the first pair (u, v) of members in some current fragment of L and then tests $u < v$. If the current fragment has fewer than two members then the computation terminates successfully using P1. Thus for the goal shown, execution will confirm $3 < 5$ in $(3, 5, 7, 9)$, then $5 < 7$ in $(5, 7, 9)$ and then $7 < 9$ in $(7, 9)$; the final fragment is the unit list (9) which according to P1 and P4 is ordered—hence the goal is solved.

Observe that Program 35 has been structured so that P1 and P2 express the logical properties of ordered lists without assuming any particular way of representing them. The specific choice of structured term representation is instead confined within both the goal and the procedures P3–P5 which access the lengths and members of fragments of L.

VI.5.2. Changing the Data Representation

Consider now the consequences of deciding to represent $L = (3, 5, 7, 9)$ in an array-like manner using the set of assertions

$$\textbf{m}(3, 1, L) \qquad \textbf{m}(7, 3, L) \qquad \textbf{length}(L, 4)$$
$$\textbf{m}(5, 2, L) \qquad \textbf{m}(9, 4, L)$$

Clearly P3–P5 must then be replaced by some new accessing procedures designed to deal with this representation, but P1 and P2 can remain unaltered.

To begin with, note that the purpose of P3–P5 is to extract either the length or the first two members of each fragment of L generated during execution. Since these fragments are themselves lists they are naturally represented by structured terms in P3–P5, since that is the chosen representation for Program 35. In deriving the new version of P3–P5 we shall need some other way of denoting the fragments which can be conveniently associated with the assertional representation of L.

One simple notation for this purpose employs terms of the form $f(x, j)$ in which x is the name of a list (such as L) and j is some position in x. The entire term $f(x, j)$ can then denote that fragment of x which remains after deleting any members of x occupying positions preceding j. So under this scheme the fragments $(3, 5, 7, 9)$, $(5, 7, 9)$, $(7, 9)$ and (9) are denoted respectively by the terms $f(L, 1)$, $f(L, 2)$, $f(L, 3)$ and $f(L, 4)$. Note that for a list x having length $m \geqslant 0$, and assuming $j \geqslant 1$, the fragment $f(x, j)$ is a unit list when $j = m$ and an empty list when $j > m$.

The new assessing procedures replacing P3–P5 must be able to extract the lengths and members of fragments represented in the form $f(x, j)$. When invoked, they will have passed to them terms such as $f(L, 2)$ which contain exactly the same sort of information—that is, a list name (L) and a position (2)—as is used in the $\textbf{m}$ assertions describing L. This suggests that the new fragment notation is well-suited to the task of accessing the assertional representation of L.

VI.5.3. Outline of the New Program

At this stage it is probably helpful to the reader to see in advance what the new program will look like. It is shown below as Program 36, although later on this will be slightly refined to improve efficiency.

Program 36

$$? \, \mathbf{ord}(f(L, \, 1))$$

P1 : as before
P2 : as before
P3' : $\mathbf{length}(f(x, j), 0)$ if $j \geqslant 1$, $\mathbf{length}(x, m)$, $j = m + 1$
P4' : $\mathbf{length}(f(x, j), 1)$ if $j \geqslant 1$, $\mathbf{length}(x, m)$, $j = m$
P5' : $\mathbf{append}^*(w, f(x, j + 1), f(x, j))$ if $\mathbf{m}(w, j, x)$
          and the assertions representing L.

The new procedures P3'–P5' serve exactly the same purposes as their respective counterparts P3–P5. Note in particular that any invocation of P3'–P5' will instigate calls of the form $\mathbf{length}(L, m)$ or $\mathbf{m}(w, j, L)$ which can be answered directly by the assertional data.

The new program behaves very much like a conventional iterative program, scanning through a linear array L sequentially under the control of an increasing index j. The initial goal effectively presets j to 1, and the incrementing mechanism is realized by P5'. The iteration terminates when it has processed the cycle dealing with the case $j = 4$ ($=$ length of L). Here is an outline of the successful computation:

$$? \, \mathbf{ord}(f(L, \, 1))$$
$$? \, \mathbf{append}^*(u, x', f(L, \, 1)),$$
$$\mathbf{append}^*(v, x'', x'), \, u < v, \, \mathbf{ord}(x')$$
$$\vdots$$
computes $x' := f(L, 2)$, $u := 3$,
          $x'' := f(L, 3)$, $v := 5$ using P5'
$$\vdots$$
$? \, 3 < 5, \, \mathbf{ord}(f(L, 2))$
$$\vdots$$
$? \, 5 < 7, \, \mathbf{ord}(f(L, 3))$
$$\vdots$$
$? \, 7 < 9, \, \mathbf{ord}(f(L, 4))$
$$\vdots$$
$? \, \mathbf{length}(f(L, 4), n), \, n \leqslant 1$
$$\vdots$$
computes $n := 1$ using P4'
$$\vdots$$
☐ solved

VI.5.4. The Specification

The relationship between Programs 35 and 36 is based upon their common specification S. In the present example it is necessary, in order to achieve the desired transformation, to invoke certain facts from the specification which could not be easily inferred from the program statements alone. Here then is the entire specification.

S1 : $\mathbf{ord}(z)$ iff $(\forall uvi)(u < v$ if $\mathbf{m}(u, i, z), \mathbf{m}(v, i+1, z))$
S2 : $\mathbf{append^*}(w, z', z)$ iff $(\forall ui)(\mathbf{m}(u, i, z)$ iff $\mathbf{m}(u, i-1, z') \vee$
$(u = w, i = 1))$
S3 : $\mathbf{length}(z, k)$ iff $0 \leqslant k, (\forall i)(1 \leqslant i, i \leqslant k$ iff $(\exists u)\mathbf{m}(u, i, z))$
S4 : $(\exists k)\mathbf{length}(z, k)$
S5 : $(u = v$ iff $\mathbf{m}(u, i, z))$ if $\mathbf{m}(v, i, z)$
S6 : $\neg\mathbf{m}(u, i, NIL)$
S7 : $\mathbf{m}(u, i, w.z')$ iff $\mathbf{m}(u, i-1, z') \vee (u = w, i = 1)$
S8 : $\mathbf{m}(u, i, f(x, j))$ iff $\mathbf{m}(u, i+j-1, x), 1 \leqslant i, 1 \leqslant j$

Sentences S1 and S2 are just straightforward definitions of the **ord** and **append*** relations. Sentences S3–S5 are standard list axioms which ensure that every list z has a non-negative length k and a unique member in every position in the range 1 to k. Membership in lists represented by the usual structured terms is described by S6 and S7, whilst membership in lists represented by the $f(x, j)$ notation is described by S8. The procedures of Programs 35 and 36 can all be derived from this specification set using first-order inference.

VI.5.5. Equivalence Substitution

Equivalence substitution is an inference rule for first-order logic which has proved especially useful for manipulating the sort of sentences typically involved in procedure derivation. In its simplest form, some sentence having the structure

$$\mathbf{F}_1 \quad \text{iff} \quad \mathbf{F}_2$$

is first either selected from S, or shown to be implied by S or shown to be a theorem (valid sentence) of first-order logic; whichever is the case, the relationship

$$S \vDash (\mathbf{F}_1 \quad \text{iff} \quad \mathbf{F}_2)$$

then necessarily holds; $\mathbf{F}_1$ and $\mathbf{F}_2$ are any logical formulae satisfying the above condition. Next, some subformula $\mathbf{F}$ of the current goal G_t is selected such that $\mathbf{F} = \mathbf{F}_1\Theta$ holds for some unifier Θ. The equivalence step then consists of substituting F_2 for F in G_t and applying Θ to the result. This produces the next goal G_{t+1} satisfying

$$S,G_t \vDash G_{t+1}$$

As an example, the precondition $S \vDash (F_1 \quad \text{iff} \quad C)$ would enable the following step to take place:

$$G_t : \quad ?(A \quad \text{iff} \quad B, F), D$$
$$G_{t+1} : \quad ?(A \quad \text{iff} \quad B, C)\Theta, D\Theta$$

provided $F = F_1\Theta$.

A useful variant of the rule is known as 'conditional equivalence substitution' and begins by establishing the slightly more elaborate precondition

$$S \vDash (F_1 \quad \text{iff} \quad F_2) \quad \text{if} \quad F_3$$

where F_1, F_2 and F_3 are any logical formulae. Here, the 'equivalence' of F_1 and F_2 is now conditional upon F_3. Once again some subformula F is selected from the goal G_t such that $F = F_1\Theta$. This time the step consists of substituting F_2 for F, adding F_3 as an extra conjunct to the goal and finally applying Θ to the result. This produces the next goal G_{t+1}, which again satisfies

$$S,G_t \vDash G_{t+1}$$

As an example, the precondition $S \vDash (F_1 \quad \text{iff} \quad C) \quad \text{if} \quad E$ would enable the following step to take place:

$$G_t : \quad ?(A \quad \text{iff} \quad B, F), D$$
$$G_{t+1} : \quad ?(A \quad \text{iff} \quad B, C)\Theta, D\Theta, E\Theta$$

provided $F = F_1\Theta$.

This brief description of the rules ignores certain petty limitations upon the allowable distribution of the variables and quantifiers occurring in G_t, F, F_1, F_2 and F_3. However, for the purpose of our example (and, in practice, most others), these limitations are not relevant and so need not be detailed here.

A useful feature of the rules is that they apply independently of both the structure of the selected goal subformula F and its context within the goal: F is simply chosen at will and replaced by some other formula which, according to S, is equivalent to F, either unconditionally (as in the first rule) or subject to the addition of an extra condition (as in the second rule); then the unifier Θ is finally applied in order to make the new goal properly dependent upon the unification necessary for replacement of F.

Applications of the rule will normally be guided by some degree of anticipation about the logical and computational features of the target procedures. This will now be illustrated by continuing our example of program transformation.

VI.5.6. Deriving the New Procedures

Here we shall just show the derivations of the new procedures P3' and P4' for the **length** relation. These deal only with the two special cases of list fragments having lengths equal to 0 or 1. Rather than developing them separately from scratch, we shall pursue just one derivation dealing with the general case of some arbitrary length n, and afterward specialize the result by considering $n = 0$ and $n = 1$. We show the derivation below in full before giving an explanation of the various steps.

G_1 :   ? $\textbf{length}(f(x,j), n)$
G_2 :   ? $0 \leqslant n,\ (\forall i)(1 \leqslant i, i \leqslant n$ **iff** $(\exists u)\textbf{m}(u, i, f(x,j)))$
G_3 :   ? $0 \leqslant n,\ (\forall i)(1 \leqslant i, i \leqslant n$ **iff** $(\exists u)(\textbf{m}(u, i+j-1, x),\ 1 \leqslant i, 1 \leqslant j))$
G_4 :   ? $0 \leqslant n,\ (\forall i)(1 \leqslant i, i \leqslant n$ **iff** $(\exists u)\textbf{m}(u, i+j-1, x),\ 1 \leqslant i, 1 \leqslant j$
G_5 :   ? $0 \leqslant n,\ (\forall i)(1 \leqslant i, i \leqslant n$ **iff** $(\exists u)\textbf{m}(u, i+j-1, x),\ 1 \leqslant i),\ 1 \leqslant j$
G_6 :   ? $j \leqslant m + 1,\ (\forall i')(j \leqslant i', i' \leqslant m$ **iff** $(\exists u)\textbf{m}(u, i', x),\ j \leqslant i'),\ 1 \leqslant j$
G_7 :   ? $j \leqslant m + 1,\ (\forall i')((i' \leqslant m$ **iff** $(\exists u)\textbf{m}(u, i', x))$ **if** $j \leqslant i'),\ 1 \leqslant j$
G_8 :   ? $j \leqslant m + 1,\ 0 \leqslant m,\ (\forall i')(1 \leqslant i', i' \leqslant m$ **iff** $(\exists u)\textbf{m}(u, i', x)),\ 1 \leqslant j$
G_9 :   ? $j \leqslant m + 1,\ \textbf{length}(x, m),\ 1 \leqslant j$

The procedure inferred from this derivation is

$$\textbf{length}(f(x,j), m-j+1) \quad \text{if} \quad j \leqslant m+1,\ \textbf{length}(x, m),\ 1 \leqslant j$$

This just states the fairly obvious relationship between the lengths of a list x and one of its fragments $f(x, j)$. The steps in the derivation rely chiefly upon equivalence substitution (ES) and conditional equivalence substitution (CES) and are explained below.

Step G_1–G_2:   Apply ES by invoking S3, choosing

$$\mathbf{F} = \text{length}(f(x,j), n)$$
$$\mathbf{F}_1 = \text{length}(z, k)$$
$$\mathbf{F}_2 = \text{definiens on right of \textbf{iff} in S3}$$
$$\Theta = \{z := f(x,j), k := n\}$$

Step G_2–G_3:   Apply ES by invoking S8, replacing $\mathbf{F} = \mathbf{m}(u, i, f(x,j))$.

Step G_3–G_4:   Apply ES by invoking the theorem

$$(\exists u)(\mathbf{A}, \mathbf{B}) \quad \textbf{iff} \quad (\exists u)\mathbf{A}, \mathbf{B}$$
where $\mathbf{B}$ does not contain u

Step G_4–G_5:   Apply CES by invoking the theorem

$$((A \text{ iff } B, C) \text{ iff } (A \text{ iff } B)) \text{ if } C$$
where C is here $1 \leqslant j$

Step G_5–G_6:   Substitute $i := i' - j + 1$ and $n := m - j + 1$, and hence replace

$$0 \leqslant n \quad \text{by} \quad j \leqslant m + 1$$
$$1 \leqslant i \quad \text{by} \quad j \leqslant i'$$
$$i \leqslant n \quad \text{by} \quad i' \leqslant m$$
$$\mathbf{m}(u, i + j - 1, x) \text{ by } \mathbf{m}(u, i', x)$$

Step G_6–G_7:   Apply ES by invoking the theorem

$$(A, B \text{ iff } A, C) \text{ iff } ((B \text{ iff } C) \text{ if } A)$$
where A is here $j \leqslant i'$

Step G_7–G_8:   This is the hardest one; invoke the implication

$$((B \text{ iff } C) \text{ if } A) \text{ if } (D, B \text{ iff } C), E$$

where

$$\begin{aligned} A \quad &\text{is} \quad j \leqslant i' \\ B \quad &\text{is} \quad i' \leqslant m \\ C \quad &\text{is} \quad (\exists u)\mathbf{m}(u, i', x) \\ D \quad &\text{is} \quad 1 \leqslant i' \\ E \quad &\text{is} \quad 1 \leqslant j \end{aligned}$$

This sentence is itself provable from S by a slightly tedious analysis of the properties of the $\leqslant$ relation. Finally, an extra call $0 \leqslant m$ can be introduced to the goal because it is implied by the existing calls $1 \leqslant j$ and $j \leqslant m + 1$, again subject to assumed properties of arithmetic implied by the specification.

Step G_8–G_9:   Apply ES by invoking S3, replacing the definiens

$$\mathbf{F} = 0 \leqslant m, (\forall i')(1 \leqslant i', i' \leqslant m \quad \textbf{iff} \quad (\exists u)\mathbf{m}(u, i', x))$$

by its definiand $\mathbf{F}_2\Theta = \textbf{length}(x, m)$.

The desired target procedures can now be obtained by choosing $n = 0$ and $n = 1$ in turn. In the first case this makes $m - j + 1 = 0$ and therefore makes $j \leqslant m + 1$ equivalent to $j = m + 1$. The derived procedure can therefore be arranged for this case in the form

$$\textbf{length}(f(x, j), 0) \text{ if } 1 \leqslant j, \textbf{length}(x, m), j = m + 1$$

which is just P3′. In the second case, putting $m - j + 1 = n = 1$ makes $j \leqslant m + 1$ equivalent to $j = m$, and so the procedure then becomes

$$\textbf{length}(f(x, j), 1) \text{ if } 1 \leqslant j, \textbf{length}(x, m), j = m$$

which is just P4′.

The guiding principle behind the derivation was the fact that the target procedure had to be able to compute the length n of any $f(L, j)$ directly from the assertional database. This data consists of a number of membership assertions and the length m of L; only the latter is likely to play any useful role in determining n. Consequently the entire derivation was motivated toward forcing a reference to **length**(x, m) into the final goal by applying a series of substitutive transformations to the definiens of **length**$(f(x, j), n)$ until the definiens of **length**(x, m) emerged at G_8.

The derivation of the new **append*** procedure P5′ is left as an exercise for the reader. It is considerably easier than the derivation above.

VI.5.7. Further Refinements of the Program

Program 36 suffers a number of operational defects. In the first place, a significant run-time overhead arises from the use of an explicit data-accessing interface P3′–P5′ interposed between the principal procedures P1–P2 and the database. Execution efficiency can be improved by applying a further simple transformation known as *macroprocessing*. In general, this replaces a pair of procedures like

$$\textbf{A} \quad \textbf{if} \quad \textbf{B}, \textbf{C}, \textbf{D}$$
$$\textbf{C} \quad \textbf{if} \quad \textbf{E}, \textbf{F}, \textbf{G}$$

by a single procedure

$$\textbf{A} \quad \textbf{if} \quad \textbf{B}, \textbf{E}, \textbf{F}, \textbf{G}, \textbf{D}$$

so eliminating the intermediary **C** call. This sort of step can be performed mechanically using resolution, prior to execution, by simply invoking the **C** procedure in response to the **C** call.

Applying this principle to Program 36, one can obtain the more compact and efficient program below.

Program 37

$$? \, \textbf{ord}(f(L, 1))$$

P1′ : **ord**$(f(x, j))$ **if** $j \geqslant 1$, **length**$(x, m), j = m + 1$
P1″ : **ord**$(f(x, j))$ **if** $j \geqslant 1$, **length**$(x, m), j = m$
P2′ : **ord**$(f(x, j))$ **if** $\textbf{m}(u, j, x), \textbf{m}(v, j + 1, x),$
                                    $u < v, \textbf{ord}(f(x, j + 1))$
and the database describing L

Here we have invoked P3′ and P4′ in turn in response to the **length** call in P1 to produce P1′ and P1″, respectively, and have also invoked P5′ in response to the **append*** call of P2 to produce P2′. Then the interface P3′–P5′ can be disposed of.

Some additional inefficiencies remain to be remedied. The conditional equivalence substitutions entailed in deriving G_5 and G_8 each introduced the condition $1 \leqslant j$ (i.e., $j \geqslant 1$) as an extra call into the current goal and hence, via P3' and P4', into the latest procedures P1' and P1". Consequences of choosing the alternative condition $j < 1$ were not explored because our intended algorithm is only concerned with processing $f(L, j)$ for $j \geqslant 1$. The $j \geqslant 1$ calls, although logically necessary, are an impediment to computational efficiency because the intended goal of the program injects the choice $j = 1$ initially and thereafter j can only increase. However, the procedures do not 'know' this, and so must redundantly test $j \geqslant 1$ whenever they are invoked.

Another source of inefficiency in Program 37 is the run-time burden of unifying structured terms of the form $f(x, j)$. The f functors serve a useful denotational purpose for specifying the logical basis of our transformation, but serve no ultimate computational purpose in the derived program.

It is possible to remedy both of these latter two defects by extending the specification with the sentence

$$S9 : \quad \mathbf{ord}^*(x, j) \quad \textbf{iff} \quad (\mathbf{ord}(f(x, j)) \quad \textbf{if} \quad j \geqslant 1)$$

and then rewriting Program 37 in terms of **ord*** instead of **ord**. This eliminates all the f functors as well as the $j \geqslant 1$ tests, giving the very efficient final version shown below.

Program 38

$$? \, \mathbf{ord}^*(L, 1)$$
$$\mathbf{ord}^*(x, j) \quad \textbf{if} \quad \mathbf{length}(x, m), j = m+1$$
$$\mathbf{ord}^*(x, j) \quad \textbf{if} \quad \mathbf{length}(x, m), j = m$$
$$\mathbf{ord}^*(x, j) \quad \textbf{if} \quad \mathbf{m}(u, j, x), \mathbf{m}(v, j+1, x),$$
$$u < v, \mathbf{ord}^*(x, j+1)$$
and the database describing L

Using non-resolution inference, it is quite easy to show (and a useful exercise for the reader) that each statement in Program 38 is implied by its counterpart in Program 37 together with the extended specification.

VI.6. Background

The history of logic program synthesis closely coincides with the history of logic program verification as outlined at the end of Chapter V. As we have seen, both can be accommodated within a single framework, based upon procedure derivation, for relating programs logically to their specifications.

The pursuit of an effective methodology for constructing logic programs was originally motivated by the more general developments in 'structured programming' for conventional formalisms during the early 1970s. These led the author (Hogger, 1975) to investigate and interrelate various logic formulations of the then popular "eight queens problem". Meanwhile, Burstall and Darlington (1977) had developed an elegant and mechanizable technique for developing programs written in the language of recursion equations, this language bearing many similarities to Horn-clause logic. Their derivation rules were first adapted to logic program synthesis by Clark and Sickel (1977).

The first application of the Burstall–Darlington methodology to the synthesis of a family of nontrivial algorithms from a common specification in first-order logic was undertaken by Hogger (1977), dealing with a number of sorting algorithms. Further studies of the derivation of these algorithms were carried out by Clark and Darlington (1980). The use of first-order deduction for deriving other families of logic algorithms has been illustrated by Clark (1977) for factorial and Fibonacci calculations, by Hogger (1979b) for string searching, by Hansson and Tärnlund (1979) for list and tree processing, by Winterstein *et al.* (1980) for unification algorithms, by McKeeman and Sickel (1980) for Hoare's FIND problem and by Clark, McKeeman and Sickel (1982) for numerical integration. More detailed expositions of the theoretical basis of logic program synthesis can be found in works by Clark (1979) and Hogger (1979a, 1981). Synthesis schemes similar to those described in this chapter have been independently discovered and further elaborated by Manna and Waldinger (1980).

No fully automated implementation currently exists which is capable of deriving necessarily efficient logic programs from arbitrary specifications, and it seems likely that none will come about in the near future. There are nevertheless a number of implementations in existence which can cooperate satisfactorily with an interacting user, being able not only to check the user's own derivations but also to exercise some initiative toward constructing derivations. These systems, discussed by Hansson and Tärnlund (1979), typically use a natural deduction inference system and can accept specifications written in unrestricted first-order logic. We do not as yet have a proper understanding of how the general problem of controlling syntheses effectively relates to the degree of restriction placed upon the specification language. Unrestricted logic inevitably requires a considerable variety of inference rules whose availability during any particular synthesis tends to give rise to a wide choice of seemingly amorphous and undirected derivations.

Some researchers, for instance Murray (1978), have instead restricted the specification language to some non-clausal subset of logic, with a consequent simplification of the inference system. One can go further than this by using Horn-clause logic exclusively for specification (as with our example in Section VI.4) and thus rely solely upon resolution inference. This achieves a pleasing coalescence both of programming language and specification language and of execution method with synthesis method, and existing logic interpreters could be easily adapted to interactive synthesizers similar to those already developed by Darlington for functional languages. The potential objection to this approach is that Horn clauses appear to be too restrictive to serve as a general specification language: this may or may not be so. In the past this allegation has often been made in the course of advocating unrestricted logic, but should perhaps be reconsidered.

An interesting research topic ripe for exploration is the derivation of programs intended for parallel execution. Approaches to the transformation of serial programs to parallel ones are considered in a paper by Hogger (1982b). It may also be worthwhile to investigate logic programming's potential for verifying and transforming conventional software. Very little work has been done on this subject, although the translation of logic programs into PASCAL-like counterparts has been investigated by Elcock (1981).

VII IMPLEMENTATION

Logic programs were first executed by computer in 1972. Since that time, much effort has been expended upon logic implementations in the quest for ever greater efficiency and usability. Indeed, the pace at which new systems are now evolving in order to service the immediate requirements of the growing community of logic users, as well as to meet the looming challenge of the next generation of machine architecture, tends to confound any attempt at proposing lasting tenets for implementation philosophy.

Thus no such attempt is made here. Instead, this chapter is intended only to provide a guide for the novice implementor, who would otherwise— unless working in the company of seasoned gurus— have to figure out a lot of basic material for himself or else resort to the research literature: in either case he could expect a hard time. The presentation given here nevertheless leaves many aspects incompletely specified and so relies upon the reader's presumed general programming competence to fill in the various gaps.

There is a commonly held view that logic is itself the best language in which to describe and implement logic interpreters. This may well hold true for individuals already possessing mastery of logic and experience in language implementation, since they can easily envisage ways of fulfilling, at the concrete level, the various abstractions employed by a high-level logical description, whereas to the uninitiated such abstractions can appear only as so much vagueness and fail to convey any real feeling of understanding. Therefore, in view of the introductory purpose of the present text, the material here has deliberately been made as concrete as space allowed. It must be stressed that the purpose of this concreteness is to build just one workable model in the mind of the reader, who can afterward reformulate the practical details, or even the overall design, to any extent which suits his convenience.

VII.1. Representing the Control State

In the *interpretive* mode of execution, all events are instigated and supervised by an *interpreter* executing in fast access memory. This program chiefly accesses two important data areas in memory. The first one contains some suitably compacted and codified facsimile of the input logic program and remains unchanged (or 'static') throughout execution. The second area is highly dynamic and is used by the interpreter to record the history of its own actions. These areas are generally called the *input heap* and the *execution stack*, respectively. The stack effectively represents both the execution's *control state* (its progress through the computation space) and its *data state* (the data currently assigned to the program's variables). This section deals with the control state and so begins by reviewing the events occurring in the standard execution of a logic program.

VII.1.1. Review of the Execution Mechanism

A logic program's execution can be described conveniently in terms of the procedure entry and procedure exit mechanisms introduced in Chapter II. The description is made more uniform by treating the program's initial goal

$$G : \quad ?\,\mathbf{R}_1, \ldots, \mathbf{R}_k$$

as just another procedure: execution is initiated by entering G and terminated by exiting from it after computing all possible solutions.

The execution process successively selects calls from the input program, beginning with the first call $\mathbf{R}_1$ in G, with the object of solving them. As the interpreter transfers its attention from one call to another it traces out a path through the program referred to as the *locus of control*. Each extension of the locus of control results from either a procedure entry or a procedure exit.

A procedure entry occurs in the course of performing a procedure-calling step. At the beginning of any such step the locus of control will have progressed as far as some call $\mathbf{P}_i$ in some procedure (possibly the initial goal)

$$P : \quad A \quad \text{if} \quad \mathbf{P}_1, \ldots, \mathbf{P}_i, \ldots, \mathbf{P}_m$$

Assuming throughout that the standard strategy applies, the position at this moment is that the calls in P preceding $\mathbf{P}_i$ have already been solved (though not necessarily in all possible ways) and $\mathbf{P}_i$ is now being activated with the intention of solving it.

In general, several procedures may *potentially respond* to $\mathbf{P}_i$ and are called the *candidates* for $\mathbf{P}_i$. It is up to the implementor to decide how to characterize a candidate. The simplest way, which also results in the simplest but often least efficient implementation, is to treat every procedure whose name matches that in P_i as a candidate; in other words, no discrimination is applied on the basis of parameter matching. However, as discussed in Chapter IV, it is usually much more efficient to employ an indexing scheme for storing and selecting procedures based upon parameter classification. This arrangement is more selective in its identification of candidates for P_i. However, it is important to realise that any discrimination scheme which falls short of the extreme strategy of attempting to match (unify) P_i fully with the headings of all available procedures will usually yield some candidates which will not actually respond to P_i when they are eventually tried. The implementor has to balance the advantage of pre-empting future mismatches against the immediate cost of applying discrimination schemes aimed at minimizing the candidate set.

In the present example, it is possible that some candidates for P_i have already been tried in earlier attempts to solve it. Those that currently remain untried can be denoted Q, Q', Q'', etc., in order of their decreasing priority for selection. Thus the next one to be tried is Q and we shall assume that this one does indeed respond to P_i. It will have the general form

$$Q : \quad \mathbf{B} \quad \textbf{if} \quad Q_1, \ldots, Q_n$$

where P_i unifies with $\mathbf{B}$. Suppose then that Q is now invoked by P_i. This procedure-calling step extends the locus of control from P_i to the first call Q_1 in Q, thus effecting an entry into the Q procedure. At the same time, certain facts about this step, explained presently, are recorded by the interpreter. After this, the next step can be performed in turn.

The invocation of Q by P_i initiates an attempt to solve that call, which, in due course, may either succeed or fail. It succeeds if execution eventually solves all the calls in Q. If this happens then the interpreter makes a *successful exit* from Q and transfers control back into P to the call P_{i+1}, which will then be the next call activated.

On the other hand, the attempt to solve P_i fails if it turns out to be impossible to solve some call in Q. If this happens then the interpreter makes a *failure exit* from Q and transfers control back into P to the call P_i. This call is then reactivated and the next untried candidate Q' is tried in order to initiate a fresh attempt to solve P_i. This behaviour is called *backtracking after failure* (i.e., after the failure to solve P_i using Q); in terms of the search tree it corresponds to the interpreter backtracking from a failure node ■ . If, after this backtracking operation, it turns out that neither Q' nor any of the remaining untried candidates Q'', etc., yield any solutions to P_i, then further backtracking will be necessary in order to seek new ways of solving P_{i-1} or its predecessors.

If execution eventually solves all the calls in G then the interpreter first reports the solution and then transfers control back to the most recently activated call, if any, for which some candidates remain untried and reactivates it in order to seek new solutions. This behaviour upon a successful exit from G is called *backtracking after success*; in terms of the search tree it corresponds to the interpreter backtracking from a success node □. If no such call exists after a successful exit from G then all calls have been investigated in all possible ways and so execution terminates.

VII.1.2. Frames

As execution proceeds, the interpreter has to remember a variety of facts about the events which have so far taken place. First and most obviously, it must remember what data has been assigned so far to the variables in order that the ultimate objective of evaluating the goal's variables can be fulfilled. We defer consideration of this matter to the next section, and concentrate meanwhile upon the second category of remembered facts dealing with the management of the locus of control.

The need to record details of how the locus of control has evolved to its current state is due partly to the interpreter having to deal with the *return* operation following every successful procedure exit; this operation transfers control back to the call immediately following the one which originally invoked the exited procedure. The need also arises from having to deal with backtracking, since that operation has to recall previously discovered opportunities still open to exploration.

The recording of such details is customarily achieved by arranging that in each procedure-calling step the interpreter creates and stores a *frame* containing certain facts about the step. Each frame can be thought of as *signifying entry* into the procedure invoked by the step. A procedure which has been entered but not yet exited is said to be *active*, and for this reason a frame is sometimes called an *activation record*—it records a step at which some procedure becomes active.

One can infer what items ought to occur in a frame by considering how the frame could usefully inform the interpreter's decisions about extending the locus of control. Suppose, then, that a frame F is to be created for the step in which the call P_i in

$$P : A \text{ if } P_1, \ldots, P_i, P_{i+1}, \ldots, P_m$$

invokes

$$Q : B \text{ if } Q_1, \ldots, Q_n$$

Thus F will signify entry into Q. At some later time, control may exit

successfully from Q having just solved the call Q_n. In order that the interpreter can then identify the next call P_{i+1} to be activated, we arrange that
the frame F contains a *return (R) pointer* to P_{i+1}; more concretely, this
pointer might consist of the address at which this call is stored within the heap
representation of the input program. Of course, in order to access this
pointer, the interpreter must first be able to identify the relevant frame F
amongst those already generated during the execution. This is achieved by
further arranging that every frame also contains a *parent-frame (PF) pointer*
which points to the frame's *parent frame*. Using the current example, we
define the latter as follows. Consider all those steps which activate calls in Q;
then the frame for each one has F as its parent frame by virtue of F signifying
entry into Q.

In order to see how procedure exit is managed using these pointers we
refer to Fig. VII.1. In each frame there the first two cells contain, respectively,
the PF pointer and the R pointer. The other cells, depicted as vacant, may
actually contain further pointers for controlling backtracking and are
explained later on.

Imagine that the interpreter has just created the frame F' upon invoking
some assertion T in response to the call Q_n. Since Q_n is the last call in Q, the
R pointer in F' will in this case just point to an imaginary position beyond Q_n
referred to as Q's success exit. The PF pointer in F' will point to frame F.
Since T contains no calls the interpreter's next action must be to exit successfully from T. By consulting the R pointer in F' it ascertains that control must

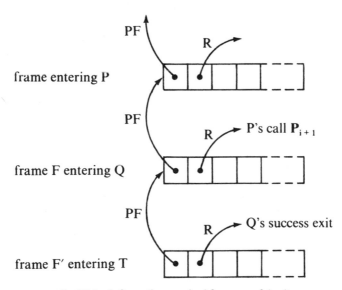

Fig. VII.1.   Information required for successful exit.

be returned to some position in the Q procedure. However, since this position turns out to be the success exit of Q, a second return operation is necessary, specifically one which returns control to whatever procedure invoked Q. The PF pointer in F′ identifies the earlier frame F at which Q was entered and that frame's R pointer in turn identifies P_{i+1} as the call to which control must be returned; normal execution then resumes by activating that call.

Observe that Fig. VII.1 represents three steps (entering P, Q and T) forming part of the following computation segment:

$$\text{enter P :}\quad ? P_1, \ldots, P_m, \ldots$$

$$\begin{aligned} &? P_i, P_{i+1}, \ldots, P_m, \ldots \\ \text{enter Q :}\quad &? Q_1, \ldots, Q_n, P_{i+1}, \ldots, P_m, \ldots \end{aligned}$$

$$? Q_n, P_{i+1}, \ldots, P_m, \ldots$$

$$\begin{aligned} &\text{enter T :} \\ &\text{exit T :} \\ &\text{exit Q :}\quad ? P_{i+1}, \ldots, P_m, \ldots \end{aligned}$$

There is therefore a 1:1 correspondence between the goals in the conventional goal-sequence representation of a computation and the frames constituting the interpreter's representation of it.

It should be clear from the foregoing that the creation, storage and consultation of return pointers and parent-frame pointers provides an adequate basis for managing those extensions of the locus of control arising from procedure entry and successful procedure exit. Similar mechanisms are used for controlling the execution of many conventional procedural-language programs. However, the additional feature of non-determinism in logic programs makes it necessary to cater also for backtracking, as explained next.

VII.1.3. Backtracking

Referring to the same procedures P and Q as before, suppose instead that after Q has been entered in response to P_i some call Q_j turns out to be unsolvable. The interpreter must then be capable of recalling the most recent step, if any, which has left open one or more untried opportunities, and must also be able to determine exactly what those opportunities are. In order to satisfy the former requirement, a single register named MRB is maintained throughout execution which always points to the most recently created frame whose associated step yielded at least one untried candidate in addition to the candidate actually invoked. Such a frame is called a *back-track point*: MRB is so named because it always points to the most recent backtrack point.

Consider the moment immediately before creating the frame F signifying entry into Q. MRB points to some earlier frame F* which is currently the most recent backtrack point (see Fig. VII.2a). Immediately after F is created, MRB must be updated to point to F, because our assumption of the existence of the untried candidates Q′, Q″, etc., makes F a new backtrack point. The position then becomes that depicted in Fig. VII.2b.

The existence and updating of MRB is not in itself adequate for controlling backtracking. Consider what happens when Q_j is found to be unsolvable. For simplicity's sake, and without any loss of generality, assume

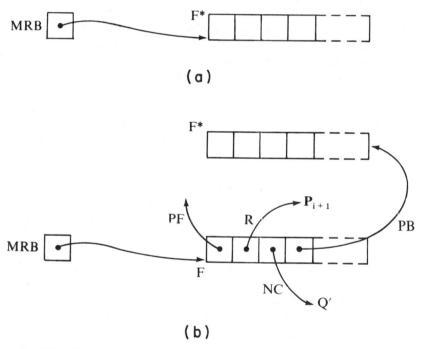

(a)

(b)

Fig. VII.2. Creating a new backtrack point F: (a) immediately before creating F, (b) immediately after creating F.

Key: MRB: most recent backtrack point register;
       PF: parent-frame pointer;
        R: return pointer;
      NC: next candidate pointer;
      PB: previous backtrack point pointer;
      F*: previous most recent backtrack point.

that no backtrack points have meanwhile arisen since creating F, so that MRB still points to F. The interpreter must now be capable of recalling that Q′ is the candidate for P_i to be tried next.

A simple way of arranging this is to construct, at the time F is created, a *next candidate (NC) pointer* pointing to Q′ and store it in the third cell of F. So when Q_j fails, the interpreter can consult MRB to identify F and then use the NC pointer in F to identify Q′. The call P_i to be reactivated with this new candidate is itself identified from the fact that the R pointer in F points to the successor P_{i+1} of P_i. Once this information has been retrieved from F, both F and all its descendant frames, representing the attempt to solve P_i by using Q, can be discarded. This completes the operation of backtracking after failure, and execution can then continue in the normal way by attempting a new step. Backtracking after success proceeds in a similar fashion except that the goal solution must be reported first.

One further provision remains necessary for the management of backtracking. Consider the moment at which frame F is about to be discarded by the backtracking operation just described. At this moment F is the most recent backtrack point (according to our earlier assumption) and MRB currently points to it. Upon discarding F, MRB must be reset to point to the previous backtrack point F*, in order that the interpreter shall not lose track of its untried opportunities. So that F* can be identified for this purpose, we arrange that at the time F is created the setting of MRB (which at that time points to F*) is copied to a fourth cell of F known as the *previous backtrack-point (PB) pointer*. When backtracking occurs later on, this pointer is retrieved from F and copied back into MRB, thus ensuring that the interpreter's knowledge of its own progress is properly preserved when F is discarded.

Figure VII.2 indicates the information handling entailed in the creation of the new backtrack point F representing the invocation of Q by P_i. The PF cell points to the frame created on entering P; the R cell points to the call to be activated after solving P_i; the NC cell points to the next candidate Q′ to be tried in response to P_i; and the PB cell points to the preceding backtrack point F*. Since F is a backtrack point, MRB has been updated to point to F. If F had not been a backtrack point then it would have neither NC nor PB cells and MRB would have remained pointing to F*.

VII.1.4. The Procedure-Calling Step

At the beginning of each attempt to perform a procedure-calling step, the interpreter will have selected some call for activation. We arrange that a register named CC ('current call') contains a pointer to this call. Another register named NCA ('next candidate') points to the next candidate procedure to be tried in response to this call. In order to avoid repeated mention of pointers, these register names can be used loosely as though they referred directly to the objects pointed to; thus, for example, a reference to 'the call CC' really means 'the call to which CC points'.

The interpreter's immediate task is to seek a procedure which responds to CC. Exactly how it does this depends upon the implementor. Let us suppose, however, that some sort of indexing scheme is used. By examining CC's parameters the interpreter can identify, amongst all the available procedures having the correct name, some subset (possibly empty) of ones which potentially respond. Scanning through these candidates, in their original textual order, it then seeks the first one which (a) does respond to CC and (b) occurs at or beyond (in a textual sense) the position of the candidate NCA.

The effect of this search is twofold. First, it stores a pointer in another register named CP ('current procedure') which then points to the selected responding procedure if one is found, but otherwise is the null pointer $\dashv$. Second, if a responding procedure is found then NCA is updated to point to the next candidate beyond that procedure if one exists, but is otherwise set to $\dashv$. So, if some procedure CP responds to CC then the updating of NCA ensures that, in the event of the interpreter backtracking later on and reactivating CC, CP cannot then be reinvoked in response to it—instead, some new choice must be sought at or beyond the new setting of NCA.

We can then distinguish three possible outcomes to the current activation of CC as follows.

(i)   CP $= \dashv$. No procedure responds to CC at or beyond NCA, and so no immediate step is possible; backtracking is necessary in order to seek an earlier call eligible for reactivation (i.e., having an untried candidate); if this succeeds then CC is updated to this earlier call and a new attempt at procedure calling is attempted, but otherwise execution terminates.

(ii)   CP $\neq \dashv$ and NCA $= \dashv$. A deterministic step takes place in which CC invokes CP, creating a new frame signifying entry into CP; this frame only needs PF and R cells.

(iii)   CP $\neq \dashv$ and NCA $\neq \dashv$. A (potentially) non-deterministic step takes place in which CC invokes CP, creating a new frame signifying entry into CP; this frame is a backtrack point and requires all four control cells.

VII.1.5. The Control Algorithm

The control algorithm for an elementary interpreter implementing the standard strategy is very simple, consisting of the mechanisms necessary for call selection, procedure selection and backtracking. The administration of these activities depends upon appropriate creation and consultation of the frames representing the execution state.

Frames can be conveniently stored in chronological order on a *stack* in the computer's fast access memory. Every procedure entry adds a new frame to the stack, whilst backtracking deletes one or more frames from it. (Other opportunities for deleting frames are discussed later in the chapter.)

In addition to the information stored on the stack it is useful to employ a few single registers holding important details about the execution state. Some of these have already been introduced. Immediately after creating a new frame their contents are as follows. MRB points to the most recent backtrack point, if any, but is otherwise ⊣; CP points to the procedure entered upon creating the frame; CC points to the call which invoked this procedure; NCA points to the next untried candidate for CC, if any, but is otherwise ⊣. A new register named MRP ('most recent parent') points to the frame's parent frame; and another new register f is used to hold the frame's position in the stack—thus a subscripted name such as PF(f) denotes this frame's PF cell.

The complete control algorithm is presented in Fig. VIII.3 using a conventional ALGOL-like notation. Blocking of statements is indicated by

Step 1 (Initialization)	Comments

f   := 1

CP   := →input goal

MRP := ⊣

MRB := ⊣

PF(1) := ⊣

R(1) := exit

Create first frame for entry into goal (assumed to have at least one call). This frame is not a backtrack point.

Step 2 (Call selection)	Comments

if CP→ is an assertion

then   CC := R(f)

     while CC = exit **and** MRP ≠ 1

      do CC := R(MRP)

         MRP := PF(MRP)

     if CC = exit

     then   output goal solution

         go to Step 5

else   CC := →first call in CP→

      MRP := f

If CP is an assertion, then next call must be sought by one or more return operations—if this fails, then the goal has been solved. Otherwise CC is chosen as the first call in CP. Since the current frame f signifies entry into CP, it will become the most recent parent after the step now being attempted, so MRP must be updated to f.

Fig. VII.3. The control algorithm.

if   no candidates exist for CC→
then go to   Step 5
else   NCA := →first candidate

If CC has no candidates, then
backtrack, but otherwise set
NCA to the first of them.

Step 3 (Procedure selection)

Using current states of CC and NCA,
seek responding procedure and other
untried candidates as described in
Section VII.4, thus updating CP and
(possibly) NCA. Then
if   CP = ⊣
then go to   Step 5

Comments

Unification is attempted between
CC and the headings of its
candidates, starting with NCA.
Failure causes backtracking, but
success determines CP as the
first invokable candidate and
NCA as the next untried one,
if any.

Step 4 (Frame creation)

f := f + 1
PF(f) := MRP
if   CC→ is the last call in
a procedure
then   R(f) := exit
else   R(f) := →call following CC→
if   NCA ≠ ⊣
then   NC(f) := NCA
PB(f) := MRB
MRB := f
go to   Step 2

Comments

Create frame for step in which
CC invokes (enters) CP. Frame is
put in position f + 1 of the stack,
and its PF and R cells are
constructed using MRP and CC.
If NCA ≠ ⊣, then untried
candidates exist for CC, so the
new frame is a backtrack point;
in this case, the NC and PB cells
are constructed using NCA and
MRB, and MRB is then updated
to point to this new frame.

Step 5 (Backtracking)

if   MRB = ⊣
then   terminate execution
else   NCA := NC(MRB)
CC := →call preceding R(MRB)
MRP := PF(MRB)
f := MRB − 1
MRB := PB(MRB)
go to   Step 3

Comments

If MRB = ⊣, then backtracking
is impossible and execution
terminates. Otherwise the most
recent backtrack point is used to
identify the call to be reactivated
and the next candidate to be tried
for it. The reduction of f to
MRB-1 effectively discards all
frames at and beyond this
backtrack point.

Fig. VII.3.   (*Continued*)

common indentation rather than by **begin** . . . **end** delimiters. The symbol 'exit' denotes the success exit position at the end of any procedure; the symbol := denotes destructive assignment; the notation r→ denotes the object to which some register r points, whilst → x denotes a pointer to the object x. Note that although CC and the R cells ostensibly identify calls, they also implicitly identify the procedures containing those calls. In particular, when they are assigned the value 'exit', this position must incorporate the identity of the procedure whose exit is being referred to.

VII.2. Representing the Data Assignments

The question of how best to deal with the assignment of data to the program's variables has preoccupied implementors for a long time and probably has no simple answer. Choosing a method involves deciding how to balance the respective costs of constructing, storing, accessing and discarding data, and this balance is in turn related to the kind of programs that the interpreter is expected to execute. The principal considerations are outlined in this section using some simple concrete examples of logic program execution.

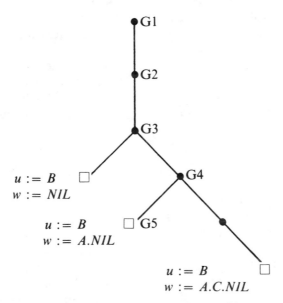

Fig. VII.4.   Computations from Program 39.

VII.2.1. The One-Stack Representation

The first example, Program 39 below, is adapted from Program 13 (Chapter III) and has the goal of finding all strings of the form $u.A.w$ which are prefixes of the string $B.A.A.C.NIL$. A prefix of any string S is either the empty string NIL or any substring of S beginning at the first member of S.

Program 39

$$
\begin{aligned}
&G1 : \quad ? \, \textbf{prefix}(u.A.w, B.A.A.C.NIL) \\
&P1 : \quad \textbf{prefix}(NIL, y) \\
&P2 : \quad \textbf{prefix}(v.x, v.y) \quad \textbf{if} \quad \textbf{prefix}(x, y)
\end{aligned}
$$

The search tree explored by applying the standard strategy is shown in Fig. VII.4 and reveals three distinct solutions. In particular, the computation G1–G5, which yields the second solution, has been singled out for a detailed examination of its data assignments. The successive goal states and assignments to goal variables in the computation G1–G5 are as follows.

$$
\begin{aligned}
&G1 : \quad ? \, \textbf{prefix}(u.A.w, B.A.A.C.NIL) \\
&\hspace{6cm} \{u := B\} \\
&G2 : \quad ? \, \textbf{prefix}(\quad A.w, \quad A.A.C.NIL) \\
&G3 : \quad ? \, \textbf{prefix}(\quad w, \quad A.C.NIL) \\
&\hspace{6cm} \{w := A.x\} \\
&G4 : \quad ? \, \textbf{prefix}(\quad x, \quad C.NIL) \\
&\hspace{6cm} \{x := NIL\} \\
&G5 : \quad \square \quad \text{answer is } u := B, \, w := A.NIL
\end{aligned}
$$

The first three steps each invoke procedure P2, whose variables are v, x and y. Since each entry into P2 instigates a new use of these variables, it follows that each entry must entail a fresh allocation of memory to hold whatever data becomes assigned to them. More precisely, every procedure entry must allocate fresh memory for that procedure's variables, if any. (Although in practice there are occasions when a variable—having some special context within the procedure—need not have any long-term memory allocated to it, since its value, used only transiently during the entry step's unification, is never afterward referred to.) Since each such allocation accompanies the creation of a frame, it is usual to arrange that the frame itself accommodates the variables' values, one per cell. Thus in general each frame contains variable cells as well as control cells. This arrangement yields the *one-stack representation* of execution, which forms an adequate basis for a workable, if unsophisticated, interpreter.

The principal contents of the single stack representing the computation G1–G5 are shown in the tabulation below. A symbolism there such as $\uparrow$(P2) denotes the success exit position of the quoted procedure.

Procedure entered	Frame position	Frame contents				
		PF	R	NC	PB	Variables
G1	1	$\dashv$	$\dashv$	—	—	$u_1 := B,\ w_1 := A.x_4$
P2	2	1	$\uparrow$(G1)	—	—	$v_2 := B,\ x_2 := A.w_1,\ y_2 := A.A.C.NIL$
P2	3	2	$\uparrow$(P2)	—	—	$v_3 := A,\ x_3 := w_1,\ y_3 := A.C.NIL$
P2	4	3	$\uparrow$(P2)	—	—	$v_4 := A,\ x_4 := NIL,\ y_4 := C.NIL$
P1	5	4	$\uparrow$(P2)	$\rightarrow$P2	$\dashv$	$y_5 := C.NIL$

The states of the registers immediately after creating frame 5 are

$$\text{MRP} = 4 \text{ (frame 4 is the most recent parent frame)}$$
$$\text{MRB} = 5 \text{ (frame 5 is the most recent backtrack point)}$$
$$f = 5 \text{ (frame 5 is the most recently created)}$$
$$\text{CP} = \text{pointer to P1 (the procedure just entered)}$$
$$\text{CC} = \text{pointer to first call in P2 (which invoked CP)}$$

Each line in the tabulation depicts a frame on the stack. That part of the frame allocated to variables actually consists of a collection of cells, one for each distinctly named variable occurring in the procedure entered. At any time during the stack's development, the content of a variable cell may be just a special symbol, say $*$, denoting 'currently unassigned'. Alternatively, some data value may have been assigned to the variable; if that value is sufficiently simple (e.g., a short constant) then it can be stored directly in the variable's cell, but otherwise it has to be stored elsewhere in memory and the variable's cell then merely contains a pointer to it. Observe also that the value stored in a variable's cell may be a pointer to some other variable's cell; for instance, a pointer to the cell for w_1 becomes stored in the cell for x_3.

The names of the variables, although shown in the tabulation to help the reader, are not explicitly stored in the frames. Instead, any variable's identity is determined implicitly by its cell's position within the frame. Thus the variables v, x and y of P2 can be deemed by the interpreter always to correspond respectively to the first, second and third variable cells in any frame signifying entry into P2. Note that, by allocating new sets of variable cells upon each procedure entry, there can be no confusion between, say, the value of 'x' upon one entry into P2 and the value of 'x' upon another. In each case the variable's identity incorporates the identity of its frame as indicated by the names x_2, x_3, etc., tabulated above. This arrangement automatically satisfies the naming requirements originally advocated in Chapter I for preventing muddles over the identities of variables.

When a frame has just been created, its variable cells will, at that moment, be variously assigned or unassigned (set to *) depending upon the unification entailed in the step. In fact u_1, w_1 and x_4 are all unassigned when their cells are first allocated, but are later assigned the respective values B (upon creating frame 2), $A.x_4$ (upon creating frame 4) and NIL (upon creating frame 5). This shows that the creation of a frame may assign data to cells in earlier frames: assignments of this kind are called *output assignments* because they each pass output data from an entered procedure to the invoking call.

Recalling the behaviour of the control algorithm, observe that the procedure (P1) entered at frame 5 is an assertion. This circumstance triggers a chain of procedure exits which reverts right back to the exit of G1, indicating that the goal has been solved. The goal's solution is recovered from the contents of both the variable cells in frame 1 and any other cells to which they refer. Thus the cells for u_1, w_1 and x_4 must all be consulted in order to construct and report the solution $u_1 := B$, $w_1 := A.NIL$.

After this the interpreter has to backtrack. We know, from previous consideration of this process, that all frames at and beyond the most recent backtrack point (consisting of just frame 5 in the example, since MRB happens to point to it) will then be discarded. A new problem now arises: since the discarding of a frame signifies forgetting its step's contribution to the execution, how do we arrange to forget any output assignments produced when the frame was created? More specifically, the creation of frame 5 caused the assignment $x_4 := NIL$; this assignment has to be 'undone' by resetting x_4 to * when frame 5 is discarded. We next describe how the interpreter remembers that it must do this.

VII.2.2. The Trail

A backtracking operation deletes from the stack both the most recent backtrack point (pointed to by MRB) and any frames occurring beyond it (i.e., more recent than it). The assignments which have to be 'undone' as part of the operation are those, if any, which assigned data to the variable cells of frames preceding the backtrack point during the creation of those frames now to be deleted. The interpreter's remembrance of these assignments relies upon another run-time structure called the *trail* (or 'reset list'). This records the identities of the variables to which such assignments have been made. A register TT ('top of trail') is maintained throughout execution, which always points to the top of the trail, that is, to its most recent entry. At the start of execution the trail is empty and TT just contains the null pointer ⊣.

The precise details of adding new entries to the trail are as follows. Suppose some frame is being created. First, if it is a backtrack point then a *trail (TR) pointer*, set to the current state of TT, is stored in a fifth control cell of the frame. Second, whether it is a backtrack point or not, if its creation entails (as a consequence of the step's unification) assigning data to a variable whose cell occurs in a frame preceding that to which MRB currently points, then that variable's identity (more concretely, a pointer to its cell) is entered on the trail and TT is incremented accordingly.

These arrangements are illustrated in a general way by Fig. VII.5. This shows two backtrack points on the current stack, each one containing a TR pointer indicating some position in the trail.

If a backtracking operation now occurs (i.e., immediately following the state shown in Fig. VII.5) then all cells for variables whose identities appear in the trail beyond (but not at) the position indicated by TR(MRB) must be reset to ∗. In the figure the trail segment C′ contains these identities. The cells themselves all occur in various frames in the stack segments A and B (but not C), and were formerly assigned data by the creation of the frames in the C segment. After the resetting operation, TT is itself reset to TR(MRB) (effectively discarding the trail segment C′), then MRB is reset to PB(MRB) and the C segment is deleted from the stack. The backtracking operation is now

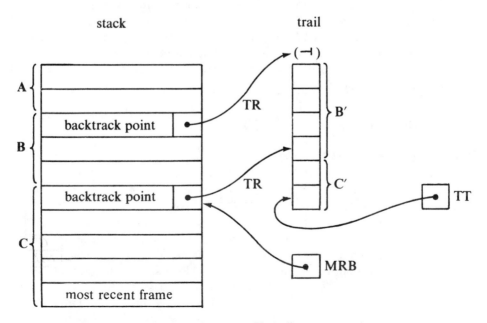

Fig. VII.5.   The trail.

complete and execution resumes in the normal way. The reader should have no difficulty in seeing how these arrangements can be incorporated in the control algorithm in Fig. VII.3.

Returning to our former example, the state of the trail after creating frame 5 is such that it contains just one entry identifying the cell for x_4, and TT points to this entry. MRB points to frame 5, whose trail pointer TR(MRB) is ⊢. When backtracking occurs, the trail segment identifying the variable cells to be reset consists of just the entry x_4. That cell is accordingly reset to *, TT is reset to TR(MRB) = ⊢, then MRB is reset to PB(MRB) = ⊢ and finally frame 5 is discarded.

VII.2.3. Data Representation

The data item assigned to a variable by unification may be a constant or a variable or a structured term, depending upon the circumstances. In general, an assigned constant can be stored directly in a variable's cell unless it is too large, in which case it must be stored elsewhere and a pointer to it placed in the cell. A variable-to-variable assignment such as $x_3 := w_1$ is dealt with simply by storing in the x_3 cell a pointer to the w_1 cell.

The assignment of a structured term is a more elaborate business. The simplest scheme stores a pointer in the variable's cell to some cluster of contiguous cells representing the term. As an example, consider some arbitrary assignment $z := A.B.C.NIL$. Figure VII.6a shows a representation of $A.B.C.NIL$ using seven cells. Each one contains either a (short) constant or

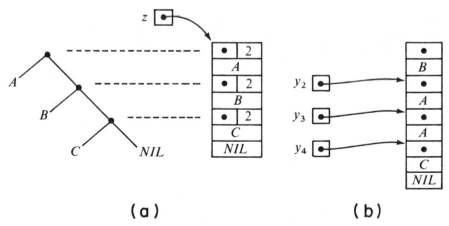

(a)   **(b)**

Fig. VII.6.   Representing structured terms: (a) representing $z := A.B.C.NIL$; (b) representing $y_2 := A.A.C.NIL$, $y_3 := A.C.NIL$, $y_4 := C.NIL$.

else a functor together with its argument count. The first cell identifies the outermost functor as 'dot' and indicates (by the '2') that the following two cells represent that functor's arguments; these are identified in turn as the constant A and another structured term whose representation begins, in the same manner, at the third cell. In general, then, a variable's cell may contain either the 'unassigned' symbol (∗) or a short constant or a pointer to another variable cell or a pointer to a cluster representing a structured term. Since the interpreter must be able to distinguish these possibilities, a few bits of each cell can be reserved for holding a 'type code' describing the type of the item encoded by the remaining bits.

Examine once more the frames generated by the prefix program. Clearly there exist among them a number of replicated substructures within the assigned terms, notably appearing in the assignments $y_2 := A.A.C.NIL$, $y_3 := A.C.NIL$ and $y_4 := C.NIL$. In fact all of these assigned terms turn out to be subterms of the term $B.A.A.C.NIL$ occurring in the input program. This suggests a useful way of economizing on the memory allocated for data values: appropriate parts of the representation of $B.A.A.C.NIL$ in the heap storage holding the input program can be simply pointed to by the cells for y_2, y_3 and y_4, as shown in Fig. VII.6b. As well as the obvious space-saving benefit of using one stored structure to represent several substructures, this scheme demonstrates a much more important general principle—when a logic program is executed, the representation of the data values assigned to its variables does not necessarily require any allocation of memory beyond that initially allocated for storing the input statements. This observation makes it appropriate now to discuss an important method of representing structured data very compactly, known as structure sharing, which is used by many existing implementations.

VII.2.4. Structure Sharing

The benefits of structure sharing can be demonstrated by examining a new program which performs iterative list reversal and is adapted from Program 4 (Chapter III).

Program 40

G1 :   ? **reverse***$(NIL, A.B.C.D.NIL, y_1)$
P1 :   **reverse***(z, NIL, z)
P2 :   **reverse***$(x, u.w, y)$ **if**   **reverse***$(u.x, w, y)$

Here a predicate **reverse***(v_1, v_2, v_3) expresses that the list v_3 is the reverse of the list obtained by appending v_2 to the reverse of v_1. Thus the goal G1 effectively asks for the reverse y_1 of $A.B.C.D.NIL$.

Since this program is deterministic it yields exactly one computation

G1 :	? **reverse***(	$NIL, A.B.C.D.NIL, y_1$)	(by entering G1)
G2 :	? **reverse***(	$A.NIL,$ $B.C.D.NIL, y_1$)	(by entering P2)
G3 :	? **reverse***($B.A.NIL,$	$C.D.NIL, y_1$)	(by entering P2)
G4 :	? **reverse***($C.B.A.NIL,$	$D.NIL, y_1$)	(by entering P2)
G5 :	? **reverse***($D.C.B.A.NIL,$	NIL, y_1)	(by entering P2)
G6 :	$\square$ answer is $\underline{y_1 := D.C.B.A.NIL}$		(by entering P1)

The computation generates six frames, one for each procedure entry, and the assignments recorded by them are as follows.

Frame	Assignments
1	$y_1 := *$ initially, but $D.C.B.A.NIL$ finally
2	$x_2 :=$ $NIL,\ u_2 := A,\ w_2 := B.C.D.NIL,\ y_2 := y_1$
3	$x_3 :=$ $A.NIL,\ u_3 := B,\ w_3 :=$ $C.D.NIL,\ y_3 := y_1$
4	$x_4 :=$ $B.A.NIL,\ u_4 := C,\ w_4 :=$ $D.NIL,\ y_4 := y_1$
5	$x_5 :=$ $C.B.A.NIL,\ u_5 := D,\ w_5 :=$ $NIL,\ y_5 := y_1$
6	$y_1 := D.C.B.A.NIL$ (output assignment), $z_6 := y_1$

Once again there are clearly many replicated substructures within the data assigned to the y_1, x_i and w_i variables. The w_i data can be represented compactly by storing pointers in the w_i cells to appropriate components of a cluster representing the input term $A.B.C.D.NIL$, in the manner shown in Fig. VII.6b for the **prefix** example. However, the same technique cannot be applied to the data for the y_1 and x_i variables, because the term $D.C.B.A.NIL$ occurs nowhere in the input program. Superficially this suggests that extra memory must be allocated for accommodating this data. Yet this turns out not to be the case: we shall see that the structure-sharing method has the re- markable quality of representing structured data using only the heap storage holding the input program together with the variable cells on the stack.

In order to see how this is possible, consider how the value $A.NIL$ assigned to x_3 originated in the course of creating frame 3. The associated procedure-calling step invoked P2 in response to the call **reverse***($A.NIL$, $B.C.D.NIL, y_1$). How did that call arise? A previous entry into P2 created frame 2 and assigned $x_2 := NIL$, $u_2 := A$, $w_2 := B.C.D.NIL$ and $y_2 := y_1$; the next call activated was therefore the P2 call **reverse***($u.x,w,y$) with those data values distributed to its variables, giving **reverse***($A.NIL, B.C.D.NIL$, y_1). The unification entailed in creating frame 3 then assigned to x_3 this call's actual parameter $A.NIL$, which, as we have just seen, is the result of distrib- uting to the input program's term $u.x$ the data values stored in the u and x

cells of frame 2. Thus all that is needed in order to represent the assignment $x_3 := A.NIL$ is a pointer in the x_3 cell to the term $u.x$ in the heap representation of the input program together with a second pointer in the x_3 cell to frame 2.

The first pointer is called a *skeleton pointer* because it points to a *skeleton* $u.x$ which, in general, can be any structured term occurring in the input program. The second pointer is called an *environment pointer* because it points to the *environment* (i.e., the context) in which the skeleton was used. When a frame is created upon entering a procedure, a new environment is thereby created consisting of the values of the procedure's variables. The initial values of these variables are determined by the unification entailed in the procedure entry, but thereafter may be modified by output assignments produced by solving the procedure's calls. When one of those calls is activated, its actual parameters at that moment are the result of substituting, for all those variables occurring in the input form (or 'pure code') of the call, their values as determined by the call's current environment, and this is just the current state of the variable cells stored in the procedure's entry frame. Thus when the call **reverse***$(u.x,w,y)$ is activated after entering P2 at frame 2, its environment is $\{x_2 := NIL, u_2 := A, w_2 := B.C.D.NIL, y_2 := y_1\}$ and its first actual parameter is therefore $A.NIL$. Assigning this value to x_3 consists simply of making x_3 point to both the skeleton $u.x$ and the frame 2 environment. A pointer pair of this kind is called a *molecule* and can be regarded as a data item whose concrete value is only ascertainable by following its pointers.

A more complete picture of the structure-sharing method is provided by Fig. VII.7, which shows the final state of the data assigned to the variables when Program 40's computation has terminated. Here each variable cell contains either a constant or a pointer to another variable cell or a pointer to a variable-free cluster or a molecule. In particular, the y_1 and x_i cells (except x_2) all contain molecules; for presentation's sake their environment pointers are indicated simply as the ordinal positions on the stack of the frames containing those environments—in reality the pointers would be stack addresses directly locating the frames. Although the figure shows the cells in contiguous groups, they are, of course, actually situated in their own frames.

The concrete value of a molecule can be determined at any stage of execution by evaluating the components referred to by its pointers, which may in turn require referring to other molecules. For instance, the final value of x_4 in Fig. VII.7 can be obtained by substituting in the skeleton $u.x$ the values of u and x determined for u_3 and x_3 by the frame 3 environment. This process is sometimes called 'fleshing out' or 'interpreting' the skeleton. The value of x_3 is B whilst that of x_3 is another molecule whose value turns

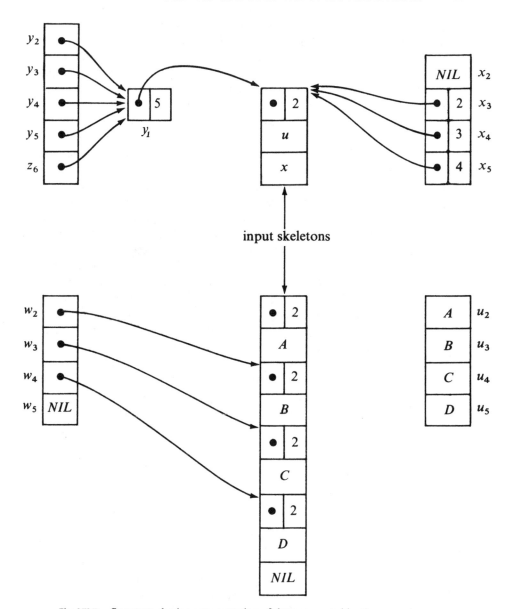

Fig. VII.7.   Structure-sharing representation of data computed by the reversal program.

out to be *A.NIL*. So the value of x_4 is *B.A.NIL*. The evaluation of data by replacing pointers (references) to its components by the components themselves is more generally known as *dereferencing*. An obvious case in which complete dereferencing is necessary is when a structured goal solution has to be output to the user. For example, the final value computed by Program 40 for y_1 is, in the structure-sharing representation, *delocalized* over several linked frames, and must be fully dereferenced in order to present the user with the intelligible value *D.C.B.A.NIL*.

The term 'structure sharing' reflects the fact that, for instance, the values of x_3 and x_4 *share* the common input skeleton $u.x$—this is the fundamental origin of the great compactness which the method brings to data storage. It is obviously most useful when run-time memory is especially limited or expensive to acquire. Set against this is the potential penalty of increased processing time necessary for performing unification, which may require the interpreter to probe through arbitrarily long chains of molecules in order to compare actual and formal parameters. This penalty is negligible for any program whose execution seldom involves such unifications, or for any host machine endowed with particularly efficient indirect addressing mechanisms. The former condition depends upon the kind of program executed. Some programs may *construct* large structured terms when executed, yet impose little or no *accessing* burden upon the unification routine. Others may make no use of structured terms at all, perhaps processing only data in assertional form. The problem of choosing between structure-sharing and non-structure-sharing techniques in the light of the host machine and the expected range of application has exercised the minds of many skilled implementors and continues to be the subject of much discussion.

VII.3. Conserving Memory

The stack space demanded by the interpreter during execution may grow to unacceptable proportions if insufficient attention is paid to conserving memory. It is the joint responsibility of the programmer and the implementor to curtail the interpreter's run-time demand for memory as much as is practicable, for no programmer can program effectively for a grossly inefficient interpreter, and no implementor can design an interpreter which elicits optimal behaviour from all conceivable programs.

Structure sharing is itself a conservative method of using memory to represent the execution state. Nevertheless, the elementary interpreter outlined so far would, if implemented without further amendment, utilize memory rather poorly. The general reason for this is that it would tend to leave information on the stack for much longer than necessary, deleting it only when backtracking. In fact, during the growth of any individual computation no contraction of the stack would ever occur, even though much of the data stored on the stack would become redundant soon after being put there. This section describes ways of overcoming this defect and so constraining stack growth.

VII.3.1. Reclaiming Space after Success Exit

When control exits successfully from a procedure, the only information which needs to be retained from amongst all that generated since entering it is—as far as the current computation is concerned—just the set of data values assigned to the variables of the invoking call. This suggests considerable scope for deleting information on the stack whenever a success exit occurs. In order to see more clearly what this involves, consider a program whose procedures include the following (in which only the procedures' names are shown).

Program 41 (fragment)

$$
\begin{array}{llll}
P1 : & A & \text{if} & B, C \\
P2 : & B & \text{if} & G \\
P3 : & C & \text{if} & D, E \\
P4 : & D & \text{if} & F \\
P5 : & E & & \\
P6 : & F & & \\
P7 : & G & &
\end{array}
$$

Figure VII.8 shows a segment of the stack containing the frames generated by solving a call to **A**—that is, from the moment when control enters P1 to the moment when it exits successfully from P1. The stack positions of the frames have been arbitrarily numbered 10–16 for easy reference. The net effect of solving the **A** call is the assignment of data to its variables, whose cells all reside in frames preceding frame 10. This data accumulates in the course of creating frames 10–16. When the call has become solved, those frames can—subject to two conditions described presently—be deleted from the stack (more concretely, they can be overwritten by new frames). We then say that their space on the stack has been *reclaimed*.

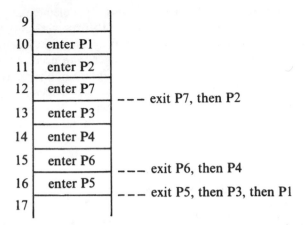

Fig. VII.8.   Frames generated by solving call to **A**.

In practice, stack space is reclaimed one frame at a time—each procedure exit instigates (if possible) the reclamation of that procedure's entry frame. In the example, when control exits from P1, frame 10 can be reclaimed provided two conditions hold:

(a)   no variable cells in frame 10 (i.e., variables of P1) are pointed to by earlier cells (in frames preceding frame 10);

(b)   the most recent backtrack point precedes frame 10.

For suppose instead that frame 10 were deleted with condition (a) contravened. A subsequent unification needing to look up the value of one of those earlier cells might then encounter a pointer to one of the cells in frame 10; since these have, by assumption, already been deleted, that pointer would 'dangle' (its intended referent would no longer exist) and thus wreck the execution process.

Alternatively, suppose that frame 10 were deleted with (a) satisfied but (b) contravened. Subsequent backtracking, seeking new ways of solving the A call, might then encounter references on the trail to some of the variables of P1 requiring their (now discarded) cells to be reset to ∗; this would also wreck the execution process.

Condition (b) is easy to test at run time by a simple inspection of the MRB register. Condition (a), however, cannot be tested at run time without consuming a lot of processing time. For this reason several implementations employ a more elaborate representation of the execution state which guarantees that condition (a) holds, as we next describe.

VII.3.2. The Two-Stack Representation

The purpose of the two-stack representation is to eliminate certain pointers which might otherwise be left dangling after performing the reclamation mechanism. In a standard structure-sharing system such pointers are of a very specific kind. As an example, suppose that the A call invoking P1 at frame 10 has an unassigned variable x as one of its actual parameters; this means that a cell, currently set to $*$, will have already been allocated for x in some frame preceding frame 10. Suppose further that the corresponding formal parameter in the heading of P1 is a structured term $f(y, z)$. When frame 10 is being created, the invocation of P1 by the A call must entail (by unification) the assignment $x := f(y, z)$. As we have seen previously, the one-stack structure-sharing system represents this assignment by storing, in the cell for x, a molecule whose environment pointer points to frame 10. The latter is exactly the sort of pointer which would perilously dangle if frame 10 were subsequently deleted after exiting from P1 : it is a pointer used for representing an output assignment of structured data from the procedure whose entry frame we wish to delete after a successful exit.

The two-stack representation was developed by David Warren for the DEC-10 PROLOG system at Edinburgh University. It overcomes the dangling-pointer problem by using an auxiliary stack, more often called the *global stack*, to accommodate the cells for those variables occurring within structured terms of the input program. The example just considered would then be dealt with by placing cells for the P1 variables y and z in a frame on the global stack and making the x-cell environment pointer point to this frame instead of to frame 10.

The general organization of the two-stack system is therefore as follows. The main stack, called the *local stack*, is very similar to that of the one-stack system. Each of its frames contains the usual control cells and also contains cells for just those variables of the entered procedure whose values could never be referred to by cells in earlier local frames. On the global stack, each global frame contains cells for all other variables in the entered procedure. This scheme is thus based upon a discrimination between the variables occurring in the input program, classifying them as either local or global. When a procedure is entered, a local frame is always created. If the procedure contains global variables then a global frame is also created and linked to its local partner by storing a pointer in the latter; more precisely, a sixth control cell is allocated in the local frame and is assigned a *global-frame (GF) pointer* which points to the global partner. The two frames jointly determine the environment for that procedure's calls. Backtracking causes the local stack to contract in the normal way and whenever a local frame is deleted in the course of backtracking then so is its global partner (if any). Figure VII.9 gives an indication of the stacks' relationship.

The permissible contents of the cells for a procedure's variables in the two-stack representation can then be summarized as follows. Denote the local and global frames accommodating these variables' cells by L and G, respectively. Then:

(i)   any cell in L or in G may contain * (unassigned) or a constant or a pointer to a variable-free term in the heap;

(ii)   any cell in L may point to another variable cell (variable-to-variable binding) provided the latter is either in any global frame or in any local frame not more recent than L;

(iii)   any cell in L may contain a molecule provided the latter's environment pointer points either to any global frame or to any local frame not more recent than L;

(iv)   any cell in G may contain a pointer to any other global cell (variable-to-variable binding) or may contain a molecule whose environment pointer points to any global frame.

The net effect of these restrictions is that, no matter what unifications occur upon or after entering P1, neither L nor its constituent cells can ever be pointed to either by global cells or by cells in local frames preceding L; in other words, condition (a) for the deletion of local frame 10 is necessarily satisfied when control exits from P1. The restrictions themselves arise partly

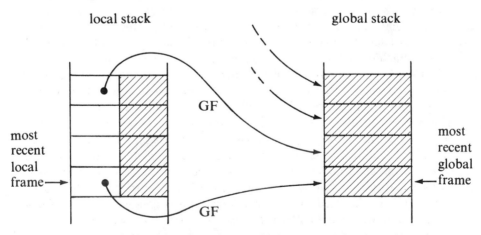

Fig. VII.9.   Local and global stacks.
Key: shaded sections—variable cells
clear sections—control cells.

from the criterion used to distinguish local from global variables, partly from the treatment of variable-to-variable bindings (always assigning the call's variable to the heading's variable) and partly from adopting the convention that all pointers between the local and global stacks invariably point from the former to the latter.

VII.3.3. The Reclamation Mechanism upon Success Exit

The satisfaction of the reclamation condition (a) depends upon appropriate mechanisms being implemented for unification and local/global memory allocation. Whether or not the other condition (b) is satisfied depends upon the current status of the MRB register: it holds provided that MRB is either ⊣ or pointing to some local frame preceding frame 10 (the frame to be reclaimed). The implementation both of this test and the reclamation mechanism can be accomplished by a simple reorganization of Step 2 in the control algorithm of Fig. VII.3 as follows:

Step 2 (Call selection)

if   CP→ is an assertion
then   CC := R(f)
     if   MRB = ⊣   **or**   MRB < f   **then**   f := f−1
     while   CC = exit   **and**   MRP ≠ 1
       do   **if**   MRB = ⊣   **or**   MRB < MRP   **then**   f := f−1
         CC := R(MRP)
         MRP := PF(MRP)
     if   CC = exit
     ⋮
     exactly as before

The consequence of this modification is that whenever a procedure exit occurs (possibly within a chain of exits driven by the loop in Step 2) and satisfies conditions (a) and (b) for reclaiming the procedure's local entry frame, that frame will necessarily be in the current top-of-stack position and can be immediately deleted—this just involves decrementing (f := f−1) the local top-of-stack position f.

When applied to the execution of Program 41, positions 12 and 11 are reclaimed by the respective exits from P7 and P2, so that the next two frames (for P3 and P4) will then occupy positions 11 and 12 instead of 13 and 14. Further similar reclamations occur by exiting from P6, P4, P5 and P3. The eventual exit from P1 will finally reclaim the entry frame of P1 at position 10 and the entire process of solving the **A** call will have never extended the local stack beyond position 13. The only remnant, if any, of that process surviving after reclamation of frame 10 will be data assigned to the variables of the **A** call.

Note that the mechanism never contracts the global stack, and so data stored on that stack generally has a much longer lifetime than that stored on the local partner. This feature imposes further burdens upon the implementor, for it is possible for data on the global stack to become redundant during execution. This is not harmful in itself, but if the global stack is approaching overflow and contains much redundant data then it may be worthwhile for the interpreter to trigger a *garbage-collector* routine which will track down that data and delete it. A competent routine for this task will consume much processing time if the triggering policy is ill-chosen. Moreover the composition of such a routine is a significant programming project in its own right.

Whatever arrangements are made for garbage collecting from the global stack, they must obviously be backed up by a good policy for determining the local/global status of variables in the first place. Since local stack reclamation is operationally simple and (usually) occurs very frequently, it is clearly desirable to accord local status to as many variables as possible. However, the task of deciding at run time exactly which variables *have* to be global cannot be accomplished at the moment the procedure is entered. In principle, the interpreter can make a provisional local/global allocation of cells at that moment which, though suboptimal, is sufficiently discriminating to prevent potentially dangling pointers from arising later on. It is further possible for these cells to be reallocated (and all references to them appropriately amended) later on in the computation in the light of the assignments taking place, but this consumes much extra processing time and can still fall short of optimality. Thus the local/global discrimination of a procedure's variables is normally decided instead at compile time, relying upon a simple syntactical rule: variables are allocated global cells if and only if they occur in structured terms anywhere within the procedure. This rule is suboptimal in that it generally makes certain variables global even though making them local instead would still not harm subsequent execution. On the other hand the rule is cheap to apply, gives all the entry frames for any particular procedure exactly the same structure independently of the run-time context in which the procedure's invocations take place and guarantees that the reclamation condition (a) is satisfied.

VII.3.4. Last-Call Optimization

Reclaiming a procedure's local entry frame need not always be delayed until control exits successfully from the procedure. Subject to certain conditions being satisfied, reclamation of this local frame (though not its global partner) can in fact take place at the instant the procedure's *last call* is activated—in other words, as soon as the interpreter begins its attempt to solve that call rather than (as previously) as soon as it has succeeded in solving it. This tactic is called *last-call optimization* and can bring substantial improvements to both memory utilization and processing speed.

Consider Program 41 again in conjunction with Fig. VII.8 and assume that control has just exited from P2. Assume also that the entry frames for P2 and P7 have been deleted by the operation of either the standard success exit reclamation mechanism or the last-call optimization. The current top-of-stack position on the local stack is therefore position 10, which currently holds the local entry frame of P1; henceforth the latter is called the *deletable frame* for brevity. Since the next immediate task of the interpreter is to activate the last call (to **C**) in P1, the scene is now set for operating the last-call optimization, henceforth abbreviated to LCO. If LCO takes place, its effect will be to make the next created local frame overwrite the deletable one, which is tantamount to reclaiming the latter's space as required; that next frame will be the local entry frame for P3, that is, for the procedure which responds to the last call of P1.

The conditions for performing the LCO are then as follows:

(c) the deletable frame must not be a backtrack point;
(d) neither must the new local frame which will overwrite it;
(e) the new local frame must contain no pointers to the deletable one.

These are similar in both form and motivation to conditions (a) and (b) for success exit reclamation, essentially preventing references to the deletable frame from arising later on in the execution. The first two can be tested at run time by suitable consultation of **MRB**. The last one (e) can be ensured in a structure-sharing system by making appropriate local/global allocations at compile time as explained presently.

Creating the local and global frames for the next step (entering P3) entails a unification which, in general, needs to consult the environment of last call **C** held in the local and global P1 entry frames. The unification may also generate data for the variables of the new local frame which must eventually occupy the stack space currently occupied by the deletable one. So, in order to prevent 'read–write' conflicts (writing data to a memory area whose original contents might need to be consulted later on), it is advisable first to copy selected data from the deletable frame into temporary registers. A large number of very low-level optimizations (not detailed here) are then feasible which minimize the flow of data between these registers, the old cells and the new cells, yielding substantial reductions in the processing time consumed by both unification and frame building.

The satisfaction of condition (e) poses an interesting problem for the implementor. One approach is simply to make the interpreter inspect the results of the new step's unification and then decide whether or not to perform LCO. However, this can consume a great deal of processing time and so partly defeat the optimization's objectives. Alternatively one can try to prevent the offending pointers from arising in the first place by appropriate compile-time provisions.

In order to see how such pointers could arise, consider the task of unifying some parameter $T1$ in the (input form of the) C call in P1 with the corresponding formal parameter $T2$ in the heading of the invoked procedure P3. If $T1$ is not a variable then any variables within it have necessarily been allocated global cells; therefore any pointers to them generated by the unification cannot dangle when the deletable frame is deleted. If $T2$ is not a variable but $T1$ is some variable x then the unification assigns $x := T2$; whatever the form of $T2$, this never produces a pointer to the x cell. These arguments narrow our consideration to the case where $T1$ is a variable x and $T2$ is a variable z, as indicated below.

$$P1 : \quad A(\ldots) \quad \textbf{if} \quad B(\ldots), C(\ldots, x, \ldots)$$
$$P3 : \quad C(\ldots, z, \ldots) \quad \textbf{if} \quad D(\ldots), E(\ldots)$$

The last call $C(\ldots, x, \ldots)$ in P1 is activated in the context of its environment and this will contain a cell for x. Now consider four exhaustive circumstances *immediately prior* to performing the unification.

(1)   Suppose x is global (occurring in a structured term); then any pointer stored in its cell by the unification cannot point to the deletable frame because of the convention governing local-to-global stack pointers.

(2)   Suppose x is local and that its cell contains some value t (so is already assigned) which does not point to, or into, the deletable frame; then the unification's assignment $z := t$ cannot create a pointer to the deletable frame.

(3)   Suppose x is local but unassigned; then the unification's assignment $z := x$ (note: $z := *$ is not good enough) stores in the z cell a potentially dangling pointer to the x cell in the deletable frame.

(4)   Suppose x is local and is assigned a value containing a pointer to, or into, the deletable frame. This could only be a pointer to the cell of some other variable y of P1 (it could not be a molecule since the latter's environment pointer would point to a global frame); thus the unification's assignment $z := y$ stores in the z cell a potentially dangling pointer to the y cell in the deletable frame, unless y is global.

This analysis establishes that cases (3) and (4)—both of which assume that x is local—must be eliminated if LCO is to be performed safely. A remedy inferred by David Warren and implemented in his DEC-10 PROLOG system consists of granting global status to x if x does not occur in the heading of P1. In this event any pointer to the x cell which the unification might assign to the z cell cannot possible dangle and so LCO can be performed with impunity. Otherwise, if x is local and does occur in the heading of P1 then the standard conventions of unification ensure that x is immediately assigned upon entry to P1, so that case (3) does not then arise.

Finally, consider case (4). Its assumptions require that an assignment $x := y$ took place some time prior to the activation of the C call. No such assignment could ever occur upon entry to P1. Therefore the solution of the B call must have assigned $x := y$ and this would in turn require x to be unassigned after entry to P1 (since a variable cannot be doubly assigned). This would mean that x could not occur in the heading. Thus case (4) arises only if x is both local and does not occur in the heading, a possibility eliminated by Warren's remedy.

What all this amounts to is that a simple compile-time discrimination of the P1 variables, supplementing the normal local/global rules by the new one, is sufficient to ensure that condition (e) holds. Condition (c) requires only that before the new step takes place, MRB be either ⊣ or point to a position preceding the deletable frame. Condition (d) requires only that the new step yield no untried candidates (NCA = ⊣) after selecting the new procedure (P3) to be invoked.

When LCO takes place, the deletable frame's R (return) pointer is, in principle, lost along with the rest of the frame. The eventual return operation which it anticipated will remain feasible provided that the new frame adopts that return pointer rather than (as previously) the success exit position following the optimized last call. This suggests that the implementation of LCO should be accompanied by a more general reorganization of the control algorithm, such that any frame's return pointer always points directly to the next call in the program waiting to be solved, and so never points to a success exit other than the goal's. This arrangement significantly improves the speed and continuity of call selection, because it eliminates the inefficiency of tracing through chains of success exits. However, the result of such a modification is that a frame's return pointer will not then be a sufficient basis (as previously) for inferring which call was activated when the frame was created. Yet this information would be needed if the frame were a backtrack point, since after some later backtracking operation that call needs to be identified in order to be reactivated. These considerations suggest that each frame (or at least, each backtrack point) should also explicitly record, in yet another control cell, the identity of the call invoking the entered procedure. The would-be implementor who has properly understood the control mechanism of the elementary interpreter should encounter no difficulty in incorporating all these modifications in order to support LCO.

It is worth noting that whilst LCO reclaims the space occupied by redundant control cells and local variable cells, it never contracts the global stack where structured data accumulates—this only contracts upon backtracking or garbage collecting. On the other hand, LCO can, when programmed as tightly as possible in order to avoid superfluous data flow between frames and registers, greatly reduce the processing time consumed by iterative computations. Program 40, for example, yields such a computation by repeated invocation of the (deterministic) iterative **reverse*** procedure. The effect of LCO upon its execution is that each frame after the first becomes overwritten by its successor, so that the local stack never expands beyond position 2, whereas formerly it expanded to a length proportional to the length of the input list. However, a second likely improvement is much greater speed, because the unification and frame building entailed in each overwriting operation can be 'tightened up' by the implementor (after engaging in sufficient analysis and programming effort). The resulting behaviour closely emulates that of a conventional program exercising destructive assignment to iterate over a fixed area of memory whilst constructing structured output in another; in the logic implementation these areas are respectively the local stack and the global stack.

Note that in the two-stack implementation of the **reverse*** program, the u_i, x_i and w_i cells shown in Fig. VII.7 will all reside in frames on the global stack because the variables u, x and w of P2 all occur in structured terms. However, the figure shows that none of the cells are ever assigned potentially dangling pointers, so that none of them strictly need to be on that stack. This shows how a simple compile-time syntactic ruling on the status of variables generally overloads the global stack as the price of enabling the interpreter to reclaim with impunity whatever remains on the local one. Consequently it has been argued that LCO is not especially effective as a space-conserving measure unless supplemented either by garbage collection or by better schemes for discriminating variables.

VII.4. Conserving Processing Time

Compared with the execution speeds attainable by writing programs in assembly languages or in somewhat low-level languages like BASIC and FORTRAN, the executions of equivalent logic programs are generally slow. To some extent this is due to the mechanisms needed for supporting nondeterminism, but to a larger extent is due to insufficient development of techniques for efficient data handling. Much of the implementation effort in the early years of logic programming was preoccupied with improving the processing of structured term representation, with the result that the development of powerful control mechanisms for handling large, irregular data structures represented in other ways has received much less attention.

It is likely that this situation will change as interest in logic programming, initially concentrated within academic artificial intelligence circles (where familiarity with kindred formalisms like LISP is second nature), gradually pervades other domains such as scientific and commercial computing. The demands made by these application areas will doubtless modify the style of logic programming—and hence its implementation technology—as much as they will themselves be changed by it.

The evolution of new computer hardware from serial, process-directed von Neumann machines toward multiprocessor architecture supporting parallelism, data-flow regimes and built-in mechanisms (such as pattern matching) specially designed for the needs of inferential formalisms will also bring radical change to the way logic is implemented.

For all these reasons no prescription of any supposedly optimal processing strategies can be expected to have enduring validity in the short term. This section therefore only describes a small selection of options available to the implementor for influencing processing speed in the context of current programming style and machine architecture.

VII.4.1. Non-Structure-Sharing Systems

Logic implementations can be broadly classified as either structure-sharing (SS) or non-structure-sharing (NSS) systems. Here we give a brief outline of NSS systems and then compare the two approaches.

NSS systems, which currently form the minority of existing implementations, generally employ two principal dynamic storage areas. The first of these is the *local stack*, which is virtually identical in character to the local stack of a SS system, except that each frame provides a local cell for *every* distinct variable in the entered procedure as well as the usual control cells. The other stack serves the auxiliary purpose of accommodating literal (or 'concrete') representations of the structured terms assigned (by unification) to the local variables. This storage area is organized more as a heap than a stack, but is usually referred to as the *global stack* (or 'copy stack').

As an example, suppose some call **reverse***$(t, z, v.v.z)$ is activated, with t, z and v currently unassigned, and invokes our procedure

$$\text{P2} : \quad \textbf{reverse*}(x, u.w, y) \quad \textbf{if} \quad \textbf{reverse*}(u.x, w, y)$$

The resulting assignments $\{x := t, z := u.w, y := v.v.z\}$ might then be represented in a typical NSS system as shown in Fig. VII.10. In the figure the

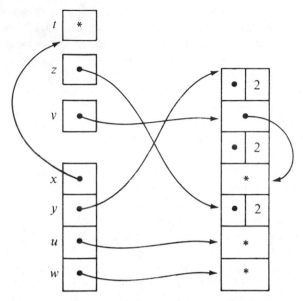

Fig. VII.10.   NSS system's use of local and global cells.

cells for t, z and v reside in various local frames for earlier steps. The new local frame created upon entering P2 is allocated cells for x, y, u and w. The cell cluster on the right is a new contribution to the global stack and is a literal representation of the term $v.v.u.w$. The pointers to it from y and z respectively signify $y := v.v.z$ and $z := u.w$. Note how a pointer chain connects the local cell for v to two associated global cells in the cluster. Thus NSS uses a total of three cells for v whereas SS would use just one (global) cell. If a later step assigns some structured term to v then that term is in turn placed, in literal form, on the global stack and a pointer to it is stored in the fourth cell of the former cluster.

The chief distinction between SS and NSS is that NSS represents the assignment of a structured term to a variable by simply associating the variable's local cell (using a pointer) with a global cluster containing a compact literal copy of that term, whereas SS represents the term more diffusely as a hierarchy of 'pure code' skeletons requiring interpretation in the context of various binding environments delocalized over the two stacks. Thus NSS generally provides virtually direct access (i.e., minimal use of pointers) to the structured data it has already computed, whilst SS does not. In fact, structure sharing can be viewed as a lazy constructor of data. When representing a set of linked assignments such as

$$\{x_i := f(y_j), y_j := g(z_k), z_k := NIL\}$$

generated by unifications in various steps i, j and k, it makes no attempt to construct the literal (fully dereferenced) values $g(NIL)$ and $f(g(NIL))$ of y_j and x_i. The pointers or molecules which it stores in the variables' cells are instead only a recipe for constructing those literal values should they ever be required (for instance, to report a goal solution). Besides this, a SS system frequently needs to access the components of structured terms when it attempts to unify those terms with others. In these various circumstances the implementation is in effect being forced to confront the low-level constructive operations which it previously evaded.

This assessment must be counterbalanced by observing that many executions generate structures which will not be involved subsequently either in producing dereferenced output or in attempting unifications. So one consideration when choosing between SS and NSS is the question of whether the expected executions will predominantly access structured data or merely construct it. SS broadly favours executions in the latter category because the task of building a molecule is trivial (very fast) compared with the tasks of dereferencing it or accessing its deep components during unification.

The choice must also take account of the potentially low memory consumption of SS systems. However, this feature should not be overrated: comparative studies have show that, in the absence of global stack garbage collection, SS may well consume more total memory than would NSS. This is because its compile-time stack allocation policy—always suboptimal and sometimes very much so—allocates global stack space to variables which, on purely syntactical grounds, *might* become components of structured terms computed during execution. By contrast, NSS allocates global stack space at run time, and only to the structured terms *actually* computed. Both approaches are in any case suboptimal if some global data becomes redundant as execution proceeds, since it will then be overlooked by the normal processes of local stack reclamation (other than backtracking).

In applications where individual computations are likely to occupy much less memory than that physically available, the relative memory demands of SS and NSS may be of little consequence (often differing by only 10–50% anyway). When this is so, one's choice should be based more strongly upon a comparison of expected processing speeds. Any comprehensive assessment of these is necessarily multifactorial, having to consider the input programs' accessing–constructing characteristics, the opportunities for optimizing the unification process and the host machine's address space, word structure and addressing mechanisms.

VII.4.2. Compilation

Most existing logic implementations execute programs interpretively. Consequently they are especially conducive to program development where the user frequently wishes to alter and rerun programs without confronting the tedious and time-consuming demands of repeated compilation. Tracing and debugging facilities are also easier to incorporate and use in an interpretive environment.

On the other hand, the compilation (translation) of a logic program into directly executable machine code offers, in principle, much greater opportunities for achieving efficient execution. The main reason for this is that an interpreter has to rely upon a single, general unification routine capable of handling any (call, heading) pair submitted to it. Usually, the more general a routine is, the less efficient it is in dealing with specific cases, because it always has to exercise provisions for circumstances which may not actually arise. A compiler can dispense with this general routine and instead produce, for each input procedure heading, a machine code unification segment specifically tailored to the heading's formal parameters. The basic run-time system then consists of the control routine, the input procedures with their headings compiled into machine code and any library routines, also in compiled code.

The only fully operational logic compilers currently available are those developed by David Warren for the DEC-10 machine. Their effectiveness in producing efficient object programs is particularly enhanced by the addition of *mode declarations* to input programs. These declare the expected forms of the actual parameters transmitted to the procedures during execution. For instance, the compilation of Program 40 would be made more effective by adding to it the declaration

$$\textbf{mode}\quad \textbf{reverse*}(+, +, -)$$

This declares that every time a **reverse*** call is activated, the first two actual parameters are not variables and the third one is. The compiler uses this knowledge to specialize the code generated for the headings of P1 and P2, effectively optimizing it for its intended mode of use.

A useful technique for implementing a sophisticated logic compiler which avoids the burden of writing the compiler itself in machine code is that known as *bootstrapping*. The compiler C is first written as a set P of logic procedures which describe all the standard compilational tasks of source inputting and compaction, parsing, symbol-table building, error diagnosis and code generation. Thus P is capable of solving any call of the form **compile**(*procedure-set, corresponding code*). A goal G is next composed which requests, as output, the code corresponding to P itself. The resulting program (P, G) can then be executed using any logic implementation already available and thus produces as output a machine code version of C—in other words, an effective, operational compiler for any other logic procedure set.

VII.4.3. Unification

Substantial opportunities for improving execution speed lie in the implementation of the unification mechanism. The algorithms most commonly used are variants of *Robinson's Algorithm*. In the logic programming context, this begins by loading two lists L1 and L2 with, respectively, the activated call's actual parameters and the selected procedure heading's formal parameters. A third list Θ serves to record the assignments generated in the course of matching the contents of L1 and L2. Initially Θ records—in some manner conducive to the consultation of Θ that become necessary later on in the algorithm—the currently unassigned status of the parameters' variables. If the algorithm terminates successfully, then the final state of Θ is the desired most general unifier for the step; otherwise no unifier exists.

The algorithm is essentially one principal loop, each ith cycle of which compares two expressions $t_1\Theta$ and $t_2\Theta$, where t_1 and t_2 are the ith members of L1 and L2, respectively. As usual, the postfixed Θ here denotes the application of the substitutions of terms for variables dictated by Θ in its current state. The various tests and outcomes of this cycle are as follows.

1. (a)   if either expression is a variable occurring in the other then the algorithm fails;

   (b)   if either expression is a variable not occurring in the other then the assignment of the latter to the former is recorded in Θ (thus updating Θ);

2.   if either expression is a constant and the other is either a different constant or a structured term then the algorithm fails;

3. (a)   if the expressions are structured terms having different principal functors then the algorithm fails;

   (b)   if the expressions are structured terms having identical principal functors then their argument lists are appended respectively to L1 and L2 (thus updating L1 and L2).

The algorithm terminates successfully only when all members of L1 and L2 have been compared without a failure occurring.

This description is necessarily only an abstraction of what actually takes place in a concrete implementation. The compared expressions $t_1\Theta$ and $t_2\Theta$ are not normally explicitly constructed. In particular, the nature of t_1 is ascertainable in a structure-sharing system only by analyzing the call's environment and any other environments to which the latter refers in turn.

Moreover, the updating of Θ by test 1(b) may assign values to variable cells in both this environment and preceding ones (when passing output to the call) as well as to variable cells in the new environment being created for the current step (when passing input to the procedure). These features give much scope to the implementor for optimizing the unification routine's tasks of accessing and updating the various environments on the stack(s). For instance, one design decision concerns whether to update the relevant variable cells as soon as some cycle updates Θ, or to store the assigned values temporarily in registers instead. In the former case, a failure to unify will make it necessary to identify and reset all those cells, whereas a successful outcome leaves them in precisely the state desired. In the latter case, a failure to unify leaves them in the state desired (i.e., unaltered) whereas after a successful outcome the values must be copied from the registers into the appropriate cells. Decisions of this kind are further complicated by space-saving optimizations (like LCO) which overwrite one frame by another. The research literature describes the minutiae of many such considerations.

Apart from the problems of accessing and updating variable cells, a major impediment to rapid unification is the test discriminating 1(a) from 1(b) which, given that one of the expressions is a variable, decides whether or not that variable occurs anywhere within the other expression. This test is generally called the *occur check* and serves to prevent nonsensical assignments like $x := f(x)$ from arising. The classic example often quoted poses an activated call $\mathbf{p}(f(u), u)$ and a heading $\mathbf{p}(x, x)$. The assignments $\{x := f(u), u := x\}$, whose net effect is $x := f(x)$, would give rise to infinite cycling in any subsequent attempt to dereference the value of x. Many implementations omit the occur check—or render its operation optional—on the grounds that the offending parameter structures rarely arise and that catering for them unreasonably impedes the majority of straightforward unifications. Others omit the test safely by allowing no more than one occurrence of any variable within a procedure heading, although this remedy places a rather unsatisfactory limitation upon one's programming style.

The implementor can further reduce the run-time unification burden by taking proper advantage of procedure indexing, since the compile-time construction of index tables is (implicitly) a partial match of each procedure's heading with anticipated classes of calls. A run-time attempt to unify a procedure's formal parameters with known actual parameters begins with the knowledge that some matching has already been achieved by virtue of that procedure's identification as a candidate for the call.

Futile, or otherwise undesired, attempts to unify can be eliminated to an arbitrary extent by the programmer's use of the cut operator (/), whose implementation normally entails only a simple updating of MRB and possibly some PB cells. The cut operation normally consumes much less time than the time saved through the elimination of superfluous untried candidates, provided it is used judiciously; when used with abandon the reverse may be true.

VII.5. Background

In 1972 the first practical implementation of Colmerauer's concept of PROLOG as a realization of Kowalski's idea of logic programming was undertaken at the University of Aix–Marseille by Roussel, taking advantage of the structure-sharing technique for resolution theorem proving newly discovered by Boyer and Moore (1972). It is described in a later report by Colmerauer et al. (1973). Written in ALGOL-W, it was both slow and highly consumptive of memory, chiefly because of its exaggerated anticipation of backtracking and its lack of reclamation mechanisms. Battani and Meloni (1973) then wrote an improved version in FORTRAN. This was subsequently transported to several other sites and so spawned a family of Marseille-PROLOG variants. The features and implementation of the version installed at Imperial College are described in the MSc thesis by Lichtman (1975), and the operation of Marseille-PROLOG from the user's viewpoint is explained in a reference manual by Roussel (1975).

By 1975, Marseille-like systems written in CDL for the ICL 1903A and System 4/70 computers were already operational in Hungary. A comprehensive guide to the prolific range of applications served by these and subsequent versions has been assembled by Santane-Toth and Szeredi (1982). More recent and more sophisticated Hungarian systems are now run mainly upon Siemens-7.755, IBM-3031 and VAX-11/80 machines and include the MPROLOG implementation: described by Bendl et al. (1980), this is claimed to be especially suitable for modular programming. Because of the rapidity with which these interpreters were made to serve serious computing applications, their authors felt compelled to augment the basic Marseille design with a variety of somewhat ad hoc mechanisms supporting, for instance, fast arithmetic, file handling and interfacing to utility routines compiled from lower-level languages. Those measures are seemingly implemented without particular regard for semantic purity, potentially adding corruptions to those already engendered by some of the control primitives of the Marseille design upon which the Hungarian systems were originally built. Some of the issues raised by the mixing of PROLOG with other languages are discussed by Szeredi (1981).

Important contributions to implementation technology were made in the mid-1970s by Bruynooghe (1976), who developed garbage-collection techniques for stack compaction and also implemented *tail recursion* (a variant of LCO which replaces certain recursions by iterations) in 1977. He subsequently circumvented the dangling-pointer problems of structure sharing by writing the first non-structure-sharing interpreter (Bruynooghe, 1982). His first system was written in PASCAL, but a new system written in the 'C' language for UNIX operation was implemented in 1979. Bruynooghe (1981) also initiated methods for 'intelligent backtracking', using run-time call-dependence analysis for detecting and eliminating futile computations. More elaborate schemes for selective backtracking were later devised by Pereira and Porto (1982).

Other major advances were meanwhile pursued by Warren and his colleagues at the University of Edinburgh. Marseille-PROLOG was operational there as early as 1974 and its deficiencies motivated Warren to develop his DEC-10 PROLOG compiler, now widely and justly acclaimed for its skilful design and programming techniques. The outstanding features which it pioneered include indexing and compilation of input procedures, the two-stack implementation of structure sharing and many carefully engineered optimizations aimed at reducing both processing time and memory consumption. The DEC-10 facility now comprises an interpreter as well as an in-core compiler in order to provide a dual-purpose environment for both developing and executing programs. Both components were written largely in PROLOG and rendered operational by bootstrapping. The original compiler design is described by Warren (1977a, 1977b). Later reports by Warren *et al.* (1977, 1979) include a guide for users and a comparison of the system's features with those of typical LISP implementations. The optimizing features of DEC-10 PROLOG are described by Warren (1979, 1980). His design has since been transported to other installations. For instance, both structure-sharing and non-structure-sharing derivatives from it have been established at Edinburgh University by Mellish (1982) for the PDP-11 computer, and many of its features have been incorporated into the Hungarian MPROLOG system.

Among the fastest available interpreters is Waterloo-PROLOG, created by Roberts (1977) at the University of Waterloo. Operating on IBM-370/158, IBM-3031 and IBM-4341 mainframes, it is structurally similar to Marseille-PROLOG but is more polished technically. Its impressive speed is due partly to its being written directly in assembly language and partly due to its lack of space-saving mechanisms. Like DEC-10 PROLOG, its assumption of a particular machine architecture restricts its portability. Roberts's account of his system is especially notable for its accuracy, clarity and completeness, in contrast to almost all the other literature on logic implementation.

Significant advances in implementation have also been made by Clark and McCabe at Imperial College. The first interpreter developed there was

IC-PROLOG. Written in PASCAL and established on both IBM-370 and CDC-6000 mainframes, this was used primarily for testing new control mechanisms. In particular it has served to confirm that the realization of control regimes governing sophisticated modes of execution (for example, coroutining and concurrency) can be achieved without mutilating the formalism's logical semantics. IC-PROLOG is variously described in papers by Clark, McCabe *et al.* (1979a, 1979b, 1980, 1982).

More recent work by Clark and McCabe has been directed toward microcomputer implementations. Their micro-PROLOG interpreter was initially designed to run under CP/M on Z80 chip machines such as the Research Machines 380Z and the North Star Horizon. Written in Z80 assembly code, it is non-structure-sharing and supports LCO. It is currently being adapted to a wide range of other small machines. Self-teaching primers for micro-PROLOG have been published by Clark and McCabe (1984) and by Ennals (1984). Micro-PROLOG supports Horn-clause logic augmented with pure extensions which usefully capture some of the syntactical generality of full FOPL; the standard version will run in 64 Kbytes with about 16 Kbytes occupied by the kernel interpreter.

The Japanese Fifth Generation Project has added a major impetus to implementation technology for logic programming. Because this project has such substantial implications for the field as a whole, it is discussed separately in Chapter VIII.

VIII BROADER CONTRIBUTIONS TO COMPUTING

Logic programming has many contributions to make to the general discipline of computing beyond the mere provision of yet another programming language. Logic had, of course, a history of usage in computing previous to the advent of logic programming, but that usage did not fit easily into the mainstream of computing activities, mainly because we did not then possess a simple and implementable computational interpretation of logic. The position now is entirely different. Logic can be used to represent data, programs, specifications and the relationships between them; it can be used for both object-level and metalevel descriptions; it can be used to describe the management of software as well as the software itself. The significance of logic programming is that it makes all these uses of logic mechanizable as well as founded upon a common computational theory, and thus brings unity to many formerly disparate activities and tools. This chapter surveys some of the contributions which logic programming has so far made to the theory, practice and technology of computing.

VIII.1. Computing Theory

The theory of computing contains that part of mathematics concerned with the study of effectively computable relations. It investigates the mathematical properties of the relations themselves, their definability in particular formalisms, their computability on particular machines and their meanings relative to particular schemes of interpretation. These and other aspects of the theory have traditionally been developed in a somewhat compartmentalized manner under such headings as recursive function theory, computability theory, formal semantics and so forth. A central tenet held by many proponents of logic programming is that it is capable of unifying, underpinning and rationalizing these various subtheories. It is held not merely in the theoretical sense that logic underlies mathematics in general, but in the more practical sense that logic programming seems able to subsume, in a natural way, the representational and operational characteristics of a wide range of computing formalisms and associated theories. In this section we briefly outline some of the ways in which logic programming has contributed to the theory of computing.

VIII.1.1. Representability and Computability

In respect of any proposed computing formalism it is natural to ask what it is capable of representing and computing. A minimal requirement for almost all practical purposes is the representation of number. In logic programming the requirement can be met by providing any fixed constant symbol, such as 0, to represent 'zero' and any fixed functor, such as s, to represent 'successor of'. The natural numbers can then be represented by the terms 0, $s(0)$, $s(s(0))$ etc. Less trivially, we also want to be able to define on any such representation all those relations which one might wish to compute over numbers. It was Robert Hill who first proved that all such relations could be so defined; specifically, he showed that Horn-clause logic is sufficient for defining all effectively computable functions over the domain $\{0, s(0), \ldots\}$ and that no functors other than 0 and s are required for this purpose. A more general account of the adequacy of Horn-clause logic is given in his report (Hill, 1974).

It is rather more usual in the study of computable functions to define them over domains constructed from a richer class of symbols than $\{0, s\}$. From any finite sets ('alphabets') of constants, say $\{a, b\}$, and functors, say $\{f, g\}$, one can build a domain by pooling together all those terms constructible from those alphabets' constants and functors; this domain $\{a, b, f(a), g(a), f(b), f(g(a)), \ldots\}$ is called a *Herbrand universe*. Andreka and Nemeti (1976) have shown that every computable function over any Herbrand universe can be defined by some Horn-clause logic program. This generalization of Hill's result was proved using the fact that every Herbrand universe is countable, that is, can be put in 1:1 correspondence with the natural numbers. Andreka and Nemeti showed further that a logic program for computing a function over a Herbrand universe can be constructed using no other constants or functors than those in the alphabets of that universe.

The most well-rehearsed notion of computability is that of *Turing computability*: the class of all functions which can be computed 'effectively' (i.e., systematically and finitely) in any machine implementation of any formalism is identified (by an empirically true conjecture known as Church's Thesis) as the class of all functions computable by a universal Turing machine (UTM). It was Tärnlund (1977) who first investigated the computability theory of logic programs in the UTM paradigm. He constructed about half a dozen simple Horn clauses representing the essential mechanism of the UTM and then proved that every Turing-computable function could be computed by resolution from those clauses in response to appropriate goals. In addition, the well-known fact that no algorithm exists which is capable of deciding whether an arbitrary Turing computation will terminate (the 'halting problem') is then transformed to the equivalent fact that no algorithm exists which is capable of deciding whether an arbitrary Horn-clause program offers a finite successful resolution computation; this is in turn just a variant of the fact that the validity of arbitrary sentences of first-order logic is not totally decidable.

The class of effectively computable functions can also be characterized as the class of *partial recursive functions*; these are constructible from a set of base functions using the operations of composition, primitive recursion and minimization. Sebelik and Stepanek (1980) have shown that all partial recursive functions are computable in Horn-clause logic; their proof was achieved simply by representing the base functions and construction rules for partial recursive functions in Horn-clause logic. Both they and Tärnlund showed that computational universality was also attainable within a restricted form of Horn-clause logic ('binary' form) in which no procedure has more than one call. In a similar fashion, Horn-clause formulations of the computable functions representable by Kleene recursion equations and Herbrand–Gödel equations have been given by van Emden (1977b) and Kowalski (1983b).

One of the simplest universal formalisms to describe is the class of *Markov algorithms*. Any such algorithm repeatedly rewrites a current character string x as a new string z by replacing some occurrence of a substring u in x by another string v in accordance with a given set of replacement rules, continuing to do so until some replacement v contains a special terminator symbol; the given rule set characterizes the function computed between the string's initial state x and final state y. It is easy to cast this scheme in Horn-clause logic by using top-level clauses of the form

rewrite(x, y) **if**   **replace**(u, v), **substitute**(u, v, x, z), **proceed**(y, z, v)
proceed(y, z, v) **if**   **has-terminator**(v) **then** $y = z$
                                                    else   **rewrite**(z, y)

with appropriate clauses defining **substitute** and **has-terminator**. The only additional ingredient is then a set of **replace** assertions, such as

$$\mathbf{replace}(A.x.B.NIL, C.x.NIL)$$

characterizing the function to be computed. As it happens, the standard logic program execution strategy corresponds directly to the rule-selection strategy customarily prescribed for Markov algorithms. The execution is initiated by posing a goal? **rewrite**(x, y) with some concrete input string in place of x. The theoretically inclined reader may wish to complete the details of this formulation [a brief and simple exposition of Markov algorithms is given by Elson (1973)] and then provide a formal proof of its Markov equivalence and hence its universality.

These various studies all lead to the reassuring, if unsurprising, confirmation that Horn-clause logic is a universal computing formalism: it is equivalent in computational power to all the other universal (and mutually equivalent) formalisms traditionally studied in the theory of computability. Because of this, and because logic programming is now so well-established in both theory and practice, it is strictly unnecessary—and possibly of no particular benefit—to deploy non-standard logics (such as fuzzy, temporal or modal logics) for computational purposes; it is more worthwhile to seek first to achieve their desired function by formulating and implementing them in standard logic.

VIII.1.2. Semantics

The study of programming language semantics is concerned fundamentally with the assignment of meaning to the constituents of programs. In general the meaning of any such constituent is relative both to its context within a given program and to some prescribed way of evaluating it using that program. For instance, from any set P of logic procedures we may select any one of its predicate symbols, say **p**, and ask what **p** 'means' according to P. This question presupposes a correspondence, partly determined by P, between the predicate symbols and some other entities constituting their meanings. Thus the meaning of **p** will be some such entity e. We call e the *denotation* of **p** in P: according to P, **p** denotes (means) e. What might such entities usefully be? For a computational semantics the effectively computable relations are an obvious choice.

The first comprehensive investigation of the semantics of logic programs was undertaken by van Emden and Kowalski (1976). They developed and related three distinct kinds of semantics, each of which determines a computable relation as the denotation of a predicate symbol. The first kind, called the *operational* (or procedural) *semantics*, gives the denotation of **p** in P as the relation whose every tuple t is such that $\mathbf{p}(t)$ is provable from P using some sound inference system, that is, the relation $\{t \mid P \vdash \mathbf{p}(t)\}$. The provability of $\mathbf{p}(t)$ from P is equivalent to the existence of a refutation demonstrating the inconsistency of the program (P, G : ? $\mathbf{p}(t)$). By regarding a refutation as a computation and by observing that systems such as resolution exist for generating such computations, the term 'operational semantics' becomes both justified and analogous to the traditional way of establishing the semantics of conventional programming languages—namely by defining an execution mechanism (typically on some abstract machine) and then explaining a program's meaning in terms of what is computed by applying that mechanism to the program. In summary, the meaning of **p** in this treatment is the relation computed by the program (P, G) using sound inference. The most attractive feature of this semantics is that, although operational in character, it does not suffer the complexities entailed in formulating the operational features of typical procedural languages, because the description of an inference step is so much simpler than the description of those languages' control mechanisms.

The second semantics given by van Emden and Kowalski is unique to logic programming. This gives the denotation of **p** in P as the relation whose every tuple t is such that $\mathbf{p}(t)$ is logically implied by P, that is, the relation $\{t \mid P \vDash \mathbf{p}(t)\}$. Note that this treatment is entirely free of operational concepts, and so is called a *non-procedural semantics*. In Chapter I it was shown that the concepts of interpretation and model underpinned the notion of logical implication. To say that P implies $\mathbf{p}(t)$ is to say that every satisfying interpretation (model) for P is also a satisfying interpretation for $\mathbf{p}(t)$. Consequently this second treatment is called the *model-theoretic semantics*. It has a most attractive simplicity: the meaning of a logic program consists of what its statements logically imply.

The third semantics is also non-procedural but is directly analogous to the semantics usually provided for programs written in the language of recursive function definitions. It depends for its formalization upon concepts somewhat more intricate than those required for the other two semantics, which are perhaps best introduced in relation to a simple, if artificial, example. Consider the following procedure C selected from some procedure set P:

$$C : \quad \mathbf{p}(x, y) \quad \textbf{if} \quad \mathbf{q}(x), \mathbf{r}(y)$$

An instance C' of C is obtained by uniformly substituting terms for the variables of C, as in

$$C' : \quad \mathbf{p}(x, B) \quad \textbf{if} \quad \mathbf{q}(x), \mathbf{r}(B)$$

(substituting B for y). A ground instance of C is an instance of C containing no variables, so that every atom (predicate) in it is a ground atom, as in

$$C' : \quad \mathbf{p}(A, B) \quad \textbf{if} \quad \mathbf{q}(A), \mathbf{r}(B)$$

Consider next the set P* of all ground instances of all the procedures in P that can be obtained by substituting for the variables just those terms occurring in the Herbrand universe H(P) constructed from just the constants and functors in P. Thus if, for example, A and B were the only constants in P and there were no functors in P, then H(P) would be just the set of terms $\{A, B\}$ and the ground instances of C in P* would be

$$\mathbf{p}(A, A) \quad \textbf{if} \quad \mathbf{q}(A), \mathbf{r}(A)$$
$$\mathbf{p}(A, B) \quad \textbf{if} \quad \mathbf{q}(A), \mathbf{r}(B)$$
$$\mathbf{p}(B, A) \quad \textbf{if} \quad \mathbf{q}(B), \mathbf{r}(A)$$
$$\mathbf{p}(B, B) \quad \textbf{if} \quad \mathbf{q}(B), \mathbf{r}(B)$$

In following this course we are preparing an interpretation of P, over domain H(P), in the manner outlined in Chapter I. Freely assign to every antecedent atom in P* a value of t or f, subject only to the restriction that identical atoms are assigned identical values. Next, for every instance in P*, if the antecedent atoms have all been assigned t then assign t to the consequent atom. Finally, all consequent atoms in P* which have not been assigned t are then assigned f. Let I denote the set of all antecedent atoms assigned t and let J denote the set of all consequent atoms assigned t. It can then be shown that the interpretation of P on the basis of these truth assignments is a model for P **iff** $J \subseteq I$.

The assignment of truth values to those instances of P formed, as above, from the substitution of terms from H(P) for the variables is called a *Herbrand interpretation*. [In much of the technical literature a Herbrand interpretation is defined as any set of ground atoms formed by substituting terms from H(P) for variables in atoms of P, as an abbreviated way of talking about ground atoms which have been assigned t.] A Herbrand interpretation which satisfies P is then called a *Herbrand model* for P.

In the treatment above, once I has been chosen J becomes uniquely determined by the rules given; in other words, there exists a function T mapping atom sets to atom sets such that $T(I) = J$ and generally referred to as the *transformation* associated with P. We now come to an important theorem: for any procedure set P there exist atom sets I satisfying $T(I) = I$ known as the *fixpoints* of T, and amongst them there exists exactly one which is a subset of all the others and is known as the *least fixpoint* of T, denoted lfp(T). In summary, every procedure set P has many models, including Herbrand models I all of which satisfy $T(I) \subseteq I$. The smallest such I, called the least Herbrand model, also happens to be the smallest one satisfying $T(I) = I$ and is therefore the least fixpoint of T.

The denotation of any predicate symbol **p** in P can then be defined as the relation $\{t \mid \mathbf{p}(t) \in \mathrm{lfp}(T)\}$. This definition, developed by van Emden and Kowalski, characterizes the *fixpoint semantics* of logic programs. In this semantics a procedure set P is viewed in terms of its associated fixpoint equation $I = T(I)$, which can be read as saying that the tuples computable from P (loosely, the solutions of its consequent atoms) are exactly those that can be evaluated by the calls (antecedent atoms) of P; the collective meaning of all the predicate symbols in P is taken to be the collection of relations formed from those tuples which constitutes the smallest I satisfying the fixpoint equation. This reading is directly analogous to the fixpoint interpretation of a program of the form $\mathbf{f}(z) := T[\mathbf{f}](z)$ in the language of recursive function definitions: the meaning of **f** in the program is taken to be that unique function which is the least fixpoint of T.

Some useful insight into the nature of T can be gained by considering the following way of accumulating a collection of ground assertions (atoms). Let this collection initially be just the empty set $\varnothing$. Then $T(\varnothing)$ adds to our collection all the ground instances of the assertions occurring in P. Applying T in turn to this contribution gives $T(T(\varnothing)) = T^2(\varnothing)$, which comprises those ground assertions immediately derivable by resolving the procedures of P bottom-up with the assertions in $T(\varnothing)$. More generally, each successive application of T yields those assertions which are immediate logical consequences of P together with those assertions already accumulated. For this reason T has come to be known as the *immediate consequence function* associated with P. The set of all ground atomic logical consequences of P is then the union of all sets $T^i(\varnothing)$, with i ranging over the natural numbers. These consequences are, of course, exactly those calls solvable by using P; the union therefore embraces the entirety of the tuples computable from P. Since we have already required this set to be $\{t \mid \mathbf{p} \text{ occurs in P}, \mathbf{p}(t) \in \mathrm{lfp}(T)\}$ it follows that we must have $\mathrm{lfp}(T) = \cup_i T^i(\varnothing)$, which is in exact accordance with the well-known Kleene (1952) characterization of least fixpoints.

The main achievement of the van Emden–Kowalski study is to provide elegant proofs that the operational, model-theoretic and fixpoint semantics for Horn-clause programs are equivalent in the sense of determining identical denotations for the predicate symbols. The equivalence of the first two is owed to Gödel's Completeness Theorem for FOPL relating provability to validity. The equivalence of the second two is established by showing that lfp(T) is the least Herbrand model of P and that $P \vDash \mathbf{p}(t)$ if and only if $\mathbf{p}(t)$ is true in that model.

In a subsequent paper, Apt and van Emden (1982) present the least-fixpoint semantics in the formal setting of complete lattice theory and then use it to prove the soundness and completeness of the standard execution strategy for Horn-clause programs. They also define the *greatest fixpoint* of T and use it to characterize unsolvable programs which fail in finite time owing to the absence of successful computations in the search space.

Systematic and formal presentations of the applications of the fixpoint theory of logic programs can be found in the monographs by Clark (1979) and Lloyd (1984), whilst a recent semantic analysis of logic programs based upon *optimal fixpoints* has been given by Lassez and Maher (1983).

VIII.1.3. Correctness of Execution Strategy

A major attraction of logic as a programming language from the viewpoint of implementation technology is that execution strategies for it can be analysed rigorously within the well-established framework of proof theory. In particular, interpreters purporting to implement variants of the standard strategy can be verified by exploiting known results in the theory of resolution inference systems. In what follows we present some of the soundness and completeness results established for resolution as an execution strategy.

In its most general form resolution applies to general clauses of the form $L_1 \vee L_2 \vee \ldots \vee L_m$, where each L_i is either a positive literal (atom, predicate) or a negative literal (negated atom). Each step takes two clauses (the parents) such that some positive literal in one of them and some negative literal in the other contain predicates unifiable by some Θ; we say that these literals have been 'resolved upon'. The step produces a third clause (the resolvent) $C\Theta$, where C is the disjunction of all the literals, if any, in the parents other than those resolved upon. The selection of parents and literals resolved upon is arbitrary. Robinson (1965) showed that resolution is correct—that is, both sound and complete—in that the empty clause $\square$ is derivable from an input set S of clauses by some finite sequence of resolution steps if and only if S is unsatisfiable.

For the most part, present-day logic programming systems restrict the input set S to Horn clauses each of which has no more than one positive literal, and also impose upon each resolution step the restrictions that (i) one parent must be an assertion or implication (i.e., a procedure of some sort), (ii) the other must be the most recent resolvent and must be a goal statement and (iii) there must exist some fixed selection rule which determines uniquely the call resolved upon in the latter parent. Since (i) selects as parents, clauses known as Definite clauses (having exactly one positive literal whilst (ii) and (iii) characterize SL-resolution (Linear resolution with Selector function), this inference system is technically described as *SLD-resolution* (or, formerly, *LUSH resolution*) and was first described by

Kowalski (1974b); a more comprehensive introduction of variants of SL-resolution is given in the paper by Kowalski and Kuehner (1971). The correctness of general resolution makes it reasonably easy to prove, as a special case, that SLD-resolution is also correct in the simple sense that $\square$ is derivable from S if and only if S is unsatisfiable.

A rather more detailed characterization of SLD's correctness is obtained by incorporating consideration of both the goal solutions (answer substitutions) computable through the derivation of $\square$ and the computation rule used to compute them. As a preliminary, a correct answer substitution Θ for a program $(P, G : \quad ?\mathbf{g}_1, \ldots, \mathbf{g}_n)$ is defined as a substitution Θ such that P implies the universal closure of $(\mathbf{g}_1, \ldots, \mathbf{g}_n)\Theta$. For instance, if G is the goal $?\mathbf{g}(x)$ and P implies $(\forall y)\mathbf{g}(t(2, y))$ then $\Theta = \{x := t(2, y)\}$ is a correct answer substitution for (P, G). A computation rule is any fixed rule which determines uniquely which of the current goal's calls is resolved upon in each SLD-step; for example, standard PROLOG's computation rule is 'select first call'. The following (weak) SLD-completeness result was then established by Hill (1974):

> Every correct answer substitution Θ of a logic program is computable using some computation rule by SLD-resolution.

Note that this theorem does not say that any one computation rule exists which delivers all the correct answer substitutions for the program; it only says that the totality of available computation rules covers all the correct Θ's.

A stronger result known as (strong) SLD-completeness does in fact prevail, which establishes that the set of computable correct answer substitutions is independent of the computation rule used: this result is especially useful for guaranteeing the completeness of sophisticated call-selection strategies such as dataflow coroutining. Combined with the definition of soundness of resolution, the result yields the following theorem ensuring the correctness of SLD-resolution:

> For any particular computation rule applied to a program, every Θ is a correct answer substitution for the program **iff** it is computable through the derivation of $\square$ by SLD-resolution.

Various proofs of this and associated theorems have been given by Apt and van Emden (1982), by Clark (1979) and by Lloyd (1984). Of particular interest is the use which these proofs make of the fixpoint and model-theoretic properties of logic programs; the verification theory for the execution strategy draws strength directly from the rigorously established and interrelated characterizations of the programming language's semantics.

It is important to note that these various correctness results apply to the SLD inference system rather than to any particular proof procedure constructed from it by stipulating a search strategy. As observed in Chapter V, the standard PROLOG proof procedure is *unfair* in that its depth-first backtracking search rule, when confronted with an infinite search space, fails to do justice to the completeness of the underlying SLD inference system, although it does safeguard soundness. The practical import of this is that the verification of any logic interpreter requires analysis of its search rule as well as reliance upon the standard correctness results for resolution. An example of an implementation which does realize a fair execution, through the use of breadth-first search, is the LOGLISP system described by Robinson and Sibert (1980), which embeds logic within LISP.

VIII.1.4. Negation

In Chapter III we noted that a logic interpreter can, with some restrictions, safely execute quasi-negated ($\sim$) procedure calls by treating failure as negation: $\neg p$ is inferred from failure to infer p. This device is very effective operationally and spares the programmer the tedium of encoding explicitly 'negative' information in his programs. Instead, whatever he omits to say in the program is treated as logically false. This economy in programming style is clearly essential in such applications as databases: we want to say what is in the database, but do not want to enumerate the infinitude of things that are not in it.

The deductive power obtained through the use of the *negation-as-failure* rule is nonetheless not as great as that provided by strict classical negation ($\neg$) and considerable research effort has been devoted to the problem of making a precise determination of the discrepancy between $\sim$ and $\neg$. Observe that a general clause, which is any disjunction of literals, can be presented in the following equivalent forms:

$$A_1 \vee \ldots \vee A_m \vee \neg B_1 \vee \ldots \vee \neg B_n$$
$$A_1 \vee \ldots \vee A_m \quad \text{if} \quad B_1, \ldots, B_n$$
$$A_1 \qquad\qquad \text{if} \quad B_1, \ldots, B_n, \neg A_2, \ldots, \neg A_m$$

The restriction to Horn clauses ($m \leqslant 1$) is equivalent to disallowing the negated calls $\neg A_i$ in the third form of the above clause. It might be thought that, since clausal form is expressively equivalent to standard FOPL, this restriction must entail some loss of expressiveness relative to FOPL. However, this clearly cannot be the case, since we know from Section VIII.1.1 that Horn-clause logic defines all computable relations. What we lose instead is some freedom of style. Negation-as-failure succeeds partially in making up for this loss. It is one candidate solution to the so-called 'negation problem' of logic programming—the problem of finding extensions to

Horn-clause logic which (i) make the result closely approximate to general clausal form, (ii) can be implemented effectively, (iii) can be reconciled with the standard procedural interpretation and (iv) respect the semantics of logic (and hence do not violate the correctness requirement).

Negation-as-failure was first justified by Clark (1978), who proved that the rule preserved soundness subject to the *closed-world assumption* (CWA), according to which the program's procedure set P represents all the knowledge to be had about the relations named in it. This is equivalent to assuming that P is implicitly augmented with the so-called *completion* of P, written comp(P), which consists of the only-if counterparts of all the procedures together with an axiomatization of the identity ($=$) relation. For instance, if P is the set

$$P1 : \quad \mathbf{a}(y) \quad \mathbf{if} \quad \mathbf{b}(y)$$
$$P2 : \quad \mathbf{a}(2)$$
$$P3 : \quad \mathbf{b}(3)$$

then comp(P) contains the sentences

$$C1 : \quad (\mathbf{b}(y) \vee y = 2) \quad \mathbf{if} \quad \mathbf{a}(y)$$
$$C2 : \quad y = 3 \quad \mathbf{if} \quad \mathbf{b}(y)$$

so that P and comp(P) then jointly imply the following **iff**-definitions of the relations **a** and **b**:

$$D1 : \quad \mathbf{a}(x) \quad \mathbf{iff} \quad (\exists y)(x = y, \mathbf{b}(y)) \vee x = 2$$
$$D2 : \quad \mathbf{b}(x) \quad \mathbf{iff} \quad x = 3$$

Note that this augmentation strictly implies negative facts such as $\neg \mathbf{b}(1)$ which are not strictly implied by P alone. Clark's justification of negation-as-failure rests on the view that the programmer intends his program to declare D1–D2, but only actually writes P1–P3 and leaves C1–C2 to stand by default, since they are computationally superfluous.

The correctness results for the rule require two preliminary definitions. The *Herbrand base* B(P) of P is the set of all ground predicates (atoms) constructible by substituting, for variables in the predicates of P, terms from the Herbrand universe H(P) of P; in essence it encompasses all the ground calls which one might conceivably wish to investigate using P. The *finite failure set* F(P) of P is the set of those ground predicates in B(P) which, when posed as goals and executed with P using SLD-resolution, fail (i.e., are unsolvable) in finite time—that is, yield finite search spaces containing no refutations. Negation-as-failure is then sound in that, for a standard Horn-clause procedure set P, we have

$$\text{comp}(P) \vDash \neg A \quad \mathbf{if} \quad A \in F(P)$$

What this means is that if a ground goal ? $\sim$A is executed in the standard way by attempting to solve **A**, and if that attempt finitely fails, then it is sound to infer $\neg$A from the closed-world assumption. (Clark's proof of this is actually more generous in allowing $\sim$ calls to appear in the clause bodies in P as well as in the initial goal.) This is because comp(P), implicitly part of the executing program, then implies $\neg$A.

The restriction of this analysis to ground calls is not critical. If a goal ? $\sim$A contains variables then finite failure of the ensuing call **A** solves the goal with no difficulties; however, if **A** is solved with some binding to at least one of its variables, then (as explained in Chapter III) a control error ought to be issued—this outcome potentially entails loss of completeness, though not of soundness.

The completeness properties of negation-as-failure have proved to be much more problematic. Jaffar, Lassez and Lloyd (1983) have recently presented an intricate proof that negation-as-failure is complete for a standard procedure set P in that

$$A \in F(P) \quad \text{if} \quad \text{comp}(P) \vDash \neg A, \ A \in B(P)$$

which says that a ground goal ? $\sim$A is necessarily solvable by the finite failure of the call **A** whenever the closed-world assumption implies $\neg$A. The potential loss of completeness when $\sim$A contains variables has already been observed. Worse still, completeness is further compromised when $\sim$ calls appear in clause bodies in P. This is because the operational treatment of $\sim$ in the negation-as-failure rule does not make **A** and $\sim\sim$A and **A if** $\sim$A all equivalent as does the classical interpretation of $\sim$ as $\neg$. Consequently a call $\sim$A which ought to be solvable according to the CWA may actually give rise to a non-terminating execution, in which case we do not have $A \in F(P)$. This shows clearly that although negation-as-failure is justified by using the CWA, it is actually weaker than that assumption. An excellent exposition of these matters is given by Lloyd (1984), whilst examples of simple pathological programs which expose the problems arising from allowing $\sim$ in clause bodies can be found in the book by Kowalski (1979a).

A most interesting alternative approach to the negation problem has recently been put forward by Gabbay and Sergot (1984). They point out that negation-as-failure is restricted to either confirming or denying any particular call, and is incapable of catering for the third option of concluding that the call is neither confirmable nor deniable. They propose a new form of negation, here denoted by $\neg^*$, which means 'leads to undesirable consequences (such as inconsistency)'. The database of facts and rules over which a goal is executed is, in their treatment, comprised of two parts P and N; P contains positive (true) facts, whilst N contains negative (false) facts. The meaning of $\neg^*$ can then be specified as follows:

$$(P, N) \vdash \neg^*A \quad \textbf{iff} \quad (P, A) \vdash B \text{ where } B \in N$$

Thus the negation of **A** cannot be inferred simply from failure to show **A** using (P, N); instead, it can only be inferred by showing that the assumption of **A** and P leads to some negative fact in N.

This scheme is called *negation-as-inconsistency* by its authors, since the inferral of $\neg^*A$ is made upon determining that **A** is inconsistent with P in the sense that their joint assumption implies some statement **B** which the programmer has explicitly arranged to be false according to N. Gabbay and Sergot show that negations-as-failure and -inconsistency coincide when N is restricted to just those predicates **A** which belong to the finite failure set of P, and they also show that negation-as-inconsistency is weaker than classical negation by pointing out that it is still possible to construct (P, N) such that $(P, N) \vdash A$ but $\neg^*\neg^*A$ finitely fails from (P, N).

VIII.1.5. Metalevel Reasoning

One of the most interesting and potentially far-reaching features of logic is its capacity to represent *metalevel* concepts. A simple example of such a concept in the logic programming context could be the notion of what is computable (inferrable) from a set of procedures. Consider, for instance, the following sentence describing the negation-as-failure rule:

$$\textbf{infer } \neg x \textbf{ from } y \quad \textbf{if} \quad \neg \textbf{infer } x \textbf{ from } y$$

Here y, x and $\neg x$ refer to constituents of an object-level system, in this case to various program statements in the Horn-clause *object language* (OL). The symbols **infer**, $\neg$**infer** and **if**, on the other hand, are constituents of the *metalanguage* (ML) in which we describe features of the object-level system.

If we regard OL as the language in which concrete programs are composed and executed then ML becomes a language for reasoning about the composition and execution of programs; that is, it becomes a language in which we can construct program-manipulating tools such as interpreters, verifiers, editors or operating systems. The metalanguage clearly has much to contribute to the formalization and implementation of such tasks as program construction, analysis and execution—in short, to software technology. What is especially interesting is the fact that ML can itself be simply Horn-clause logic and thus realizable through the logic implementations already available. This powerful dual role of logic was recognized and exploited even in the early days of logic programming: simple interpreters written in conventional languages were used to bootstrap into existence more refined versions which were themselves written (more conveniently) in logic, these versions constituting metalevel descriptions of how other logic programs were to be executed.

All interpreters in existence today offer the programmer some capability for writing logic programs which manipulate other programs, through the simple expedient of using particular kinds of terms to represent program constituents. For example, a structured term $p(x)$ appearing in a metalevel program may be used to represent a predicate **p**(x) in some object-level program. A number of powerful program manipulations enabled by the passing of such terms through metavariables are explained by Clark and McCabe (1984) for the micro-PROLOG system, whose design philosophy is strongly based upon metalevel capability.

The use of a single language to serve the roles of both OL and ML is called *amalgamation*, and in order to be effective needs to make use of some definition Pr (written in the language) of the *provability relation*. The construction and analysis of Pr for Horn-clause logic was pioneered by Kowalski (1979a). The foundation of his construction, in the simplest formulation of provability, is a predicate **demo**("x", "y") which is read as

> the sentence x named by "x" is provable from
> the sentence y named by "y"

The purpose of Pr is then to provide a definition of the **demo** relation. The condition for this being achieved correctly is expressible as

$$\text{Pr} \vdash \textbf{demo}("x", "y") \quad \textbf{iff} \quad x \vdash y$$

and is identified by Kowalski as a *reflection principle* of the kind proposed by Weyrauch (1980); it expresses the requirement that the metalevel *simulation* (of the proof of y using x) which results from executing the program (Pr, ? **demo**("x", "y")) at the metalevel shall be equivalent to the direct execution of the program $(x, ?\,y)$ at the object level. Using Horn-clause logic, the metalevel statement of the negation-as-failure inference rule would be somewhat as follows, where "$not(x)$" and "y" would be replaced by some suitable concrete terms representing, respectively, a negated ($\neg$) predicate and a procedure set : —

$$\textbf{demo}("not(x)", "y") \quad \textbf{if} \quad \sim \textbf{demo}(x, y)$$

Such a statement might then form part of a logic interpreter itself written in logic, describing an object-level execution strategy through the use of the **demo** relation.

A more up to date account of the metalogical capability of Horn-clause logic and its applications to program reasoning is given by Bowen and

Kowalski (1982). They also discuss the potential of the OL-ML amalgamation for resolving certain long-held criticisms of classical logic, specifically its monotonicity (e.g., see Minsky, 1975; Bobrow, 1980) and its susceptibility to the frame problem (e.g., see Raphael, 1971). These problems are briefly outlined in turn below.

Classical logic is *monotonic* in that the result of augmenting any set S of sentences with some other sentence s never reduces, and quite possibly increases, the set of provable consequences. We can express this fact symbolically as

$$\text{for all S, s and } \mathbf{c}, \ S \cup \{s\} \vdash \mathbf{c} \quad \textbf{if} \quad S \vdash \mathbf{c}$$

from which it is apparent that monotonicity is a property of the logic's provability relation ⊢. The basic objections to monotonicity are usually raised in connection with applications involving dynamically changing knowledge bases. As a trivial example, suppose that the current state of a knowledge base S enables us to infer some conclusion **c**. Depending upon the inference system used, it may be that **c** is a necessary logical consequence of S or it may be that **c** is merely inferred as plausible in default of contrary knowledge. Suppose that the system is now explicitly informed that ¬**c** holds, for example, by adding to S the sentence s = ¬**c**. In this new state of the system we might require that **c** now be uninferrable, that is, require non-monotonic behaviour. But classical logic does not behave in this way since its montonicity insists that **c** shall continue to be inferrable from $S \cup \{\neg \mathbf{c}\}$. In fact, if $S \vdash \mathbf{c}$ then the augmented base $S \cup \{\neg \mathbf{c}\}$ is necessarily inconsistent. Kowalski (1979a) has argued that the naive objection to classical logic's monotonicity might be overcome by treating inconsistency as a natural and useful outcome of certain kinds of transition in knowledge base evolution and using it positively to guide the subsequent restoration of consistency, for instance, by using it to identify assumptions which ought now to be abandoned, modified or otherwise reduced in status. The paper by Bowen and Kowalski (1982) gives an interesting illustration of the contribution which OL-ML amalgamation makes to this thesis in the context of a simple database management system. Unfortunately, the effects of monotonicity have tempted others to resort to other (typically many-valued) forms of logic or even to abandon logic altogether.

Confusingly, perhaps, existing interpreters may not, in any case, behave monotonically. For instance, negation-as-failure is non-monotonic because it is always possible to augment a sentence set so as to make some conclusion **c** inferrable when formerly it was not, in which case the former consequence ∼**c** is no longer a consequence. Thus logic programming in practice has been variously criticized both for being monotonic and for not being so, depending upon the accuser's viewpoint.

The *frame problem* of logic can also be regarded as a problem associated with representing and achieving change in knowledge bases. A simple example will suffice. Suppose we wish the base to represent a dynamically varying list, which at some instant might be $L = (A,B,C)$ and represented by the following array-like assertion set:

item(A, 1)
item(B, 2)
item(C, 3)   **length**(3)

Suppose next that we want the list to be extended by adding a fourth element D, so that the next state should become representable by

item(A, 1)
item(B, 2)
item(C, 3)
item(D, 4)   **length**(4)

The frame problem arises in the attempt to describe this extension process in logic. For then it is apparently necessary to name and relate the old and new states of the base. So instead of writing, in general, **item**(u, i) we write **item**(u, i, L) to express that L is the state in which u is the ith element, and write **length**(L, n) in place of **length**(n) to express that the length of the list is n in state L. If the state which results from adding v to L is named $ext(L, v)$, the contents of this new state can be related to the old contents by the sentences

item(u, i, $ext(L, v)$) **if** **item**(u, i, L)
item(v, i, $ext(L, v)$) **if** **length**(L, $i-1$)
length($ext(L, v)$, i) **if** **length**(L, $i-1$)

The first of these sentences is an example of a *frame axiom*: it serves to identify those facts in the base which are preserved (carried over) during a state transition. Large state-space problem formulations may require many classes of facts to be so preserved. In the present example we are declaring that if u is the ith element in one state then it continues to be whenever the list is extended to yield the new state.

Kowalski (1979a) identifies two aspects of the frame problem: first, the multiplicity of frame axioms required for realistic applications, and, second, the difficulty of controlling them efficiently when invoking them bottom-up in order to reason forward from the initial state toward the goal state. His suggested remedies are, respectively, the use of a single generalized frame axiom capable of accessing a separate database identifying all properties to be preserved under various kinds of state transition, and the proposal that this frame axiom be executed top-down so as to make its use immune to the combinatorial explosion of facts unrelated to the goal which characterizes bottom-up reasoning.

Studies of the frame problem can be cast as investigations about provability and naming. In an ideal implementation of the extension of the list (A, B, C) to (A, B, C, D) we might require the system to recognize that the extension process preserves the original members and their associated positions, rather than redundantly recompute them through the frame axiom. In effect we want the system to recognize and exploit an (approximately) monotonic aspect of the extension process by which most of what was provable in the old state remains so in the next. The implementation might also be capable of recognizing those situations (typically deterministic ones) in which only the current state need be maintained, yielding up both its name and its allocated memory to its successor. This behaviour is, of course, exactly what conventional programmers achieve using destructive assignment, although the economies thereby attained are offset by the resulting loss of semantic clarity. Kowalski (1983b) has indicated ways in which this mechanism might be invisibly elicited from a program by incorporating appropriate **demo** calls in it which express the justification for implementing destructive assignment on the grounds of what remains provable through a state transition. At present, however, there is no well-developed metalevel formulation on which we might build satisfactory programming styles and optimally efficient implementation techniques conducive to such updating mechanisms. The discovery of such a formulation is regarded as a high-priority research objective.

Finally, logic as a programming language, or rather its manifestation in the guise of PROLOG, has often been criticized for offering weak control mechanisms. It is true that, for the most part, logic programmers have had to make do with a rather arbitrary and incoherent range of control annotations and built-in calls in order to procure the desired run-time effects. It is now generally accepted that development of the uses of the metalanguage will largely nullify these criticisms. Accounts of *metalevel control* over program execution can be found in papers by Pereira (1982) and by Gallaire and Lasserre (1982).

The significance of the Horn-clause metalanguage in the wider computing context lies in its special contribution to software tools through amalgamation, and is comparable to the importance of the role played by higher-order functions in the management of functional languages such as LISP and HOPE. The amalgamation feature is unique to the declarative languages and reinforces the case for their eventual ascendancy over non-declarative formalisms.

VIII.2. Computing Practice

In this section we survey the impact which logic programming is making upon programming methodology, and illustrate some of the applications which its use makes possible.

VIII.2.1. Programming Methodology

Programming methodology encompasses those aspects of software engineering directly concerned with the composition of computer programs. Whilst many 'craft' professions have evolved their tools to fit the requirements of their practitioners, the position with computer programming has been rather the reverse: programming languages and tools have been dominated largely by predetermined features of machine architecture rather than by consideration of the best ways in which humans might represent computational problems and methods of solution. These features have themselves been dictated by technical and economic constraints in the manufacture of logic circuitry.

Conventional computers, spanning the first four 'generations', are now commonly referred to as *von Neumann machines* in recognition of their dependence upon that model of mechanized computation which was brought into physical reality in the earliest computers through the energy and vision of John von Neumann. In this model the machine's operation is a sequence of state transitions effected upon discrete memory cells, each transition replacing some cell's current state by a new state. The object of any computation is then to transform some initial state to some final state by making the machine follow a prescribed sequence of transitions. A program is needed in order to specify this sequence and must itself be stored in the memory. The program should therefore consist of discrete instructions detailing both the transitions and their sequencing. Thus one arrives at the von Neumann concept of programming languages as languages for instructing the machine. Nearly all languages in common use today are of this kind; it is as true for PASCAL and ADA as it is for BASIC, FORTRAN and COBOL, and as true for them as it is for symbolic assembly languages. The only notable feature which changes across the spectrum of von Neumann languages is the extent to which their descriptions of state transitions and the decisions controlling them are abstracted from the details of individual types of real machine. Thus there is no difference in concept between the assembly instructions

$$\text{LOAD I}$$
$$\text{ADD ONE}$$
$$\text{STORE I}$$

for a specific real machine and the FORTRAN instruction $I = I + 1$ for some abstract machine which, by suitable interpretive mechanisms, can be realized on the real one.

The machine-oriented approach to programming might have proved unobjectionable had it been the case that humans were naturally adept at reasoning about von Neumann processes. However, this is manifestly not the case: how many programmers would readily face the prospect of determining whether a randomly selected assignment deep in the middle of a FORTRAN program could be safely deleted or modified? The reasons why such a task is so daunting have been much rehearsed in computing science circles, but are worth restating here for readers unfamiliar with the central argument, which is this: in such a program the role of each operational statement can be understood only in relation to its run-time context, that is, in relation to the state of the machine at the moment control arrives at the statement. That state is itself a function of the history of the entire execution up to that moment.

The significance of this can be shown up very easily. Imagine that a program contains somewhere within it the assignment S1 : $A := B + C$ and elsewhere the assignment S2 : $P := 10 * A$. Perhaps we want to analyse some proposition about the value of P computed by S2. Clearly P is evaluated by using A, which is itself evaluated by S1 as $B + C$. Can we therefore treat the proposition as being about $10 * (B + C)$? Certainly not, because if control arrives at S2 then it may not have previously passed through S1, and even if it has, the value of A may yet have been altered by other statements along the path from S1 to S2. We cannot know without comprehensively identifying and analysing that path, which is tantamount to executing the program—merely to investigate one or two statements having a bearing upon P!

The substitution of $(B + C)$ from S1 for A in S2 is unsound in that it fails to preserve the *referent* of A—what A refers to in S1 cannot be equated with what A refers to in S2. This is a direct consequence of the statements being destructive assignment instructions. By contrast, consider a logic program containing two statements

$$\text{S1 :} \quad \textbf{parent}(x, z) \quad \textbf{if} \quad \textbf{mother}(x, z)$$
$$\text{S2 :} \quad \textbf{grandparent}(x, y) \quad \textbf{if} \quad \textbf{parent}(x, z), \textbf{parent}(z, y)$$

In both S1 and S2, **parent**(x, z) identically expresses the membership of an arbitrary pair (x, z) in the **parent** relation determined by the program as a whole. We may therefore substitute for **parent**(x, z) in S2 its referent **mother**(x, z) as determined by S1 to obtain

$$S3 : \quad \textbf{grandparent}(x, y) \quad \textbf{if} \quad \textbf{mother}(x, z), \textbf{parent}(z, y)$$

This substitution is sound in that S3 is implied by S1 and S2 jointly. Logic and other pure *declarative languages* therefore enjoy what is called *referential transparency*; what any of their constituents refers to in a program can be ascertained by exploiting the soundness of *substitutivity*, taking no account of the irrelevant run-time context. That grandparenthood refers in S3 to a certain combination of motherhood and parenthood has been determined by considering what grandparenthood and parenthood each refer to according to S1 and S2.

Curiously, and regrettably, the pernicious effects of *destructive assignment* upon program analysis, which have been cogently argued in the paper by Backus (1978), have not registered very strongly in the consciousness of many programmers. This is partly because the operation has been taken deeply for granted since the dawn of computing: indeed, some programmers may have little awareness of other ways of associating data with variables. Another reason may be that many proponents of '*structured programming*', initiated by Dijkstra (1976) in the late 1960s, were diverted into concentrating unduly upon tidying up control flow constructs rather than seriously questioning the underlying semantics of conventional languages, thus mistakenly believing that fundamental defects were being remedied. Even today one still sees numerous publications of inconsequential controversies over whether one dialect of BASIC is more 'structured' than another. Given the dimensions of the problems currently facing software management this is, to borrow a phrase, arguing over deckchairs while the Titanic is sinking.

The advantages conferred by the alternative use of declarative languages have of course, long been appreciated by certain groups of programmers, particularly within the artificial intelligence community. Perhaps one reason why these languages received little attention during the turmoil of the structured programming era is that artificial intelligence was at exactly the same time, in the United Kingdom at least, experiencing a forced contraction. However this may be, their recently elevated roles in major initiatives such as the Fifth Generation Project (Japan), the Alvey Programme (U.K.) and the ESPRIT Programme (European Community) are owed partly to the now recognized necessity of raising rigour and productivity in the software engineering process, partly to the demands posed by new machine architectures and partly to recent advances in computational logic and artificial intelligence. Nonetheless, even before these new generation initiatives began, the advancement of declarative systems was being postulated by many [e.g., see the collection of papers edited by Wallis (1982)] as paramount to the resolution of long-standing problems in software engineering.

A concise assessment of the potential of declarative languages and associated system architectures has recently been given by Darlington and Kowalski (1983). They point out the essential features which distinguish these languages from wholly procedural ones, namely, their dual functions of both knowledge representation and problem solving, their dual functions of both specification and computation, their inherent parallelism and their conduciveness to software systems subject to frequent modification.

It is not hard to construct simple examples illustrating these distinctions. For instance, consider the following rule R declaring a relation in a database D of assertions of the form x **likes** y:

$$R : \quad \textbf{friends}(x, y) \quad \textbf{if} \quad x \textbf{ likes } y, y \textbf{ likes } x$$

The rule makes sense in its own right as a statement of our knowledge about friendship independently of its possible uses for problem solving. In a non-declarative language we cannot even state the rule—the most we can do is write a procedure whose behaviour simulates a particular use of the rule, for example, to show that a given pair (x, y) are friends. If we want to support other uses we have to write yet more procedures even though they all encode no more knowledge than is specified by R; such a methodology is ludicrously redundant and inflexible.

Next, consider a specification of any set z of friends x in D:

$$S : \quad \textbf{friends-of}(x, z) \quad \textbf{iff} \quad (\forall y)(x \textbf{ likes } y,$$
$$y \textbf{ likes } x \quad \textbf{if} \quad y \in z)$$

By implementing the full standard form of FOPL as a programming language (e.g., see Bowen, 1980), S can be executed directly, if inefficiently, to solve computational problems about D. Even if this is unsatisfactory for large-scale data, its very possibility provides us with a means of rapid *prototyping* on small-scale experimental versions of the database. Alternatively, S can be used as a specification in order to derive Horn-clause procedures

friends-of$(x, \varnothing)$
friends-of$(x, y:z')$ **if** x **likes** y, y **likes** x, **friends-of**(x, z')

offering better executions. The prospects for executing logic specifications as programs have been recently expounded by Kowalski (1983a).

Further, consider the significance of the fact that, for any particular x, the database simultaneously determines all individuals in the set z of friends of x. If the resources are available then it is obviously more natural and more efficient to determine them in parallel than to do so sequentially. Existing parallel architectures such as ALICE (see Darlington and Reeve, 1983) can elicit such behaviour from declarative programs without demanding that the programmer specify how the execution is to be organized.

Darlington and Kowalski (1983) argue that the distinctive features of declarative systems hold much promise for a wide range of computing activities. As examples, commercial data-processing programs could be constituted directly from rules declaring the properties of the data; natural and graphical languages, which are inherently conducive to declarative representation, offer major benefits in the important field of man–machine interfacing; declarative representations of shapes, components, assemblies, plans and design objectives clearly have much to offer to computer-aided design and manufacture.

Although major efforts are now under way to promote awareness and investment in such opportunities, it is at present too early to identify a broad prospectus of proven commercial or industrial achievements based upon declarative systems. It is, however, possible to identify very significant progress in the field of intelligent knowledge-based systems; these are the principal applications described in the next section.

VIII.2.2. Applications

Logic programs were first used for representing and analysing subsets of natural language. It was this application which largely motivated Colmerauer and Roussel to develop the first PROLOG implementation. Soon afterward, other researchers in artificial intelligence readily found applications of their own, early examples of which were plan formation and compiler writing by Warren (1977b), geometrical proofs by Welham (1976) and problem solving in mechanics by Bundy *et al.* (1979). Reported applications have since multiplied enormously—for instance, an astonishing range of uses in Hungary up to 1980 has been documented by Santane-Toth and Szeredi (1982). In what follows, we concentrate upon a selection of important classes of application: *intelligent knowledge-based systems*, database systems, expert systems and natural language processing systems. The reason for emphasizing these is that they are widely predicted to be the principal new applications of computers during the next decade.

INTELLIGENT KNOWLEDGE-BASED SYSTEMS (IKBS)

IKBS are systems which apply intelligent reasoning mechanisms to explicit representations of knowledge. The IKBS field has been identified by some as simply applied artificial intelligence. Database systems, *rule-based systems* and expert systems are distinct but overlapping examples of IKBS. IKBS technology has been identified by the U.K. Alvey Report (1982) as one of the four enabling technologies necessary to the full exploitation of the next (fifth) generation of computer systems. The others are man–machine interfaces (MMI), very large scale integrated (VLSI) circuitry and software engineering; again, there is much overlap amongst the four fields. The relationship between IKBS and new generation computers is in fact highly symbiotic: each is necessary for realizing the full potential of the other. Nonetheless the present state of development of declarative systems already makes many useful IKBS applications feasible even on small conventional computers.

It needs to be emphasized that one does not obtain an IKBS merely by constructing a knowledge base and a processing mechanism for it. Whilst virtually any composition of, say, a logic program might properly be called an instance of 'knowledge-based programming', it could not be said that a **PROLOG**-like implementation of the program necessarily constituted an IKBS. Intelligent processing certainly entails much more than basic provisions for inference and search; at the very least it requires strategic mechanisms (such as *heuristics*) which can reduce unnecessary search, for instance, by being sufficiently knowledgeable about the class of problems being investigated. Intelligent strategies can be built directly into an interpreter, giving high degrees of efficiency, when they are sufficiently general to justify this. Alternatively, object-level application programs can be invoked through the agency of metalevel programs describing the strategies; the latter programs, being decoupled from the interpreter, can then be reprogrammed at will to suit the circumstances. This approach can exploit all the power and generality conferred by the amalgamation of object language and metalanguage.

Sloman (1983) has identified a broader role of IKBS in that, as well as putting into practice those artificial intelligence techniques already known, they may themselves help to illuminate and advance general theories about knowledge representation and intelligence. For instance, he argues their role as tools for investigating such capabilities as discovery, learning, creativity, communication, self-improvement and self-awareness, and suggests that they may need to be deployed within a variety of representational frameworks besides logic. Since the above capabilities are typical of those now being postulated for new generation computers, we may say that the traditional objectives of artificial intelligence are in the process of becoming the standard expectations of the computing community as a whole. Thus we might expect that artificial intelligence, far from remaining a small subset of computing science, might soon become a superset of most of it.

Database Systems (DBS)

A particularly well-defined application of IKBS which is currently receiving much attention is to *database systems*. Conventional DBS have traditionally treated data as collections of relations stored extensionally in the form of tables. For example, a simple database recording average prices in the London property market might contain the following data:

> *Chelsea, semidetached, 7, freehold, £250,000;*
> *Kensington, bedsitter, 1, rental, £65;*
> *Knightsbridge, apartment, 5, leasehold, £80,000;*
> etc.

The rows in this table are *n*-tuples of the form

$$(area, \ type, \ room\text{-}count, \ tenancy, \ price/charge)$$

and jointly constitute an *n*-place relation.

The *relational model of databases* has led to the implementation of many query systems through relational calculi providing standard relational operators such as joins and projections. The query processor of a conventional DBS typically derives from an input query some specific conjunction of these algebraic operations which a manager program then applies to the tables in order to retrieve responding *n*-tuples.

The potential of logic programming for representing and querying databases was investigated in early studies by van Emden (1978), Kowalski (1978) and Tärnlund (1978), all of whom established the fundamental point that data retrieval in the conventional DBS model is intrinsic within the standard inference mechanisms of logic interpreters. Van Emden's paper demonstrates this directly by using logic to reformulate the Query-by-Example system of Zloof (1975). Another account of this system's formulation in PROLOG is given by Neves *et al.* (1982). The state of the art in logic databases up to 1978 is covered by the collection of papers edited by Gallaire and Minker (1978), whilst more recent appraisals of logic's contribution to this field have been given by Dahl (1981), Gallaire (1981) and Kowalski (1981a).

In the logic formulation of DBS, retrieving *n*-tuples in response to a query becomes a theorem-proving process which treats the database (which might be simply a set of ground assertions) as an assumption set and the query (some goal statement) as the theorem. Retrieval is then identified with the standard answer-extraction mechanism.

Besides these elementary observations there are other important points to be made about logic as a database language. Chief among these is that the content of a logic database, unconstrained by any assumptions about internal table representations, need not be confined to ground assertions: it may also include general knowledge in the form of rules such as

tenancy$(x, RENTAL)$ **if**   **type**$(x, BEDSITTER)$

A conventional (relational) DBS has no satisfactory way of incorporating these rules in the database itself—instead it must encode their operational effects within specially programmed procedures. An arrangement of this sort may then become very heterogeneous, employing distinct formalisms for representing data, rules, queries and query analysis procedures. The claim made for logic is that it deals uniformly with all these requirements. In particular, it makes no distinction between data represented by specific assertions and data represented by general rules. Likewise it makes no distinction between rules treated as data and rules treated as procedures. Thus it eliminates the artificial and obstructive distinction often alleged between programming languages, query languages and data-description languages.

The fundamental disparity between the theorem-proving and relational approaches to DBS has been characterized by Nicolas and Gallaire (1978). They argue that the former approach, through its admittance of rules generalized by the occurrence of variables, treats a database as a theory possessing many possible satisfying interpretations, whilst the latter, confined to dealing only with tables of ground n-tuples, treats it as one particular interpretation. Characteristic defects of the relational approach then become manifested in its difficulties both in accommodating recursive access and in handling incompletely specified (partially instantiated) n-tuples in queries and responses.

The advantages of logic are beginning to encourage a shift away from the relational calculus approach to DBS implementation, and much work is now in progress to determine how best to make logic serve the higher-level requirements of DBS methodology. A major strand of this effort concerns *query optimization* and analysis. It is generally agreed that DBS query languages need to be usable by naive users who should not need to concern themselves with storage and retrieval mechanisms. This view treats a query as a specification, devoid of procedural bias. The problem for the implementor is then how best to impose the query upon the database. One difficulty raised by the standard PROLOG execution of queries represented by goal statements is, as Warren (1981) points out, that PROLOG, by default, blindly follows the textual ordering of the query's subgoals, which may be grossly inefficient. Worse still, it fails to economize on superfluous non-determinism: given a query, say **find**(x), which reduces to a conjunction, say **p**(a), **r**(a, y) with $x := a$, it will (in the absence of 'cut' directives) redundantly output the solution $x := a$ for every instance of y satisfying **r**(a, y). Warren shows how these deficiencies are mitigated in his CHAT-80 DBS by augmenting PROLOG with capabilities for query planning (e.g., intelligent reordering of subgoals) and query optimization (e.g., observing independences between subgoals).

Query processing has been further investigated by Chakravarthy *et al.* (1982), who demonstrate the role of metalevel control in the management of query evaluations. They present an interesting synthesis of the inferential and relational calculus approaches to DBS implementation by showing how bindings accumulated during the deductive evaluation of queries can be stored in table-like structured terms whose internal representations can be highly compacted through schemes directly analogous to conventional structure sharing. A concise account of this and related DBS research at the University of Maryland is given by Minker (1983).

Many researchers have also stressed the need for *indexing* in order to access data efficiently from clausal-form representations. This is possibly of even greater importance to DBS than it is for ordinary logic programs which, usually, are less preoccupied with accessing large volumes of ground data. In particular, indexing in the DBS context must normally be targeted on data held in secondary rather than primary storage. Methods for efficient indexing, such as *multikey hashing* techniques, are discussed in a paper by Lloyd (1983).

Apart from these directly pragmatic considerations, a number of important theoretical issues in the use of logic as a database language remain open for investigation. Amongst these we may briefly cite the familiar frame problem arising in the representation of time, state and change, and the interaction of non-monotonic reasoning (e.g., default reasoning over incompletely specified data) with database integrity constraints. These problems are discussed in papers by Kowalski (1983c), Sergot (1983a) and Minker (1981).

Expert Systems (ES)

An *expert system* is a form of IKBS specially designed to emulate human expertise in some specific domain. Typically it will possess a rich knowledge base of facts, rules and heuristics about that domain, together with a capability for engaging in an interactive consultation with its user much as a human expert might. In addition it should be able to account to the user for any advice or decisions which it gives, and may also be able to improve its own skill through the experience of such interaction. Detailed expositions of the properties and uses anticipated for ES are given in the book edited by Michie (1979).

ES form an obvious and attractive application for logic programming, and a good overview of logic's role in this field is given by Kowalski (1983d). He stresses the point that ES should be distinguished from mere rule-based systems, which are often wrongly credited with expertise solely because they contain object-level facts and rules correctly capturing some subset of an expert's knowledge. The distinction lies in the fact that a human expert is able to summon—as a consequence of experience, insight and intuition—a variety of domain-specific heuristics enabling him to cut intelligent routes through large search spaces and respond sensibly to any inconsistencies or incompletenesses which he perceives in the course of deploying his knowledge. In short, as well as knowing the facts and rules pertinent to the domain, he knows how to use them effectively.

The latter point underlies Kowalski's thesis that human expertise is typically incapable of complete formalization (being in some respects a replacement for it) and so cannot be expected to have a precise specification to which it must conform. The process of encapsulating it within a computer program must therefore—in contrast to rigorous development of a well-specified ordinary program—be expected to proceed by trial and error. Successive adjustments must be made as the knowledge base evolves and as new demands are made upon the system's competence, in much the same way as a program's specification might need to evolve in order to accommodate corrections, finer detailing or new requirements. Logic programming, more than any other existing computing formalism, is naturally equipped for the tasks of detecting inconsistencies (e.g., by refutation procedures) and incompletenesses (e.g., by default inference rules) for the purpose of motivating an expert system's refinement, whilst its metalanguage provides for mechanizable descriptions of the criteria and mechanisms for the refinement.

Logic as an expert system language was investigated by Hammond (1980) and subsequently elaborated upon by Clark and McCabe (1982). They identified a number of basic requirements: logical inference as the basis of query processing, ability to add what has been learned to the knowledge base (lemma generation), ability to account to the user as to how or why a particular conclusion was reached and ability to elicit knowledge from humans (the '*interactive symmetry*' principle). Clark and McCabe implemented these features chiefly by adding special-purpose control features to the object-level rules of the knowledge base. A more sophisticated way of realizing those features through the use of the metalanguage has since been described by Hammond and Sergot (1983). Their system combines a Query-the-User facility with an expert system shell (APES), described respectively in earlier reports by Sergot (1983b) and Hammond (1983a). Implemented in micro-PROLOG, it provides a very flexible tool, called Ape-the-User, for building expert systems. The expert user can enter any assertion declaring that some relation is 'askable', whereupon the system treats him as an extension to the existing internal knowledge base and queries him in order to elicit further knowledge about that relation, which it then stores. In this way the system and expert cooperate in the construction of the knowledge base. The user's object-level queries can be processed directly by invoking the micro-PROLOG interpreter in the core of the system, whilst explanation-seeking queries of the 'how', 'why' and 'why not' variety are processed by invoking a metalevel interpreter (itself executed through micro-PROLOG) which constructs and outputs explanations in the form of edited proofs. Facilities for natural language structuring of queries are also provided. These features in combination offer a congenial, general-purpose environment for building, modifying and consulting expert systems.

APES has been used successfully for automating legal expert systems. For instance, Hammond (1983b) describes how, in collaboration with the Department of Health and Social Security, more than two hundred non-discretionary regulations governing entitlement to supplementary benefit were assimilated into an APES knowledge base. On a larger scale, and encountering much greater legal and linguistic complexities, it has been used to encode the 1981 British Nationality Act, which defines categories of British citizenship and includes rules for its own interpretation. The account of this work by Cory et al. (1984) makes two interesting points about the logical formalization of law: first, since all law is written down in a manner which seeks to be precise and complete (within its own terms), many of the familiar difficulties of knowledge elicitation from human experts can be avoided; second, since legislation can be viewed as a particular category of complex software, experience in its computerization may yield useful insights into the problems of software engineering in general. Another instance of the use of PROLOG for representing law has been described by Hustler (1982) in relation to the Law of Battery, and a more general overview of the role of logic in law is given by Sergot (1982).

An up to date collection of documented evidence of the utility of logic programming for ES technology is contained in the proceedings of a conference organized by the British Computer Society (1983); several contributors explain there the advantages they have found in using logic rather than the historically more popular choice of LISP, and provide comparisons with well-known LISP-based systems such as the EMYCIN medical diagnosis expert system. Expert systems in logic are also being developed at Lisbon University: an account of the ORBI system for environmental resource evaluation is given by Pereira *et al.* (1982).

NATURAL LANGUAGE (NL) PROCESSING

NL processing is of major importance to the development of tools for man–machine interfacing, and to the construction of outer layers for IKBS in particular. It is therefore an important application area for logic programming.

Computer implementation of natural language requires formalization of both its syntax and semantics. The use of Horn-clause logic for this purpose was first studied by Alain Colmerauer and subsequently in collaboration with Kowalski (1974a). They showed that Horn clauses are adequate for expressing any *context-free grammar* (CFG), that questions about NL sentence structure can be formulated as goal statements and that different proof procedures applied to logic representations of NL correspond to different parsing strategies.

A Horn-clause grammar is more generally referred to as a *definite clause grammar* (DCG) since Horn-clause assertions and implications are jointly known as definite clauses. The descriptive and operational properties of DCGs and their relationships to other NL formalizations have been investigated by Pereira and Warren (1980).

The nature of natural language is such that many of its features are best represented by *context-dependent grammars*, that is, grammars containing rules whose categorizations of certain phrase structures are dependent upon the context in which the latter appear within the NL sentence under consideration, rather than—as in CFGs—dependent only upon their own structure. The use of clausal-form logic to represent context dependence was pioneered by Colmerauer (1978) through his development of '*metamorphosis grammars*', for which DCGs constitute a normal form. Colmerauer (1982) presents the logic formulation of a useful subset of NL in terms of these grammars, in particular showing how strictly classical logic can represent extended notions of quantification in order to distinguish semantically meaningful NL sentences from meaningless ones. Overviews of work on DCGs and related grammars have been given recently by Pereira (1983) and Abramson (1983).

A more general representational framework, which accommodates NL structures as well as others, is that of *semantic networks*. Deliyanni and Kowalski (1979) showed that the traditional formulation of these networks could be generalized in order to express sets of sentences in clausal form. In this generalization, the nodes of the network represent terms and connecting arcs represent consequent or antecedent binary relations between them; the bundle of arcs emanating from any node then represents some clause. Besides providing a very compact and uniform representation, these systems are amenable to procedural interpretations yielding operational schemes for deriving information from the networks. A more recent discussion of logic-based semantic networks and the support they give to the thesis 'NL = logic + control' can be found in the book by Kowalski (1979a).

VIII.2.3. Education

Logic programming promises to contribute significantly to the educational use of computers. This proposition was first tested in 1978 when Kowalski introduced logic programming to Park House Middle School in Wimbledon using on-line access to computing facilities at Imperial College. The success of this exercise was such that a more comprehensive project 'Logic as a Computer Language for Children' was inaugurated in 1980 with support from the Science Research Council. The early aims, materials and methodology of the teaching programme are described by Ennals (1980), whilst a more recent assessment of the work is given in Ennals (1982).

This project is now founded upon the micro-PROLOG implementation. Children aged 10–12 have been taught micro-PROLOG in easy stages, progressing from simple variable-free assertional databases interrogated by single-call queries to the use of general procedures and queries. The drawing of semantic networks has assisted explanation of recursion, whilst the congenial list representation afforded by micro-PROLOG has allowed introduction of the concept of data structure.

As well as introducing children to computing in its own right, logic programming can be used to enrich academic studies across the entire school curriculum. This potential is illustrated in a variety of papers by Ennals (1981). He points out that logic is the single academic discipline common to all subjects taught at school, promoting clarity of thought and expression in all of them. Amongst the many examples he cites of logic's service to the teaching of other subjects are historical simulation games in History, molecular analysis in Science, equation solving in Mathematics and grammar formulation in French. The use of micro-PROLOG for these purposes has also admitted the use of tools built from it such as the Query-the-User system developed by Sergot (1983b); the use of this tool for teaching children how to formulate logic queries correctly has been investigated by Weir (1982). Recently Briggs (1984) has described the construction of a new interface to micro-PROLOG which specially adapts the external syntax for easy assimilation by very young pupils; in fact logic programming has now been taught to children aged 7–9.

The explosive growth of personal or hobby computing is such that many amateur programmers are, for better or worse, being self-taught rather than formally educated in the subject. At present they are mostly oriented towards BASIC in accordance with the current bias of the personal software market. However, the ready availability of micro-PROLOG and the excellent self-teaching book for it written by Clark and McCabe (1984) may begin to change this situation.

Teachers of logic programming generally agree that acceptance of logic comes more readily to those with no computing experience than to those already conditioned to a conventional formalism. Someone who for ten years has programmed in such a formalism, with the support of familiar tools and with expectations of particular standards, is likely to need a lot of convincing that logic—still in a comparative state of infancy—offers an attractive alternative. One cannot reasonably expect—or even desire—an instant conversion to follow from the demonstration of well-chosen examples which nicely show off the fancier features like multiple solutions and in-vertibility. The larger principles of programming methodology, the importance of knowledge-based applications and the proper exploitation of forthcoming new generation machine architectures are the real issues which should be used to motivate interest in logic, and all of them need to be brought home, where necessary, through proper training and educational programmes. As yet there is little publicly available literature written with the specific intention of helping existing professional programmers toward an appreciation of logic. Some of the issues which such literature would need to address, particularly in relation to the conceptual transition from procedural determinism to declarative non-determinism, have been outlined in papers by Byrd (1980) and by Kluzniak and Szpakowicz (1982).

VIII.3. Computing Technology

The next generation of computers is being designed to span a diverse range of powerful processing capabilities which are fundamentally impractical on our current von Neumann machines. These capabilities include, in particular, dataflow and reductive execution schemes which extricate and exploit the parallelism inherent in many computer programs. These new machines will implement such schemes upon highly parallel multiprocessor architecture, giving dramatic increases in processing power relative to the norm of present-day computing. Machines of this kind do, of course, already exist; probably the best-known in the United Kingdom is the Manchester Dataflow Machine, whose features are described by Gurd and Watson (1980).

Securing the benefits of parallel execution schemes nevertheless requires more than the provision of new machines. We can, after all, implement them already by simply connecting several von Neumann computers together in parallel. The reason why such an approach fails to do justice to the desired level of performance lies in the nature of the individual von Neumann machine. This sort of machine presupposes a deterministic, prescriptively controlled sequence of assignments performed primarily upon scalar numerical data; it offers a fundamentally unsympathetic environment in which to implement non-deterministic inference-directed or data-directed concurrent evaluations, and is especially unsuited to processing structured non-numerical data. Escape from these limitations requires the abandonment not only of von Neumann machines but also of those programming languages based upon them. This is why so much attention is now being focused upon the declarative languages whose features are compatible with a wide range of novel evaluation schemes and host architectures. These languages contribute directly to the advance of new generation computing technology by virtue of making its use feasible.

VIII.3.1. Logic as a Non–von-Neumann Language

The basic property which renders logic and other declarative languages unconstrained by the von Neumann concept of computation is their semantic neutrality with respect to the execution strategy. We have previously referred to this as the complete decoupling of logic from control: if a problem can be solved on a computer using a logic program then this is solely because of the implications afforded by the logical content of the program, not because of the way the computer explores them. The potential which this observation holds for coroutined and parallel execution schemes for logic programming was recognized long ago by Kowalski (1979a).

Besides consideration of its relative ease of implementation, the standard PROLOG strategy was devised in the way that it was in order to give the programmer some control over call selection and procedure selection in a single-processor environment. The first practical efforts towards the realization of a more liberal strategy concentrated upon *dataflow coroutining*, which can be viewed as a generalization of the standard computation (call-selection) rule. In this scheme the activation of calls is governed by the flow of data through the variables which they share instead of by a prescribed or implicit control sequence. Coroutining is a dominant control feature of the IC-PROLOG system described by Clark, McCabe and Gregory (1982) and developed on the basis of earlier studies by Stevens (1977) of *lazy evaluation* schemes for PROLOG. In IC-PROLOG a variable, say x, can be annotated in the source program by one of the symbols '?' or '^' to indicate the dependence of the mode of evaluation of the call containing it upon the binding state of x at the point of activation. More precisely, the annotation x? in a call specifies that control must pass immediately to that call whenever an execution step either binds x directly or binds some other variable in a term already bound to x—in other words, whenever execution increases the degree of instantiation of the computed value of x (or, loosely, transmits data to x). At this point the current (possibly uncompleted) evaluation of whatever call was previously being dealt with is suspended whilst the interpreter now proceeds to process the call to which its attention has just been transferred. It continues along this course until able to foresee that the next execution step wants to transmit data to x, whereupon the present evaluation is now suspended and control reverts to the previous suspension point. The alternative annotation x^ specifies that control must pass immediately to the call containing it, suspending the current evaluation, whenever the interpreter foresees that the next execution step wants to pass data to x; control subsequently returns to this suspension point only when an execution step in the new evaluation succeeds in passing data to x. The two annotations are therefore roughly complementary in their effects. Under this scheme, control traverses the computation space in a more arbitrary way than it does under the standard PROLOG strategy: loosely, it jumps about from one partially completed computation to another according to the dataflow through the annotated variables. The paper by Clark *et al.* cited above illustrates the efficiency improvements obtained by this richer kind of behaviour.

Since a call containing x? receives attention as soon as an execution step passes more data to x, it is called an *eager consumer* (of x). Since a call containing x^ receives attention only when its capacity to produce more data for x is demanded by some execution step, it is called a *lazy producer* (of x). The *producer–consumer protocol* is fundamental to most models of dataflow coroutining. By variously designating selected program calls to be in one category or the other, one can obtain a large spectrum of evaluation modes varying from completely lazy production to wholly eager consumption.

At about the same time as IC-PROLOG was being developed, Pereira and Monteiro (1981) took an interestingly different approach to the construction of logic interpreters for coroutined and parallel execution by defining those behaviours in Horn-clause logic itself. They therefore arrived

at metalevel control descriptions which, when executed, functioned as intermediate interpreters themselves capable of eliciting these behaviours from
standard object-level logic programs. However, instead of using dataflow
annotations to achieve coordination, they employed explicit system calls
variously capable of interrogating the binding states of variables and of
forcing process suspension.

Dataflow coroutining is subsumed by the more general concept of
dataflow execution, which operates upon a stored graph representation of
the data dependences between operations in the source program. Each
node of the graph represents some operation any one activation of which
consumes one or more data tokens arriving from its input arcs in order to
produce (by carrying out the associated operation) another data token which
is identically transmitted along all its output arcs. The arcs connecting the
nodes thus serve as unidirectional channels through which data is communicated around the graph. The graph itself has to be compiled from the
source program by determining the mutual dependences amongst the program's operations; this task is clearly easiest for languages possessing
referential transparency.

In execution the graph behaves as a network of processors cooperatively
producing and consuming data. For implementing simple computational
mechanisms the graph can remain topologically static during execution, but
the support of other mechanisms—notably recursion—may require either
dynamic graph modification or complicated token-labeling schemes.

Since any node can be activated to perform its associated operation at
any time after it has become enabled by the arrival of all necessary inputs,
the scope for parallelism is considerable. In the crudest case one can simply
force one or more initial activations and then let all the available processors
loose upon the network without attempting to coordinate the ensuing
processes. Unsurprisingly this makes the execution highly vulnerable to
various undesirable states of imbalance—for instance, one possibility is
channel saturation in which production overtakes consumption in one or
more channels, so forcing the temporary suspension of enabled producers
and thus potentially under-utilizing the available processing power until
desaturation has been accomplished.

One possible dataflow model of logic program execution has been
proposed by van Emden and de Lucena Filho (1982). They first show how
the relation computed at any node of a dataflow graph can be specified by
a Horn-clause procedure; the connection of any two nodes is then representable as a logic query conjoining two procedure calls, and process activation becomes interpretable as call activation in the query. They are then able
to formulate a (parallel) *process interpretation* of logic in contrast to the
usual (sequential) procedural interpretation. The same dataflow model has

been related, in a subsequent paper by Brough and van Emden (1984), to the logic representation of conventional flowcharts previously developed by Clark and van Emden (1981).

Dataflow execution is only one of many schemes available for exploiting parallelism between individual processes. Moreover, a given programming formalism may admit distinct kinds of parallelism each implying a particular mode of governance over the processes which realize it. The opportunities for parallel execution of logic programs fall into a number of categories. One which has turned out to be reasonably tractable from the implementor's viewpoint is *OR-parallelism*, which exploits the fact that when several procedures respond to an activated call they can be invoked and used in parallel to investigate that call. The parallel computations which ensue can proceed independently except to the extent that they might begin with shared references to unbound variables in their common parent environment and subsequently compete to bind these; special stack-management schemes can be used for ameliorating this slight impediment to truly independent OR-parallelism. OR-parallelism has a useful role to play in database retrieval, where a single query may have a large number of alternative solutions; it is a direct consequence of the non-determinism of logic programs in the sense of admitting multiple computations.

A second category is *AND-parallelism*, which exploits the fact that calls conjoined in a query can be activated and solved in parallel. AND-parallelism is the key feature of cooperative '*concurrent process*' problem-solving schemes whose efficacy depends upon fine control over process communication (e.g., through shared variables between calls) and process synchronization (e.g., through the imposition of binding precedences). Truly independent AND-parallelism is possible when the parallel calls share no variables. However, a shared variable such as x in the goal ? $\mathbf{p}(x)$, $\mathbf{q}(x)$ can be made to serve a variety of useful purposes in mediating the non-independent parallel execution of the calls in which it appears. In situations where the programmer does not wish to concern himself with the calls' coordination and offers the interpreter no guidance on this matter, the shared variable can be problematical for the implementor. Logically, the calls $\mathbf{p}$ and $\mathbf{q}$ have to 'agree' upon any binding made to x and the problem is to achieve this agreement operationally whilst still preserving as much parallelism as possible. The significance of this requirement is greatly compounded when either $\mathbf{p}$ or $\mathbf{q}$ or both can be solved non-deterministically, for then the agreement of $\mathbf{p}$ and $\mathbf{q}$ must be sought as the intersection of their individual solution sets for x. A compromise commonly used for mitigating these difficulties is to designate one AND-parallel call as the producer of the shared variable and all others as consumers, on the principle that there is probably not much problem solving motivation to have more than one producer. In addition, multiple solutions of AND-parallel calls can be disallowed (potentially sacrificing completeness) in order to achieve a more manageable allocation of processing resources.

A third category is *stream-parallelism* (or 'structure pipelining') in which the consumption by one call of some structured data—a list would be typical—produced by another call is allowed to begin as soon the first call receives some substructure of that data, whilst the producer call concurrently proceeds to generate the next substructure. This category can be viewed as a special way of dealing with shared-variable AND-parallelism. It provides an excellent vehicle for achieving process coordination based upon message-passing protocols, especially if the transmitted substructures are permitted to contain uninstantiated variables available for two-way communication.

Parallelism can be attained at a much finer grain of activity by implementing it, as far as possible, within the unification algorithm. This can bring major improvements to the efficiency even of sequential PROLOG. A precise scheme for this has been described by Tick and Warren (1984), who estimated its potential performance as approaching 450 klips (1 klip = 10^3 logical inferences/second), which represents at least a 20-fold increase over DEC-10 PROLOG. They propose that high-level PROLOG instructions compiled from source logic programs be themselves expanded into overlapping microinstructions processed by *pipelined parallelism*.

These and other species of parallelism have been classified and investigated by Conery and Kibler (1981), who have developed an 'AND/OR process model' for parallel execution of logic programs. This primarily supports OR-parallelism but also offers a limited form of AND-parallelism—independent calls are executed in true AND-parallel, but in order to deal with calls sharing variables they use the device mentioned earlier whereby one call is made a producer and the others all consumers; the producer and consumers are then executed sequentially in an order decided by the interpreter using dataflow analysis.

Earlier detailed studies of schemes for OR-parallelism were made in the doctoral theses of both Pollard (1981) and Conery (1983). As observed previously, the main implementation problems centre on the management of the binding environments of OR-parallel subcomputations. For instance, there is the housekeeping problem of minimizing redundancy amongst what those subcomputations individually inherit from the current environment upon descent from the activating parent node, and there is also the tactical problem of how to manage the binding and resetting ('trailing') of variables in that environment to which OR-parallel processes have common access; an interesting approach to the latter problem is explained in a paper by Borgwardt (1984). Pollard's thesis also considers possible methods for the ideal complete support of AND/OR-parallelism (combining both AND

and OR modes). He investigates the deployment of separate concurrent processes responsible for supervising the generation and reconciliation of bindings. No practical schemes for this have yet been implemented.

Two implementations which have recently evoked much interest are *PARLOG*, developed by Clark and Gregory (1984) and *Concurrent Prolog* (CP) developed by Shapiro (1983b). PARLOG extends the parallel relational language developed earlier by Clark and Gregory (1981). It supports species of both OR- and AND-parallelism, whilst CP currently supports the AND mode only. Both systems also support *committed-choice indeterminacy* by allowing the user to specify in any procedure that some subset of its body is to serve as a '*guard*' for the procedure. In this scheme, when several procedures respond to a call, their guards, if any, are executed in parallel; the procedure whose first guard is solved is then committed to the activating call, the others being dismissed. The scheme is inherently indeterminate in that the competition between potentially successful guards is governed by machine resource allocation and not by the program's logic or the user's direction. Both systems also provide for a wide range of concurrent process control mechanisms. PARLOG's behaviour is governed by compile-time analysis of input–output mode declarations similar to, but stronger than, those allowed by DEC-10 PROLOG, as well as various refining annotations which the user can place on selected variables. CP, on the other hand, uses just the single device of a read-only annotation on variables to achieve much the same ends but entailing substantially different programming style. The prospects for implementing PARLOG on the ALICE system, which features a *graph-reductive parallel architecture*, have been described by Darlington and Reeve (1981, 1983).

A critical comparison of CP and the relational language precursive to PARLOG is given by Shapiro (1983b), whilst a comparison of PARLOG and CP is in turn provided by Clark and Gregory (1983). Hellerstein and Shapiro (1984) have impressively demonstrated the elegance and power of CP by applying it to highly intricate parallel algorithms for network flow maximization, showing that the high-level message-passing facilities of CP can elicit the same degree of performance as is attainable in conventional languages using machine-level assignment mechanisms. More information about PARLOG, CP and other proposals for parallel logic programming can be found in the proceedings of the Atlantic City (1984) Symposium.

VIII.3.2. The Fifth Generation Project

In 1979 the Japanese Ministry of International Trade and Administration initiated feasibility studies for a new and uniquely ambitious enterprise in computing which is generally referred to as the *Fifth Generation Computer*

Systems (FGCS) Project. Its national objective is to give Japan a leading, innovative role in new computing technology. The broad technical objective, spread over a ten-year schedule, is to combined highly parallel non–von-Neumann machine architectures with knowledge-processing schemes drawn from research in artificial intelligence.

Following an international airing of its aims in the JIPDEC (1981) conference, the project proper was inaugurated in Spring 1982 under the direction of Kazuhiro Fuchi and based in the new Institute for New Generation Computing Technology (ICOT) in Tokyo. Its rationale and strategy are described in both broad and detailed terms in the JIPDEC presentations by Fuchi (1981) and Moto-oka (1981). Explaining how information technology must soon pervade virtually all industrial, administrative, educational and cultural activities, they emphasize the need for machines whose inherent sophistication will make them easily usable by a wide spectrum of users. Such machines must be capable of large-scale knowledge acquisition, intelligent learning, reasoning and problem solving functions and congenial human-oriented interaction. It is chiefly these requirements which pose the necessity for greatly increased processing power and its elicitation through extremely high-level software.

It is clear that these ambitions will call for radical changes in the education, attitudes and working practices of software engineers, programmers and users. For instance, there may be substantial psychological resistance by many conventional programmers against the adoption of declarative formalisms, as a result of the deeply ingrained procedural programming mentality. Another possible impediment to voluntary change may be the commercial truth that enormous investments have already been committed to conventional software and hardware. As pointed out by d'Agapayeff (1982), the choice facing the rest of the world in its response to the FGCS Project is one of 'innovation versus stability'. The Japanese, in clearly making their own choice, have gambled not only upon the belief that the costs entailed in converting to a new generation of technology will be outweighed in the longer term by the competitiveness of this technology in the world market, but also more fundamentally upon the very technical feasibility of that technology.

Preliminary designs for the FGCS Project were presented in the JIPDEC (1981) proceedings and in subsequent Japanese publications in the form of rather abstract diagrammatic conceptualizations whose constituents and relationships are not easy to unravel. In general terms, a fifth generation system is presented as comprising a *software system modeler* (SSM) interposed between a range of *human application systems* (HAS) and a *hardware machine system* (HMS). HAS are formulated in a wide range of human-oriented languages including speech, natural languages and graphics, and conveyed to the SSM through an interface capable of both representing and understanding the knowledge content of the HAS in a form suitable for intelligent software synthesis and manipulation. At the heart of the SSM is an intelligent programming system and a variety of knowledge base systems, equipped with which the SSM can construct a machine-processable representation of both the knowledge and the programs necessary for fulfilling the goals of the HAS. This synthesis function is the dominant feature of the SSM/HMS interface. The HMS itself comprises a problem-solving machine and a knowledge base machine, which are themselves composites of yet more machines variously adapted to symbolic, numerical and database manipulations. A detailed interpretation of all these proposals is given in a paper by Treleavan (1982).

The ultimate performance target for the FGCS Project is very high, usually quoted as in the order of 10^7 klips and elicited (conjointly) from as many as 10^4 parallel processors addressing up to 10^4 megabytes of memory. However, the short-term target of the first three-year phase of the project is a personal work station with just one processor yielding 20–30 klips and addressing 10–20 Mb of memory. In terms of inference speed this desk-top machine will achieve much the same performance as compiled DEC-10 PROLOG does on a DEC 2060 mainframe. It is intended subsequently to produce a more powerful personal work station called PIM (*parallel inference machine*) possessing 32 parallel processors conjointly yielding 10^6–10^7 klips; this will be a formidable competitor to many large existing conventional computers, and is expected to be ready well before 1990. A prototype called TOPSTAR-II comprised of 24 parallel Z80 microprocessors running a parallel inference system called PARALOG has already been built and tested.

Immediate world interest is naturally focused upon the forthcoming first machine, which is known as PSI (*personal sequential inference*); its internal features, as presently conceived, are described in an ICOT report by Nishikawa *et al.* (1983). It will feature specialized CPU hardware for rapid unification and binding lookup, as well as firmware-controlled garbage collection. Each of its 40-bit words comprises a 32-bit data field plus a 6-bit tag for dynamic type checking and a 2-bit field for garbage collection control.

Besides the ambitious hardware programme, a feature which caused much surprise when the FGCS plans were revealed was the strong commitment to logic programming as the central formalism. The rationalizations now given for this choice encompass several factors and are articulated in the JIPDEC paper by Furukawa *et al.* (1981). The factors include logic's subsumption of both functional programming and relational database formalisms, together with its uniformity in representing data, programs, specifications and metalevel concepts. In a more recent appraisal, Kowalski (1982) explains how logic provides important links between the goals of software engineering and artificial intelligence, and between rule-based programming and VLSI technology.

The PSI machine uses as its (version 0) kernel language (KL0 for short) a modified form of DEC-10 PROLOG, which features the usual apparatus of control, local, global and trail stacks supporting the conventional structure-sharing model. From the systems programming viewpoint, KL0 will serve much the same role, but with infinitely superior power, as an assembly language does on a conventional machine. KL0 will be used to write most of the PSI operating system and associated software; at the same time it doubles as a very high-level language for user interaction and problem solving. The logic-based kernel language for PIM, known as KL1, seems likely to be based upon both PARLOG and Shapiro's Concurrent Prolog. Interesting historical insights, personal impressions and anecdotes concerning the FGCS Project and logic's role in it have been documented by both Warren (1982) and Shapiro (1983a).

The FGCS Project has stimulated government-funded programmes for new generation computing in the United Kingdom (e.g., see the Alvey Debate, 1984), Europe and the United States as well as substantially raising world-wide interest in logic programming. How far this interest will spread and endure remains to be seen. If the FGCS Project comes near to achieving its stated aims, the challenge posed to the computing community in the rest of the world will be momentous: as Kazuhiro Fuchi claimed at the JIPDEC conference, the question will then be "whether to stand still or proceed, as there are no other paths to choose from."

REFERENCES

Abramson, H.
   1983   Definite clause transition grammars. Research Report, Dept. of Computer Science, Univ. of British Columbia, Vancouver.
Alvey Debate
   1984   Debate on Information Technology: The Alvey Report. House of Lords, HANSARD, January 18th.
Alvey Report
   1982   A programme for advanced information technology. The report of the Alvey Committee. HMSO, London.
Andreka, H. and Nemeti, I.
   1976   The generalized completeness of Horn predicate logic as a programming language. Research Report 21, Dept. of Artificial Intelligence. Univ. of Edinburgh, Scotland.
Apt, K. R. and van Emden, M. H.
   1982   Contributions to the theory of logic programming. *Journal of the ACM* **29**(3), 841–862.
Atlantic City
   1984   International Symposium on Logic Programming, Atlantic City, New Jersey, February 6–9. IEEE Computer Society Press, New York.
Backus, J.
   1978   Can programming be liberated from the von Neumann style? (ACM Turing Award Lecture), *Comm. of the ACM*, **21**(8), 613–641.
Balogh, K.
   1981   On an interactive program verifier for PROLOG programs. See Salgotarjan (1981).
Battani, G. and Meloni, H.
   1973   Interpreteur du language de programmation PROLOG. Research Report, Artificial Intelligence Group. Univ. of Aix-Marseille, Luminy, France.
Bendl, J., Koves, P. and Szeredi, P.
   1980   The MPROLOG system. See Logic Programming Workshop (1980).
Bobrow, D. G.
   1980   (Editor). Special issue on non-monotonic logic. *Artificial Intelligence* **13**.
Borgwardt, P.
   1984   Parallel PROLOG using stack segments on shared-memory multiprocessors. See Atlantic City (1984).
Bowen, K. A.
   1980   Programming with full first order logic. Research Report, School of Computer and Information Science (November). Syracuse University, New York.

Bowen, K. A. and Kowalski, R. A.
   1982   Amalgamating language and metalanguage in logic programming. See Clark and
           Tärnlund (1982).
Boyer, R. S. and Moore, J. S.
   1972   The sharing of structure in theorem proving programs. *In* "Machine Intelligence,"
           Vol. 7, (B. Meltzer and D. Michie, eds.) 101–116. Edinburgh University Press,
           Scotland.
   1977   A fast string searching algorithm. *Comm. of the ACM* **20**(10), 762–772.
Briggs, J.
   1984   Designing and implementing a child orientated interface to micro-PROLOG. See LP
           Research Reports.
British Computer Society
   1983   Proceedings of Conference on Expert Systems, British Computer Society, Churchill
           College, Univ. of Cambridge, December 14–16.
Brough, D. R. and van Emden, M. H.
   1984   Dataflow, flowcharts and LUCID-style programming in logic. See Atlantic City
           (1984).
Bruynooghe, M.
   1976   An interpreter for predicate logic progams: Part I. Report CW 10, Applied Mathe-
           matics and Programming Division. Katholieke Universiteit, Leuven, Belgium.
   1981   Intelligent backtracking for an interpreter of Horn clause logic programs. See Salgo-
           tarjan (1981).
   1982   The memory management of PROLOG implementations. See Clark and Tärnlund
           (1982).
Bundy, A., Byrd, L., Luger, G., Mellish, C. S. and Palmer, M.
   1979   Solving mechanics problems using meta-level inference. Proc. of 6th Int. Joint Conf.
           on Artificial Intelligence, Tokyo, pp. 1017–1027.
Burstall, R. M. and Darlington, J.
   1977   A transformation system for developing recursive programs. *Journal of the ACM*
           24(1), 44–67.
Byrd, L.
   1980   Understanding the control flow of PROLOG programs. See Logic Programming
           Workshop (1980).
Chakravarthy, U. S., Minker, J. and Tran, D.
   1982   Interfacing predicate logic languages and relational databases. See Marseille (1982).
Chang, C-L. and Lee, R.C-T.
   1973   "Symbolic Logic and Mechanical Theorem Proving." Academic Press, New York.
Clark, K. L.
   1977   The synthesis and verification of logic programs. See LP Research Reports.
   1978   Negation as failure. See Gallaire and Minker (1978).
   1979   Predicate logic as a computational formalism. Ph.D. Thesis. Imperial College of
           Science and Technology, Univ. of London, England.
Clark, K. L. and Darlington, J.
   1980   Algorithm classification through synthesis. *The Computer Journal* **23**(1), 61–65.
Clark, K. L. and Gregory, S.
   1981   A relational language for parallel programming. Proc. of ACM Conf. on Functional
           Programming Languages and Computer Architecture, Portsmouth, New Hampshire.
   1983   PARLOG: a parallel logic programming language. Report DOC 83/5. See DOC
           Reports.
   1984   PARLOG: parallel programming in logic. Report DOC 84/4. See DOC Reports.

Clark, K. L. and Kowalski, R. A.
1977   Predicate logic as programming language. See LP Research Reports.
Clark, K. L. and McCabe, F. G.
1979a Programmers' guide to IC-PROLOG. Report DOC 79/7. See DOC Reports.
1979b The control facilities of IC-PROLOG. See Michie (1979).
1980   IC-PROLOG: aspects of its implementation. See Logic Programming Workshop (1980).
1982   PROLOG: a language for implementing expert systems. *In* "Machine Intelligence," Vol. 10, (J. E. Hayes, D. Michie, and Y-H. Pao, eds.), pp. 455–470. Ellis Horwood Ltd., Chichester, England.
1984   "Micro-PROLOG: Programming in Logic." Prentice-Hall, Englewood Cliffs, New Jersey.
Clark, K. L. and Sickel, S.
1977   Predicate logic: a calculus for deriving programs. Proc. of 5th Int. Joint Conf. on Artificial Intelligence, Cambridge, Massachusetts.
Clark, K. L. and Tärnlund, S-A.
1977   A first order theory of data and programs. Proc. of IFIP-77, Toronto, pp. 939–944. North-Holland Publ., Amsterdam.
1982   (Editors). "Logic Programming" (APIC Studies in Data Processing, Vol. 16). Academic Press, London.
Clark, K. L. and van Emden, M. H.
1981   Consequence verification of flowcharts. *IEEE Transactions on Software Engineering* **SE-7**(1), 52–60.
Clark, K. L., McCabe, F. G. and Gregory, S.
1982a IC-PROLOG language features. See Clark and Tärnlund (1982).
Clark, K. L., McKeeman, W. and Sickel, S.
1982b Logic program specification of numerical integration. See Clark and Tärnlund (1982).
Clocksin, W. F. and Mellish, C. S.
1980   The UNIX PROLOG system. Software Report 5, Dept. of Artificial Intelligence. Univ. of Edinburgh, Scotland.
1981   "Programming in PROLOG." Springer-Verlag, Berlin.
Colmerauer, A.
1978   Metamorphosis grammars. *In* "Natural Language Communication with Computers" (L. Bolc, ed.) (Lecture Notes on Computer Science, No. 63) pp. 133–189. Springer-Verlag, Berlin.
1981   An interesting subset of natural language. See Clark and Tärnlund (1982).
Colmerauer, A., Kanoui, H., Pasero, R. and Roussel, P.
1973   Un systeme de communication homme–machine en Francais. Research Report, Artificial Intelligence Group. Univ. of Aix-Marseille, Luminy, France.
Conery, J. S.
1983   The AND/OR process model for parallel interpretation of logic programs. Technical Report 204 (Ph.D. Thesis) (June). Univ. of California at Irvine.
Conery, J. S. and Kibler, D. F.
1981   Parallel interpretation of logic programs. Proc. of ACM Conf. on Functional Programming Languages and Computer Architecture, Portsmouth, New Hampshire, pp. 163–170.
Cory, H. T., Hammond, P., Kowalski, R. A., Kriwaczek, F., Sadri, F. and Sergot, M. J.
1984   The British Nationality Act as a logic program. See LP Research Reports.
d'Agapayeff, A.
1982   An introduction to the fifth generation. See SPL (1982).

Dahl, V.
1980   Two solutions for the negation problem. See Logic Programming Workshop (1980).
1981   On data base system development through logic. Research Report, Dept. of Mathematics, Faculty of Exact Sciences. Univ. of Buenos Aires, Argentina.

Darlington, J. and Kowalski, R. A.
1983   (Editors). Declarative systems architecture. SERC-DOI IKBS Architecture Study, Vol. 2, U.K. Government Department of Trade and Industry, London.

Darlington, J. and Reeve, M.
1981   ALICE: a multi-processor reduction machine for the parallel evaluation of applicative languages. Proc. of ACM Conf. on Functional Programming Languages and Computer Architecture, Portsmouth, New Hampshire.
1983   ALICE and the parallel evaluation of logic programs. Invited Paper to 10th Annual Int. Symposium on Computer Architecture, Stockholm, Sweden.

Davis, M.
1958   "Computability and Unsolvability." McGraw-Hill, New York.

Deliyanni, A. and Kowalski, R. A.
1979   Logic and semantic networks. *Comm. of the ACM* **22**(3), 184–192.

De Long, H.
1970   "A Profile of Mathematical Logic." Addison-Wesley, Reading, Massachusetts.

Dijkstra, E. W.
1976   "A Discipline of Programming." Prentice-Hall, Englewood Cliffs, New Jersey.

DOC Reports
1975–   Dept. of Computing Reports, Imperial College of Science and Technology, London,
1984   England.

Elcock, E. W.
1981   Logic and programming methodology. Departmental Report No. 80, Dept. of Computer Science, Univ. of Western Ontario, London, Ontario, Canada.

Elson, M.
1973   "Concepts of programming languages" (Computer Science Series). Science Research Associates, Chicago.

Ennals, J. R.
1980   Logic as a computer language for children. See LP Research Reports.
1981   History and computing. Collection of Papers 1979–1981, Report DOC 81/22. See DOC Reports.
1982   Teaching logic as a computer language in schools. See Marseille (1982).
1984   "Beginning Micro-PROLOG" (2nd Ed.). Ellis Horwood Ltd., Chichester, England and Heinemann Computers in Education Ltd., London, England.

Fuchi, K.
1981   Aiming for knowledge information processing systems. See JIPDEC (1981).

Furukawa, K., Nakajima, R., Yonezawa, A., Goto, S. and Aoyama, A.
1981   Problem solving and inference mechanisms. See JIPDEC (1981).

Gabbay, D. M. and Sergot, M. J.
1984   Negation as inconsistency. DOC Report 84/7. See DOC Reports.

Gallaire, H.
1981   The impact of logic on databases. Proc. of 7th Int. Conf. on Very Large Data Bases, Cannes, France.

Gallaire, H. and Lasserre, C.
1982   Metalevel control for logic programming. See Clark and Tärnlund (1982).

Gallaire, H. and Minker, J.
1978   (Editors). "Logic and Data Bases." Plenum Press, New York.

Green, C. C.
   1969   The application of theorem proving to problem solving. Proc. of 1st Int. Joint Conf.
          on Artificial Intelligence, Washington, D.C., pp. 219–240.
Gurd, J. and Watson, I.
   1980   A multilayered dataflow computer architecture. Research Report, Dept. of Computer
          Science. Univ. of Manchester, England.
Hammond, P.
   1980.   Logic programming for expert systems. M.Sc. Thesis, Dept. of Computing. Imperial
          College, Univ. of London, England.
   1983a   APES: a user manual. DOC Report 82/9. See DOC Reports.
   1983b   Representation of DHSS regulations as a logic program. See British Computer
          Society (1983).
Hammond, P. and Sergot, M. J.
   1983   A PROLOG shell for logic based expert systems. See British Computer Society
          (1983).
Hansson, B. and Johansson, A-L.
   1980   Development of software for deductive reasoning. See Logic Programming Workshop
          (1980).
Hansson, A. and Tärnlund, S-A.
   1979   A natural programming calculus. Proc. of 6th Int. Joint Conf. on Artificial Intelligence,
          Tokyo.
Hayes, P. J.
   1973   Computation and deduction: Proc. 2nd Symposium on Mathematical Foundations
          of Computer Science, Czechoslovak Academy of Sciences, pp. 105–118.
Hellerstein, L., and Shapiro, E. Y.
   1984   The MAXFLOW experience. See Atlantic City (1984).
Herbrand, J.
   1967   Investigations in proof theory. *In* "From Frege to Gödel" (J. Heijenoort, ed.), pp.
          525–581. Harvard Univ. Press, Cambridge, Massachusetts.
Hill, R.
   1974   LUSH resolution and its completeness. DCL Memo No. 78, Dept. of Artificial
          Intelligence. Univ. of Edinburgh, Scotland.
Hoare, C. A. R.
   1969   An axiomatic basis for computer programming. *Comm. of the ACM* **12,** 576–580.
Hodges, W.
   1977   "Logic." Penguin, Middlesex, England.
Hogger, C. J.
   1975   Stepwise refinement for the synthesis of predicate logic programs. See LP Research
          Reports.
   1976   A logic program for the linear programming Simplex algorithm. See LP Research
          Reports.
   1977   Deductive synthesis of logic programs. See LP Research Reports.
   1978a   Program synthesis in predicate logic. Proc. of AISB/GI Conf. on Artificial Intelligence,
          Hamburg, Germany, July 18–20.
   1978b   Goal-oriented derivation of logic programs. Proc. 7th Symposium on Mathematical
          Foundations of Computer Science, Polish Academy of Sciences, Zakopane, Poland.
   1979a   Derivation of logic programs. Ph.D. Thesis. Imperial College of Science and Tech-
          nology, Univ. of London, England.
   1979b   Logical analysis of some string-matching algorithms. See LP Research Reports.

1981 Derivation of logic programs. *Journal of the ACM* **28**(2), 372–392.

1982a Logic programming and program verification. Invited Paper to Pergamon Infotech State of the Art Conference on Programming: New Directions, World Trade Centre, London, June 15–17. Republished in Wallis (1982).

1982b Concurrent logic programming. See Clark and Tärnlund (1982).

Hustler, A.
1982 Programming law in logic. Research Report, Dept. of Computer Science. Univ. of Waterloo, Ontario, Canada.

Jaffar, J., Lassez, J-L. and Lloyd, J. W.
1983 Completeness of the negation as failure rule. Proc. of 8th Int. Joint Conf. on Artificial Intelligence, Karlsruhe, Germany.

JIPDEC
1981 Proc. of Int. Conf. on Fifth Generation Computer Systems, Japan Information Processing Development Centre, Tokyo. Republished 1982. (T. Moto-oka, ed.). North-Holland Publ., Amsterdam.

Kleene, S.
1952 "Introduction to Metamathematics." Van Nostrand, New York.

Kluzniak, F. and Szpakowicz, S.
1982 PROLOG for programmers: an outline of a teaching method. Logic Programming Newsletter No. 3 (L. M. Pereira, ed.). Univ. Nova de Lisboa, Lisbon, Portugal.

Knuth, D. E., Morris, J. H. and Pratt, V. R.
1976 Fast pattern matching in strings. *SIAM Journal of Computing* **5**, 90–99.

Kowalski, R. A.
1974a Logic for problem solving. DCL Memo No. 75, Dept. of Artificial Intelligence. Univ. of Edinburgh, Scotland.

1974b Predicate logic as a programming language. Proc. of IFIP-74. North-Holland Publ., Amsterdam, pp. 569–574.

1975 A proof procedure using connection graphs. *Journal of the ACM*, **22**(4), 572–595.

1978 Logic for data description. See Gallaire and Minker (1978).

1979a "Logic for Problem Solving" (Artificial Intelligence Series, Vol. 7). Elsevier-North Holland, New York.

1979b Algorithm = logic + control. *Comm. of the ACM* **22**, 424–431.

1981a Logic as a database language. Proc. of Workshop on Database Theory, Cetraro, Italy.

1981b PROLOG as a logic programming language. Proc. of AICA Congress, Pavia, Italy, September 23–25.

1982 Logic programming in the fifth generation. See SPL (1982).

1983a The relationship between logic programming and logic specification. Invited Paper to BCS-FACS/SERC Workshop on Program Specification and Verification, Univ. of York, March 28–30.

1983b Logic Programming. Invited Paper to IFIP-83, Paris, France.

1983c The frame problem in logic databases. See LP Research Reports.

1983d Logic for expert systems. See British Computer Society (1983).

1984 The history of logic programming. See LP Research Reports.

Kowalski, R. A. and Kuehner, D. G.
1971 Linear resolution with selector function. *Artificial Intelligence* **2**, 227–260.

Lassez, J-L. and Maher, M. J.
1983 Optimal fixedpoints of logic programs. Research Report, Dept. of Computer Science. Univ. of Melbourne, Australia.

Lichtman, B. M.
  1975 Features of very high-level programming with PROLOG. M.Sc. Thesis, Dept. of
        Computing. Imperial College, Univ. of London.
Lloyd, J. W.
  1983 An introduction to deductive database systems. *The Australian Computer Journal*
        15(2), 52–57.
  1984 Foundations of logic programming. Springer-Verlag, Berlin.
Logic Programming Workshop
  1980 Proc. of Int. Workshop on Logic Programming, von Neumann Comp. Sci. Soc.,
        Debrecen, Hungary, July 14–16.
Logic Programming Workshop
  1983 Proc. of Int. Workshop on Logic Programming, Nucleo de Inteligencia Artificial,
        Univ. Nova de Lisboa, Albufeira, Algarve, Portugal, June 29–July 1.
LP Research Reports.
  1975– Logic Programming Research Reports, Theory of Computing Research Group, Dept.
  1984 of Computing. Imperial College of Science and Technology, London, England.
Manna, Z.
  1974 "Mathematical Theory of Computation." McGraw-Hill, New York.
Manna, Z. and Waldinger, R.
  1980 A deductive approach to program synthesis. *ACM Transactions on Programming
        Language and Systems* **2**(1), 90–121.
Marseille
  1982 Proc. of 1st Int. Logic Programming Conference, Faculte des Sciences de Luminy,
        Marseille, France, September 14–17.
McKeeman, W. and Sickel, S.
  1980 Hoare's program FIND revisited. See Logic Programming Workshop (1980).
Mellish, C. S.
  1982 An alternative to structure sharing in the implementation of a PROLOG interpreter.
        See Clark and Tärnlund (1982).
Michie, D.
  1979 (Editor). "Expert Systems in the Microelectronic Age. Edinburgh University Press,
        Scotland.
Minker, J.
  1981 On indefinite databases and the closed world assumption. Research Report, Dept. of
        Computer Science. Univ. of Maryland, College Park, Maryland.
  1983 AI and database research laboratory at the University of Maryland. Logic Program-
        ming Newsletter No. 5 (L. M. Pereira, ed.). Univ. Nova de Lisboa, Lisbon,
        Portugal.
Minsky, M. L.
  1975 A framework for the representation of knowledge. *In* "The Psychology of Computer
        Vision" (P. Winston, ed.), pp. 211–280. McGraw-Hill, New York.
Moto-oka, T.
  1981 Challenge for knowledge information processing systems. See JIPDEC (1981).
Murray, N.
  1978 A proof procedure for non-clausal first order logic. Research Report, School of Com-
        puter and Information Science. Syracuse University, New York.
Neves, J. C., Backhouse, R. C., Anderson, S. O. and Williams, M. H.
  1982 A PROLOG implementation of Query-by-Example. Research Report. Heriot-Watt
        University, Edinburgh, Scotland.

Nicolas, J-M. and Gallaire, H.
1978 Database: theory versus interpretation. See Gallaire and Minker (1978).
Nilsson, N. J.
1971 "Problem-Solving Methods in Artificial Intelligence." McGraw-Hill, New York.
Nishikawa, H., Yokota, M., Yamamoto, A., Taki, K. and Uchida, S.
1983 The personal inference machine (PSI): its design philosophy and machine architecture. ICOT Technical Report TR-013. Institute for New Generation Computing Technology, Tokyo, Japan.
Pereira, F. C. N.
1983 Logic for natural language analysis. Research Report, Artificial Intelligence Centre. Computer Science & Technology Division, SRI International, Menlo Park, California.
Pereira, F. C. N. and Warren, D. H. D.
1980 Definite clause grammars for language analysis—a survey of the formalism and a comparison with augmented transition networks. *Artificial Intelligence* **13**, 231–278.
Pereira, L. M.
1982 Logic control with logic. See Marseille (1982).
Pereira, L. M. and Monteiro, L. F.
1981 The semantics of parallelism and coroutining in logic programming. See Salgotarjan (1981).
Pereira, L. M. and Porto, A.
1982 Selective backtracking. See Clark and Tärnlund (1982).
Pereira, L. M., Sabatier, P. and Oliveira, E.
1982 Orbi: an expert system for environment resource evaluation through natural language. See Marseille (1982).
Pollard, G. H.
1981 Parallel execution of Horn clause programs. Ph.D. Thesis. Imperial College of Science and Technology, Univ. of London, England.
Quine, W. V. O.
1959 "Methods of Logic" (2nd Ed.). Routledge and Kegan Paul, London.
Raphael, B.
1971 The frame problem in problem solving systems. Proc. of Advanced Study Institute on Artificial Intelligence and Heuristic Programming, 1970, Menaggio, Italy. Republished (N. V. Findler and B. Meltzer, eds.), pp. 159–169. Edinburgh University Press, Scotland.
Roberts, G. M.
1977 An implementation of PROLOG. M.Sc. Thesis. Univ. of Waterloo, Ontario, Canada.
Robinson, J. A.
1965 A machine-oriented logic based on the resolution principle. *Journal of the ACM* **12**, 23–41.
1979 "Logic: form and function." Edinburgh University Press, Scotland, and Elsevier-North Holland, New York.
Robinson, J. A. and Sibert, E. E.
1980 Logic programming in LISP. Research Report, School of Computer and Information Science. Syracuse University, New York.
Roussel, P.
1975 PROLOG: manuel de reference et d'utilisation. Research Report, Artificial Intelligence Goup. Univ. of Aix-Marseille, Luminy, France.
Salgotarjan
1981 Proc. of Colloquium on Mathematical Logic in Programming, 1978, Salgotarjan,

Hungary. Republished (B. Domoki and T. Gergely, eds.). North-Holland Publ., Amsterdam.

Sammut, R. A. and Sammut, C. A.

1983a PROLOG: a tutorial introduction. *Australian Computer Journal* **15**, 42–51.

1983b The implementation of UNSW-PROLOG. *Australian Computer Journal* **15**, 58–64.

Sandewall, E.

1973 Conversion of predicate-calculus axioms, viewed as non-deterministic programs, to corresponding deterministic programs. Proc. of 3rd Int. Joint Conf. on Artificial Intelligence, Stanford, California, pp. 230–234.

Santane-Toth, E. and Szeredi, P.

1982 PROLOG applications in Hungary. See Clark and Tärnlund (1982).

Sebelik, J. and Stepanek, P.

1980 Horn clause programs suggested by recursive functions. See Logic Programming Workshop (1980).

Sergot, M. J.

1982 Prospects for representing the law as logic programs. See Clark and Tärnlund (1982).

1983a Logic databases and state transitions. Proc. of Workshop on Uses of Databases for Knowledge Bases, Univ. of Aberdeen, Scotland, April 14th.

1983b A Query-the-User facility for logic programming. *In* "Integrated Interactive Computer Systems" (P. Degano and E. Sandewall, eds.). North-Holland Publ., Amsterdam.

Shapiro, E. Y.

1983a Japan's fifth generation computers project—a trip report. Report No. CS 83-07, Dept. of Applied Mathematics. Weizmann Institute of Science, Rehovot, Israel.

1983b A subset of Concurrent Prolog and its interpreter. ICOT Technical Report TR-003, Institute for New Generation Computing Technology, Tokyo, Japan.

Sloman, A.

1983 Intelligent systems: a brief overview. SERC-DOI IKBS Architecture Study, Vol. 1 Annexes, U.K. Government Department of Trade and Industry, London.

SPL

1982 Proc. of Int. Conf. on The Fifth Generation: Dawn of the Second Computer Age. SPL International, London, July 7–9.

Stevens, C.

1977 The application of call-by-need to automatic theorem proving. M.Sc. Thesis, Dept. of Computing. Imperial College, Univ. of London, England.

Szeredi, P.

1981 Mixed language programming—a method for producing efficient PROLOG programs. Proc. of Workshop on Logic Programming for Intelligent Systems, Los Angeles, California, August.

Tärnlund, S-A.

1975a An interpreter for the programming language predicate logic. Proc. of 4th Int. Joint Conf. on Artificial Intelligence, Tbilisi, Georgia, USSR, pp. 601–608.

1975b Logic information processing. Report TRITA-IBADB 1034, Dept. of Information Processing and Computer Science. The Royal Institute of Technology and the Univ. of Stockholm, Sweden.

1977 Horn clause computability. *BIT* **17**, 215–226.

1978 An axiomatic data base theory. See Gallaire and Minker (1978).

Tarski, A.

1969 Truth and proof. *Scientific American* **220**(6), 63–77.

Tick, E. and Warren, D. H. D.
1984   Towards a pipelined PROLOG processor. See Atlantic City (1984).
Treleavan, P.
1982   Japan's fifth generation computer systems project. See SPL (1982).
Uppsala
1984   Proc. 2nd Int. Logic Programming Conference, Univ. of Uppsala, Sweden, July 2–7.
van Emden
1977a   Programming in resolution logic. "Machine Intelligence" Vol. 8 (E. W. Elcock and
         D. Michie, eds.), 266–299. Ellis Horwood Ltd., Chichester, England.
1977b   Relational equations, grammars and programs. Proc. of Conf. on Theoretical Com-
         puter Science, Univ. of Waterloo, Ontario, Canada.
1978   Computation and deductive information retrieval. In "Formal Description of Pro-
         gramming Concepts" (E. Neuhold, ed.), 421–440. North-Holland Publ., Amsterdam.
van Emden, M. H. and de Lucena Filho, G. J.
1982   Predicate logic as language for parallel programming. See Clark and Tärnlund (1982).
van Emden, M. H. and Kowalski, R. A.
1976   The semantics of predicate logic as a programming language. *Journal of the ACM*
         23(4), 733–742.
Wallis, P. J. L.
1982   (Editor). "Programming Technology: State of the Art Report." Pergamon Infotech
         Ltd., Maidenhead, England.
Warren, D. H. D.
1977a   Implementing PROLOG—compiling predicate logic programs. Research Reports
         Nos. 39 and 40, Dept. of Artificial Intelligence. Univ. of Edinburgh, Scotland.
1977b   Logic programming and compiler writing. Research Report 44, Dept. of Artificial
         Intelligence. Univ. of Edinburgh, Scotland.
1979   PROLOG on the DEC System-10. See Michie (1979).
1980   An improved PROLOG implementation which optimizes tail recursion. See Logic
         Programming Workshop (1980).
1981   Efficient processing of interactive relational database queries expressed in logic. Proc.
         of 7th Int. Conf. on Very Large Data Bases, Cannes, France.
1982   A view of the fifth generation and its impact. Proc. of Conf. on Japan and the Fifth
         Generation, Pergamon Infotech State of the Art Conference, London, September
         27–29.
Warren, D. H. D. and van Canaghem, M.
1985   Logic programming and its applications. Ablex Publ., Norwood, New Jersey.
Warren, D. H. D., Pereira, L. M. and Pereira, F. C. N.
1977   PROLOG—the language and its implementation compared with LISP. Proc. of
         Symposium on Artificial Intelligence and Programming Languages, SIGPLAN
         Notices, Vo. 12, No. 8.
1979   User's guide to DEC System-10 PROLOG. Occasional Paper 15, Dept. of Artificial
         Intelligence. Univ. of Edinburgh, Scotland.
Weir, D. J.
1982   Teaching logic programming: an interactive approach. M.Sc. Thesis, Dept. of Com-
         puting. Imperial College, Univ. of London, England.
Welham, R.
1976   Geometry problem solving. Research Report 14, Dept. of Artificial Intelligence.
         Univ. of Edinburgh, Scotland.

Weyrauch, R.
  1980   Prolegomena to a theory of mechanized formal reasoning. *Artificial Intelligence* **13**, 133–170.
Winterstein, G., Dausman, M. and Persch, G.
  1980   Deriving different unification algorithms from a specification in logic. See Logic Programming Workshop (1980).
Zloof, M. M.
  1975.   Query-by-Example. "Proceedings of AFIPS-75 National Computer Conference," Vol. 4. AFIPS Press, Montvale, New Jersey.

INDEX

A.P.I.C. Studies in Data Processing
General Editors: Fraser Duncan and M. J. R. Shave